CHILD ABUSE AND NEGLECT

CHILD ABUSE AND NEGLECT: CROSS-CULTURAL PERSPECTIVES

WITHDRAWN

Edited by

Jill E. Korbin

with Forewords by
Robert B. Edgerton
and C. Henry Kempe

University of California Press
Berkeley   Los Angeles   London

University of California Press
Berkeley and Los Angeles, California

University of California Press, Ltd.
London, England

Copyright © 1981 by The Regents of the University of California

First Paperback Printing 1983
ISBN 0-520-05070-3

Library of Congress Cataloging in Publication Data

Main entry under title:
Child abuse and neglect.

    Includes index.
    1. Child abuse--Addresses, essays, lectures.
I. Korbin, Jill E. [DNLM: 1. Child abuse. 2. Cross-
cultural comparison.   WA 320 C534015]
HV713.C3819   362.7'044   81-6

Printed in the United States of America

1 2 3 4 5 6 7 8 9

CONTENTS

v

FOREWORD

Robert B. Edgerton

Throughout the history of mankind, children have only sometimes been spared the indignities, cruelties, and horrors that human beings so often inflict upon one another. At various times, in various places, children have been abandoned, starved, beaten, enslaved, sexually assaulted, and put to death. One such horror—child abuse—has become a serious social problem in the United States and in some other industrialized societies, yet it occurs infrequently or not at all in many of the world's societies. Why? The search for an answer is overdue.

Dr. Jill Korbin is the first anthropologist to make child abuse a topic of concerted study. In several previous papers and in ongoing research projects Dr. Korbin has demonstrated that anthropological perspectives can contribute to an improved understanding of child abuse. In the present volume, Dr. Korbin has furthered this understanding by assembling nine anthropological discussions of child abuse in various parts of the world. The book provides a wealth of valuable information which serves well to identify the critical relevance of several issues, including the difficulty of providing a universally acceptable definition of what constitutes child abuse. The contributions to this book also show the many ways in which the occurrence of child abuse is related to such factors as the value placed on children, the availability of multiple caretakers, the extent to which caretakers have models for good child care, and the degree to which people accept collective responsibility for a child's welfare.

The contributors also note that while child abuse seems to increase in situations of rapid sociocultural change, urban migration, family disorganization, and the like, no clear-cut set of prognostic variables has been identified.

Indeed, it seems likely that factors that seem to predict child abuse in one society will not be predictive in another. For example, in her chapter on child abuse in the People's Republic of China, Dr. Korbin documents the ways in which fundamental social and cultural changes affect patterns of child abuse, but she questions the prevailing Western belief that abusive parents were themselves abused as children by noting that many present-day Chinese who were abused by their parents did not become abusing parents under the changed conditions of the People's Republic.

Beyond its importance for our understanding of child abuse, this volume is a reflection of the continuing maturation of anthropology as a science. In addition to its interest in the smaller, simpler societies of the non-Western world, anthropologists now study complex and urban societies. And, in addition to their interest in more normative behaviors, anthropologists have begun to study seriously much that was previously left to such disciplines as psychology, psychiatry, and sociology. Like rape, incest, wife battering, torturing of wild animals, tormenting or teasing the blind or handicapped—all of which occur in many of the world's societies—child abuse is an important subject for anthropological inquiry, not only because anthropologists can help in understanding this phenomenon, but also because until anthropologists study *all* human behaviors, however horrendous or distasteful they may be, they will fall short of their most fundamental goal—an understanding of humankind.

FOREWORD

C. Henry Kempe

Cross-cultural perspectives in the field of child abuse and neglect are largely lacking and therefore this book fills a very important void. It can, of course, be only a start, because in so many countries not much is published about child rearing and about possible child abuse and neglect. One or two official statistics are not adequate to show a low incidence of these conditions. Thirty years ago in the industrial world child abuse was thought to be uncommon. Only active public and professional concern led to the emergence of a truer picture of all forms of child abuse and neglect: physical, sexual, emotional, and failure to thrive owing to maternal deprivation.

Child rearing is the essential element in the transmission of culture in any group or society. Definitions of child abuse vary from culture to culture and evolve over time, and they may reflect the necessities for survival of the group. Not infrequently, cultural rationalizations for harmful behavior toward children are accepted blindly as proof that the treatment accorded children is neither abusive nor harmful.

It has been presumed that Western cultures have advanced to the point where the individual right of each child is not in conflict with those of the group and has come to be protected more fully in recent decades. But Western cultures continue to show competitive and violent behavior which does not yet give sufficient support to dependent individuals, such as mothers and children. Indeed, mothers are no longer thought of as "dependent" although they do require extra care and concern in order to fulfill their maternal role. In contrast, studies of non-Western groups may suggest that those cultures see some of the Western child care practices as abusive and neglectful (baby-sitting, toilet training, for example). We may need to reevaluate our own methods as well. What is needed, then, is a careful balance between those who believe that all "progress" is good for children as against those who glorify "simple" societies which are indeed highly complex and whose child care practices, while traditional, may no longer serve the best interests of their society.

Child-rearing practices transmit many cultural values at a level (non-verbal, for example) so basic as to seem innate. They all tend to favor the development of those characteristics that form character and influence behavior. Some child-rearing customs help to develop characteristics in the child which are highly valued by the culture, which are suited to perpetuate cultural values (independence or violence or filial piety or obedience to law). Erikson's work clearly shows this interplay among cultural values, child-rearing practices, and behavior characteristics.

All cultures encourage dependence and even total care for the very young for varying periods after birth as a necessity for the babies' survival as well as for attachment and socialization. How early in a child's development a shift toward more self-sufficiency and independence is made (in some groups it is as early as one year) and *how* it is made (in some groups it is gradual and kindly; in others, abrupt and harsh) have much to do with the kind of character developed in the child.

When circumstances of a nation change rapidly, as in times of sudden urbanization and industrial exploitation, there may be a serious lag and maladaptation of traditional cultural values which are then quickly reflected in difficulties in child rearing. Isolation and loss of support for mothering come through clearly as frequent concomitants of abuse and neglect in many cultures trying to adjust to rapid change brought about by external forces.

Ours is increasingly becoming one world. The recent declaration of the Year of the Child brought efforts from all members of the United Nations to address the most urgent needs of their children. Thus, for the first time in human history, has the world as a whole addressed the needs of children wherever they are. This shift in attitude should rapidly lead to more understanding of how to prevent and treat child abuse and neglect the world over. Clearly, no nation has a monopoly on superior methods of child rearing. But worldwide attention to the physical and emotional needs of the defenseless child has taken the matter out of the hands of those who regard children as chattel and is gradually identifying those in each culture who are willing to defend the defenseless baby and its often inadequately supported mother. This development is so recent as to become a landmark in the history of child welfare everywhere.

PREFACE

The chapters in this volume were prepared for presentation as a symposium at the 1978 annual meetings of the American Anthropological Association and then were revised for publication. As efforts to deal with child abuse and neglect became international in scope, our purpose was to acquaint professionals in the field of child abuse and neglect with the concept of culture and to bring the issue of deviance in child-rearing practices to the attention of the anthropological community as a valid topic for study.

I would like to acknowledge the help and support of many individuals. First and foremost, I thank the authors of this volume for their contributions at a time when anthropologists were just beginning to be concerned with issues of child abuse and neglect. These friends and colleagues have shown patience and helpfulness, in addition to their high standards of scholarship.

As seems fitting to me, C. Henry Kempe and Robert B. Edgerton have each provided a foreword for this book. Dr. Kempe, a pioneer in the field of child abuse and neglect, and Dr. Edgerton, a pioneer in anthropological attention to deviance, have not only provided me with professional training but also have been consistently supportive of and interested in my work. To them both I owe a professional and personal statement of gratitude.

Special mention must be made of Brandt F. Steele, who acted as my "mentor" during my training at the National Center for the Prevention and Treatment of Child Abuse and Neglect in Denver. During our conversations many of the issues that arise in this volume were discussed.

L. L. Langness, in addition to being a contributor, has had an important role in the appearance of this book, encouraging me to initiate it, and then assisting with advice throughout its preparation.

In the numerous forms that this volume has taken, I would like to thank Lupe Montaño and Phyllis Takayanagi for helping to type the manuscript. A debt of gratitude is also owed the staff of the University of California Press, particularly to James Kubeck for his help in seeing the book to its final form, and to Grace Stimson for her concern and conscientious editing of the manuscript.

Family and friends are often acknowledged at this time, both for their love and support, as well as for their understanding of the attention denied them while I was working on the manuscript. For their encouragement, understanding, and love, I thank them.

J. E. K.

CONTRIBUTORS

Robert B. Edgerton, Departments of Psychiatry and Anthropology, University of California, Los Angeles

Orna R. Johnson, Department of Psychiatry, University of California, Los Angeles

C. Henry Kempe, The National Center for the Prevention and Treatment of Child Abuse and Neglect, Department of Pediatrics, University of Colorado Medical Center, Denver

Jill E. Korbin, Department of Anthropology, Case Western Reserve University, Cleveland, Ohio.

L. L. Langness, Departments of Psychiatry and Anthropology, University of California, Los Angeles

Robert LeVine, Laboratory of Human Development, Harvard University, Cambridge, Massachusetts

Sarah LeVine, Laboratory of Human Development, Harvard University, Cambridge, Massachusetts

Emelie A. Olson, Department of Sociology, Anthropology, and Social Work, Whittier College, Whittier, California.

Thomas Poffenberger, School of Public Health, University of Michigan, Ann Arbor, Michigan

James Ritchie, Department of Social Sciences, University of Waikato, Hamilton, New Zealand

Jane Ritchie, Department of Social Sciences, University of Waikato, Hamilton, New Zealand

Hiroshi Wagatsuma, Institute of Socio-Economic Planning, University of Tsukuba, Sakuramura, Japan

David Y. H. Wu, Culture Learning Institute, East-West Center, Honolulu, Hawaii

INTRODUCTION

1

Jill E. Korbin

Whereas Mankind Owes to the Child the Best It Has to Give[1]

—United Nations Declaration of the Rights of
the Child, 20 November 1959

Humankind has fallen far short of the goal set by the United Nations. The lot of children the world over is not pleasant to contemplate. In both developing and developed nations, children are subject to poor prenatal and postnatal care, malnutrition, disease, and poverty. Despite this bleak picture, one of our cherished beliefs is that human nature compels parents to rear their young with tender and loving care, thus dulling or mitigating noxious environmental and societal conditions. Since Kempe and his colleagues (1962) drew attention to the "battered baby syndrome," the increasing recognition in the United States and other Western nations that children may come to great harm at the hands of their parents has forced us to acknowledge that child abuse and neglect are within the repertoire of human behavior. But are child abuse and neglect universal? Or do they occur only under certain conditions? A cross-cultural perspective can enhance our understanding of this disturbing aspect of human behavior.

Present knowledge of child abuse and neglect is based almost entirely on research and clinical experience in Western nations. Evidence for the universality of child abuse and neglect is predicated on a consideration of cultural and historical traditions similar to our own (deMause 1974; Radbill 1968; Solomon 1973; Steele 1970) Cross-cultural comparisons of child abuse and

[1]While I prefer the term "humankind," I use the quotation as it appeared in the 1959 United Nations Declaration of the Rights of the Child.

1

neglect have tended to focus on incidence rates, intervention strategies, and service delivery systems in Western nations (Kamerman 1975; Silver 1978). The literature on child abuse and neglect in Western nations reflects international cooperation and a consensus about the characteristics of abusive parents, their children, and abuse-provoking conditions.[2]

The chapters in this volume explore the issues involved in child maltreatment from the perspective of cultural groups not before considered in the child abuse and neglect literature. The cross-cultural record, a "natural laboratory" of human behavior, allows us to consider child maltreatment from a broader range of social and environmental conditions than that afforded by a consideration of Western nations alone.[3] In this volume we consider a particular behavior, child abuse and neglect, within the context of a selected number of cultures in which we have carried out anthropological, or ethnographic, fieldwork and research.

With rare exception (Fraser and Kilbride 1981; Rohner 1975), anthropologists and others engaged in cross-cultural research have not conducted studies specifically concerned with child maltreatment in non-Western cultures. Anthropological research in general has concentrated on the regularities, the cultural patterns, rather than the departures or deviations from cultural norms (Edgerton 1976). The sparse information that is available concerning parental incompetence or mistreatment must be gleaned from ethnographic materials on other subjects (Korbin 1977, 1979).

Even a cursory examination of the cross-cultural literature on child rearing presents a remarkable range of variation. This is all the more notable considering the commonality of tasks that must be accomplished in socializing the next generation:

> . . . child training the world over is in certain important respects identical. It is identical in that it is found always to be concerned with universal problems of behavior. Parents everywhere have similar problems to solve in bringing up their children. In all societies the helpless infant . . . must be changed into a responsible adult obeying the rules of his society. Child training everywhere seems to be in considerable part concerned with problems which arise from universal characteristics of the human infant and from universal characteristics of adult culture which are incompatible with the continuation of infantile behavior.
> . . . even in these important respects, child training also differs from one society to another. Societies differ from each other in the precise character of the

[2]For a perspective on international work on child abuse and neglect, see *Child Abuse and Neglect: The International Journal*, 1977 to present.

[3]It should be noted that throughout this volume "Western" culture is referred to in the singular. This usage does not connote homogeneity among Euro-American cultures, but makes for ease of presentation.

rules to which the child must be taught to conform; no society, for example, permits its children the complete sexual freedom which they might spontaneously develop, but the extent and character of the restrictions placed on sexual freedom vary tremendously. Societies differ, moreover, in the techniques that are used in enforcing conformity, in the age at which conformity is demanded to each rule of adult life . . . and in countless other details of the socialization process. [Whiting and Child 1953:63–64]

The task at this point is one of splicing together what we know about child abuse and neglect in Western nations and what we know about child rearing practices, beliefs, and behaviors in other cultures (Korbin 1977, 1979, 1980). Such a collation of materials to shed light on a problem in our own society is not unique to the history of anthropology or social science. Margaret Mead's (1928) classic, *Coming of Age in Samoa*, was an early demonstration that what may be troublesome in our culture, the *Sturm und Drang* of adolescence, is not necessarily so in another cultural context. The cross-cultural record has been useful in gaining a perspective on alcoholism, mental retardation, sexual aberrations, aging, and deviant behavior (Edgerton 1970, 1976; MacAndrew and Edgerton 1969; Myerhoff and Simic 1977; Selby 1974). Similarly, the understanding of child abuse and neglect in our culture can be expanded and enhanced by examining factors in different cultural contexts which increase or decrease the propensity for such behavior to occur.

CULTURALLY APPROPRIATE DEFINITIONS OF CHILD ABUSE AND NEGLECT

In assessing the cultural implications of child abuse and neglect, the first task is to employ culturally appropriate definitions. Conventional wisdom suggests that child maltreatment would be easily identified across cultural boundaries. As the following chapters explore cross-cultural variation in child-rearing patterns, however, it becomes clear that there is no universal standard for optimal child rearing or for child abuse and neglect. This presents us with a dilemma. If we do not include a cultural perspective, we will be entangled in the ethnocentric position of considering our own set of cultural values and practices preferable, and indeed superior, to any other. At the same time, a stance of extreme cultural relativism, in which all judgments of human treatment of children are suspended in the name of cultural sensitivity, would be counterproductive to promoting the well-being of the world's children. The present volume is a step toward resolving this dilemma by considering child maltreatment within the context of cultures very different from our own.

Each chapter in this volume addresses the issue of what is and what is not regarded as abusive or neglectful by the cultures in question. One must be cognizant of both the viewpoint of the members of the cultural group itself, and of an outside perspective. An understanding of the insider's perspective has been central to anthropology's efforts to organize and explain the diversity of human behavior which has been documented cross-culturally. Thus, the anthropologist has traditionally sought to "grasp the native's point of view, his relation to life, to realize his vision of his world" (Malinowski 1922:25). A wider frame of reference, based on an understanding of the cross-cultural record, must also be maintained so that behavior can be interpreted within the broader context of human experience. Both perspectives, that of the particular culture, and that obtained from a wider cross-cultural data base, are prerequisites to sorting out the context in which behavior, including child abuse and neglect, takes on meaning.

Three levels can be identified at which cultural considerations come into play in identifying child abuse and neglect cross-culturally (Korbin 1980). On the first level are practices viewed as acceptable by one culture but as abusive or neglectful by another. It is in this realm that cultural conflict can confound definitions of child maltreatment. All the contributors present numerous examples of practices that appear abusive or neglectful to the Westerner. These include extremely hot baths, designed to inculcate culturally valued traits; punishments, such as severe beatings, to impress the child with the necessity of adherence to cultural rules; and harsh initiation rites that include genital operations, deprivation of food and sleep, and induced bleeding and vomiting. The authors consider these behaviors within their cultural contexts, seeking to understand the reasons for and the functions of such practices. Thus, for example, the parent who "protects" his or her child from a painful, but culturally required, initiation rite would be denying the child a place as an adult in that culture. That parent, in the eyes of his cultural peers, would be abusive or neglectful for compromising the development of his child.

It is equally sobering to look at Western child-rearing techniques and practices through the eyes of these same non-Western cultures. Non-Western peoples often conclude that anthropologists, missionaries, or other Euro-Americans with whom they come into contact do not love their children or simply do not know how to care for them properly (Benedict 1938). Practices such as isolating infants and small children in rooms or beds of their own at night, making them wait for readily available food until a schedule dictates that they can satisfy their hunger, or allowing them to cry without immediately attending to their needs or desires would be at odds with the child-rearing philosophies of most of the cultures discussed. Such practices may seem to us benign in comparison with many of those described in this book. As the contributors point out, however, many of our normative child-rearing practices would be viewed as equally bizarre, exotic, and damaging to child welfare as behaviors acceptable in other cultures seem to us.

At the second definitional level, the authors make it clear that while cultures vary in their definitions of child abuse and neglect, each group nevertheless has criteria for identifying behaviors that are outside the realm of acceptable child training. This idiosyncratic abuse or neglect, which signals a departure from the range of behaviors tolerated by the culture, may more appropriately be considered child abuse or neglect than behaviors classified as such on the basis of cultural differences.

Societal abuse and neglect of children is the third level of concern. Conditions such as poverty, inadequate housing, poor health care, inadequate nutrition, and unemployment have been seen either as contributing powerfully to the incidence of child abuse and neglect in Western nations, or as so damaging to children as to outweigh the proportion of child abuse and neglect which occurs because of parental psychopathology (Gelles 1973; Gil 1970; Pelton 1978). There can be no doubt that these conditions seriously compromise the survival and well-being of children around the world. Several contributors consider these conditions, noting that they can contribute to an increase in child abuse and neglect in societies in which such behavior was previously reported to be rare. Even when recognized by parents as detrimental to their child's survival, development, and welfare, such circumstances may be viewed as unfortunate but as beyond individual parental control. Nevertheless, detrimental environmental and societal conditions must be distinguished from accepted child-rearing practices that are differentially perceived as abuse or neglect, and from idiosyncratic maltreatment of children which falls outside a culture's accepted range of behaviors. As several of the authors note, it is also well to remember that many of the detrimental environmental conditions in technologically less developed societies closely resemble past Euro-American conditions of poor sanitation, inadequate health care, and poverty of resources of all kinds.

The contributors to this volume also delineate some of the factors to be considered in reconciling cultural variability with an acceptable definition of child abuse and neglect. In formulating such culturally appropriate definitions, the authors point out the need to be aware of the socialization goals of the culture, parental intentions and beliefs about their actions, and the way a child perceives his or her treatment. The authors also indicate the importance of a real versus an ideal distinction. Parents may maintain the right to physically discipline their children, but the effectiveness of their socialization practices may diminish the chances that this right is very often translated into tangible behavior, or that punishment turns into beatings out of control.

ETIOLOGY OF CHILD ABUSE AND NEGLECT

Despite differences in emphasis and approach in explaining child abuse and neglect in Western nations, there is general agreement that child maltreatment arises from a complex interaction of parental characteristics, attributes of particular children, and environmental and social stresses. Intergenerational transmission of abusive parenting patterns and failure in attachment and bonding processes have also been importantly linked with child abuse and neglect.[4] The contributors to this volume make use of the cross-cultural record in considering factors implicated in the etiology of child abuse and neglect in Western nations.

Characteristics of abused and neglected children have been implicated in the etiology of child abuse and neglect in Western nations (Lynch 1976; Martin 1976; Milowe and Lourie 1964). These characteristics may be tangible, as in low birth weight, prematurity, prolonged illness in early childhood, or developmental delays. These characteristics may also involve perceptions on the part of parents that their child is somehow "different." The chapters in this volume point out quite clearly that while children in general may be highly valued by a cultural group, there are categories of children who are more vulnerable to mistreatment. These include illegitimate children, adopted children, deformed or retarded children, high birth order children, and female children. Vulnerability depends to a large degree on the cultural context. Adopted children, particularly girls, may be more susceptible to mistreatment in one society, for example Taiwan, but not in Polynesian cultures. Children who are the result of a difficult pregnancy or labor, children who display characteristics that are not valued or liked by their parents or their cultural group, and children whose personalities seem at odds with their parents are more likely to receive a lesser quality of care. The authors also point out that mistreatment need not be overt but may represent an "underinvestment" (Scrimshaw 1978) or a "benign neglect" of certain children. These children may not as readily receive medical attention when sick or their fair share of scarce resources.

The distinction that various cultures make concerning the competence and "humanness" of children of various ages is also an important considera-

---

[4]This volume does not extensively summarize the voluminous literature that has accumulated over the past twenty years on child abuse and neglect in the United States and other Western nations. Among the many excellent books on the subject, the reader is directed to Bourne and Newberger 1979; Garbarino, Stocking et al. 1980; Gil 1970, 1979; Giovannoni and Becerra 1979; Kempe and Helfer 1980; Kempe and Kempe 1978; Martin 1976; Straus, Gelles, and Steinmetz 1980; and Williams and Money 1980.

tion. Thus, among the Japanese, the infant's birth cry precluded the possibility of infanticide. Similarly, among the Machiguenga of South America, once a mother nursed her infant, she could no longer do away with the child. Several of the contributors point out that children below the age of seven or eight are not considered to be competent, to "have sense." Thus behaviors of these children cannot legitimately result in parental anger or punitiveness. How the maturation process is perceived in different cultures thus can mitigate the age-inappropriate expectations of children that are so often implicated in child abuse and neglect in Western nations.

The relationship between parental characteristics or psychopathology and child abuse and neglect is the component least accessible to cross-cultural comparison at this point. There remain conflicting pictures of the psychological characteristics of abusing and neglecting parents in Western nations (Spinetta and Rigler 1972). Since the classification of personality characteristics as deviant is largely dependent upon the cultural context, a definitive relationship between parental attributes and child maltreatment cross-culturally awaits further investigation. The chapters in this volume, however, indicate that not all individuals in these non-Western cultures are, or are expected to be, equally good parents.

In terms of social and environmental conditions, again the context is of primary importance. For example, although societal violence has been importantly linked with child abuse and neglect in Western nations (Gil 1970, 1979), several of the chapters suggest that societal violence and/or spousal violence are not inextricably linked with violence directed at children. Similarly, the likelihood of poverty or food scarcity leading to child abuse or neglect, is dependent upon the larger cultural context. These conditions are undeniably detrimental to child morbidity and mortality, but they do not necessarily translate into idiosyncratic abuse and neglect. Some conditions, however, are potentially hazardous in both Western and non-Western nations. Among certain African groups discussed, an increase in alcoholism leads to deterioration in child care practices and increases the likelihood of child neglect.

Embeddedness in kin and community networks arises repeatedly in the subsequent chapters as a crucial element in the etiology of child abuse and neglect. Children, because of their immaturity and dependent nature, are particularly vulnerable to the "we/they," "insider/outsider" dichotomy. The child who does not have a network of individuals beyond the biological parents who are concerned with his or her welfare is at increased jeopardy. Child rearing as a group concern rather than as the exclusive domain and responsibility of individual parents is seen by the authors as both ensuring general standards of child care and preventing idiosyncratic departure from those standards. If a wider network of individuals is concerned with and actively participates in child rearing, then the deficits and failings of particular parents may be less deleterious. Inadequate parenting, including child abuse and neglect, can be dealt with by others before the child is harmed or the parent labeled a deviant. Nearly all the subsequent chapters point out that in smaller-scale societies, others readily intervene when overly severe punishment has been inflicted. The authors also overwhelmingly indicate that a situation in which many people actively participate and assist in child rearing is a far cry from a situation in which one or two biological parents are expected to be all things at all times to all their children. The following chapters thus support the linkage between social isolation and a lack of support systems on the one hand, and child abuse and neglect on the other, which has been noted in Western nations (Elmer 1967; Garbarino 1978; Helfer 1973; Young 1964).

The flexibility of responsibility for child rearing which is closely tied to a wider network of kin and community both provides a source of alternative caretakers and allows for redistribution of children who might be at increased risk of inadequate parenting or mistreatment. Cross-culturally, mothers who are isolated in child-care tasks, without others to relieve them periodically, are more likely to be harsh with their children (Minturn and Lambert 1964; Rohner 1975). The availability of alternative caretakers relieves the biological parents from an unremitting burden of child care. Additionally, children who are not wanted by their parents are welcomed into other households where they are economic assets and emotionally valued. Mechanisms such as child lending, fostering, and informal adoption facilitate this process of redistribution.

The following chapters take us to cultures that are, for the most part, far removed from the Western nations that are most seriously grappling with problems of child abuse and neglect. For only a few of the cultures discussed were any official reporting statistics or newspaper accounts available. The nature of the cross-cultural record, and the lack of attention paid by anthropologists to deviance, including child maltreatment, have meant that the extent of information on child abuse and neglect in these societies is varied. The contributors seek to provide the information that is available on a selected number of cultures very different from our own. Each chapter includes a discussion of how child abuse and neglect are defined in the particular culture. Several also review Western child-rearing practices that are seen as abusive or neglectful by these same diverse cultural groups. The authors then examine the conditions under which child abuse and neglect occur as well as the circumstances that seem to diminish or to increase its likelihood.

While a brief description cannot do justice to each contribution, an orientation will help to set the tone. In chapter 2, Langness discusses the issue of cultural values and child abuse. He questions how it is that practices such as harsh initiation rites occur in New Guinea, in cultures that value children highly and in which idiosyncratic abuse of children is virtually nonexistent. In chapter 3, the LeVines discuss child abuse and neglect in East Africa, describing practices that would seem unduly harsh to Westerners but that correspond with the exigencies of child rearing in these societies. They also comment upon economic and social changes sweeping the continent which are recognized as being detrimental to child welfare but are often viewed as beyond the control of individual parents. In chapter 4, Johnson examines the relationship among societal violence, economic conditions, and violence directed toward children in native South America. She also discusses physically harsh practices that are aimed at inculcating culturally valued traits and behaviors. Poffenberger, in chapter 5, describes the relationship between societal child-rearing goals in rural India and the treatment of individual children. He discusses the differential treatment of boys and girls within this framework. Olson, in chapter 6, explores Turkish child-rearing practices in their social and psychological context. Her description of how Turkish villagers responded to her American-style rearing of her two-year-old daughter is particularly relevant to the issue of culturally diverse perceptions of abuse and neglect. In chapter 7, Wagatsuma presents information on an industrialized nation, Japan, in which the pattern of child mistreatment appears to be different from that in the industrialized nations of the West. He notes that maltreatment of children is likely to take the form of abandonment in infancy or infanticide rather than the recurrent battering of children seen in Western nations. He also discusses the Japanese phenomenon of joint suicides in which the parents kill their offspring when they take their own lives. Wu, in chapter 8, discusses maltreatment of children within the context of the cultural value of filial piety, suggesting that this ethic provides a background for sacrificing the younger generation for the older. He also writes about abuse of adopted daughters in light of attachment and bonding. In chapter 9, I examine the efforts of the People's Republic of China to decrease maltreatment of children and the context within which these efforts have been made. While several chapters consider socioeconomic change, the chapter by the Ritchies concludes the discussion of different cultures with a focus on the issue of how quickly changing conditions in the child-rearing milieu can produce the preconditions for child abuse and neglect. They consider how child maltreatment, which appears to be virtually nonexistent in the ethnographic record for Polynesia, is now a problem of considerable magnitude. In the final chapter I suggest some general principles that tie together the threads running through the volume.

It is hoped that this volume will assist the clinician, the theoretician, the researcher, the anthropologist, and all others concerned with children's welfare in such a way as to shed light on a path of progress in decreasing and preventing this affront to our children.

REFERENCES

Benedict, Ruth
1938 Continuities and discontinuities in cultural conditioning. *Psychiatry* 1:161–167.

Bourne, Richard, and Eli H. Newberger, eds.
1979 *Critical perspectives on child abuse and neglect*. Lexington, MA: Lexington Books.

deMause, Lloyd, ed.
1974 *The history of childhood*. New York: Harper and Row.

Edgerton, Robert B.
1970 Mental retardation in non-Western societies: toward a cross-cultural perspective on incompetence. In *Socio-cultural aspects of mental retardation*, ed. H. C. Haywood. New York: Appleton-Century Crofts. Pp. 523–559.

1976 *Deviance: a cross-cultural perspective*. Menlo Park: Cummings.

Elmer, Elizabeth
1967 *Children in jeopardy: a study of abused minors and their families*. Pittsburgh: University of Pittsburgh Press.

Fraser, Gertrude, and Philip Kilbride
1981 Child abuse and neglect—rare but perhaps increasing phenomena among the Samia of Kenya. *Child Abuse and Neglect: The International Journal*. 4(4): 227–232.

Garbarino, James
1978 Defining the community context for parent-child relations: the correlates of child maltreatment. *Child Development* 49:604–616.

Garbarino, James, Holly Stocking, and Associates
1980 *Protecting children from abuse and neglect: developing and maintaining effective support systems for families*. San Francisco: Jossey-Bass.

Gelles, Richard
1973 Child abuse as psychopathology: a sociological critique and reformulation. *American Journal of Orthopsychiatry* 43(4):611–621.

Gil, David
1970 *Violence against children: physical child abuse in the United States*. Cambridge: Harvard University Press.

1979 *Child abuse and violence*. New York: AMS Press.

Giovannoni, Jeanne M., and Rosina M. Becerra
1979 *Defining child abuse*. New York: Free Press.

Helfer, Ray E.
1973 The etiology of child abuse. *Pediatrics* 51(4):777–779.

Kamerman, Sheila
1975 Cross-national perspectives on child abuse and neglect. *Children Today* 4(3): 34–37.

Kempe, C. Henry, and Ray E. Helfer, eds.
1980 *The battered child*. 3d ed. Chicago: University of Chicago Press.

Kempe, C. Henry, Frederic N. Silverman, Brandt F. Steele, William Droegmueller, and Henry K. Silver
1962 The battered child syndrome. *Journal of the American Medical Association* 181: 17–24.

Kempe, Ruth S., and C. Henry Kempe
1978 *Child abuse*. Cambridge: Harvard University Press.

Korbin, Jill E.
1977 Anthropological contributions to the study of child abuse. *Child Abuse and Neglect: The International Journal* 1(1):7–24.

1979 A cross-cultural perspective on the role of the community in child abuse and neglect. *Child Abuse and Neglect: The International Journal* 3(1):9–18.

1980 The cultural context of child abuse and neglect. In *The battered child*, ed. C. Henry Kempe and Ray E. Helfer. 3d ed. Chicago: University of Chicago Press. Pp. 21–35.

Lynch, Margaret
1976 Risk factors in the abused child: a study of abused children and their siblings. In *The abused child: a multidisciplinary approach to developmental issues and treatment*, ed. Harold P. Martin. Cambridge: Ballinger. Pp. 43–56.

MacAndrew, Craig, and Robert B. Edgerton
1969 *Drunken comportment: a social explanation*. Chicago: Aldine.

Malinowski, Bronislaw
1922 *Argonauts of the Western Pacific*. New York: Dutton.

Martin, Harold P., ed.
1976 *The abused child: a multidisciplinary approach to developmental issues and treatment*. Cambridge: Ballinger.

Mead, Margaret
1928 *Coming of age in Samoa*. New York: William Morrow.

Milowe, I. D., and R. S. Lourie
1964 The child's role in the battered child syndrome. *Journal of Pediatrics* 65:1079–1081.

Minturn, Leigh, and William W. Lambert
1964 *Mothers of six cultures: antecedents of child rearing*. New York: John Wiley and Sons.

Myerhoff, Barbara, and Andre Simic, eds.
1977 *Life's career—aging: cultural variations in growing old*. Beverly Hills: Sage Publications.

Pelton, Leroy
1978 Child abuse and neglect: the myth of classlessness. *American Journal of Orthopsychiatry* 48(4):608–617.

Radbill, Samuel X.
1968 A history of child abuse and infanticide. In *The battered child*, ed. Ray E. Helfer and C. Henry Kempe. Chicago: University of Chicago Press. Pp. 3–17.

Rohner, Ronald P.
1975 *They love me, they love me not: a worldwide study of the effects of parental acceptance and rejection*. New Haven: HRAF Press.

Scrimshaw, Susan
1978 Infant mortality and behavior in the regulation of family size. *Population and Development Review* 4(3):383–403.

Selby, Henry
   1974 *Zapotec deviance: the convergence of folk and modern sociology*. Austin: University of
      Texas Press.
Silver, George A.
   1978 *Child health: America's future*. German Town, MD: Aspen Systems Corporation.
Solomon, Theo
   1973 History and demography of child abuse. *Pediatrics* 51(4):773–776.
Spinetta, John J., and David Rigler
   1972 The child-abusing parent: a psychological review. *Psychological Bulletin* 77(4):
      296–304.
Steele, Brandt F.
   1970 Violence in our society. *Pharos of Alpha Omega Alpha* 33(2):42–48.
Straus, Murray A., Richard J. Gelles, and Suzanne K. Steinmetz
   1980 *Behind closed doors: violence in the American family*. Garden City, NY: Anchor
      Press.
Whiting, John W. M., and Irvin L. Child
   1953 *Child training and personality*. New Haven: Yale University Press.
Williams, Gertrude, and John Money, eds.
   1980 *Traumatic abuse and neglect of children at home*. Baltimore: Johns Hopkins Univer-
      sity Press.
Young, Leontine
   1964 *Wednesday's children: a study of child neglect and abuse*. New York: McGraw-Hill.

CHILD ABUSE AND CULTURAL VALUES:
The Case of New Guinea[1]

L. L. Langness

Child abuse and neglect in the United States have recently been emphasized as serious and perhaps alarmingly increasing social problems (Kempe et al. 1962; Helfer and Kempe 1968, 1976; Light 1973; Martin 1976). As in the case of mental illness and other similar problems, we are somewhat handicapped in our understanding of child abuse by the absence of any widely accepted standard for what is "normal" or "acceptable" in the care of children. The problem is particularly difficult in so heterogeneous a nation as the United States. Radbill (1974), pointing out that what may be an unacceptable practice in one culture may be commonplace in another, has given us a useful historical perspective from which to view the remarkable variation in the human species' treatment of children. In this paper I would like to add to our knowledge of this variation by considering the case of New Guinea.

New Guinea, the second-largest island in the world, with a total population of over 2 million, with several hundred distinct languages, and with a huge number of autonomous and often small and isolated political groups and cultures, would appear to be a particularly fruitful area for the study of human variation. It is valuable for the study of child abuse and neglect specifically because we already know of extremes of variation in many aspects of culture

[1]Preparation of this paper was made possible by the Mental Retardation Research Center, University of California, Los Angeles (HEW Grant HD-04612-05). I wish to acknowledge the advice of Robert B. Edgerton, Jill Korbin, Harold Levine, and John G. Kennedy. The term New Guinea is meant to include the entire island.

which would appear to relate directly to such issues. In New Guinea one can find infanticide, initiation rites, child mutilations, sale of infants for both marriage and sacrifice, and forced homosexuality, to name only the more dramatic examples. Yet we know that the same people who practice these customs also value their children highly, and thus the practices must be seen and understood in the context of the particular belief systems that produce them. It is paradoxical indeed that although such customs were widespread in aboriginal New Guinea, child abuse, from the natives' point of view, was probably no more common than is cannibalism, from our point of view, in the United States. By western European standards some New Guinea customs were truly bizarre, but by local standards they at least "make sense." Furthermore, New Guineans do have their own ideas of what constitutes child abuse and neglect, although these have seldom been reported. They also have views on the subject of western European child-rearing techniques as they understand them. In this chapter I survey the anthropological literature on New Guinea and also draw freely and in some detail on the case of the Bena Bena of the Eastern Highlands District where I conducted field research in 1961–62 and 1970–71.[2]

Infanticide, although some might argue that, strictly speaking, it is not child abuse, was widespread in aboriginal New Guinea. The prevalence is perhaps more comprehensible when it is understood that even without infanticide the infant mortality rate was very high and that children were often not regarded as truly human until they had survived for several years. And, although it was rarely if ever consciously stated by the people concerned, infanticide was a means of population control when other means were not available. A somewhat dramatic example appears in a letter by the late Margaret Mead, written from her field station in the Mundugumor area and dated September 1932: "And we've had one corpse float by, a newborn infant; they are always throwing away infants here, as the fathers object to observing the taboos associated with their survival" (1977:132). While this particular case might be seen as idiosyncratic rather than as a custom, infanticide, especially female infanticide, was quite common throughout New Guinea. The Bena Bena, for example, often killed a newborn daughter if the mother already had a small child to care for, and they also typically killed one of a pair of twins. Their explanation is couched in very practical terms: "Girls don't stay with us

---

[2]It must be understood that most of the customs mentioned in this paper are no longer practiced by New Guineans and that those that are, are practiced by only a handful of still very isolated groups in remote regions of the nation. Most of these customs were, however, practiced at approximately the same time, just before or just after substantial contact with western Europeans. They represent legitimate variations on the child-rearing practices of the human species in both historical and geographical perspective.

when they grow up. They marry and go to other places. They don't become warriors, and they don't stay to look after us in our old age." Or, more important, I believe: "Before we fought all the time. We had to take our children and pigs and run, and we couldn't carry too many children." The Bena Bena also state that if a woman had two small children she could not look after them properly (Langness 1967). The killing of one twin also occurred in other areas (Serpenti 1965:145). In some areas children born out of wedlock were killed (Van Baal 1966:155), but killing illegitimate children was unusual. Infants that were obviously abnormal were killed at birth in the Bena Bena area, Orokaiva (Williams 1930:95), Wogeo (Hogbin 1971:178), and probably in most other areas of the country. In Banaro society, "if two boys or two girls are born in succession, the second one is usually killed" (Thurnwald 1916:272).

Still other customs can be seen as abusive by western European standards. For example, from another group in the same general area as the Mundugumor, Mead reported the following:

> It was considered necessary that every Tchambuli boy should in childhood kill a victim, and for this purpose live victims, usually infants or young children, were purchased from other tribes. Or a captive in war or a criminal from another Tchambuli hamlet sufficed. The small boy's spearhand was held by his father, and the child, repelled and horrified, was initiated into the cult of head-hunting. [1963:242]

Similar practices are also reported for the nearby Chambri peoples (Gewertz 1977:132). That the Tchambuli boys were "repelled and horrified" could be merely a supposition on Mead's part, but certainly by western European standards both the children killed and the Tchambuli boys can be seen as victims of abuse. In other areas for which head-hunting is reported it is obvious that children's heads were taken along with those of adults (Williams 1936:277).

In the Bena Bena area, as well as in other areas of New Guinea, it was not uncommon for both male and female children to be captured and kidnapped during warfare. The stolen children would be raised by the kidnapper and would eventually be incorporated into his group. Female captives were sometimes married when they matured (Berndt 1964; Langness 1969; M. Strathern 1972; Williams 1930, 1936). Children were also exchanged as hostages when groups were attempting to bring about a truce and they might be exchanged for adoption to make it more difficult to resume fighting (Serpenti 1965:92). The feelings of such children are unknown, but it is probably reasonable to assume that the experience was, at least initially, traumatic, disruptive, and unpleasant. Both male and female children could be bought and sold, at least in some areas, and girls as young as seven or eight could be betrothed without their knowledge and taken to other groups where they sometimes could not even speak the local language (Langness 1969; Williams 1936).

In areas where cannibalism occurred children were sometimes killed and consumed along with adults. According to Van Baal (1966:746), "those of Sangase, for instance, also killed children, roasted human flesh in sago and gave it to their children, telling them that it was cassowary meat."

Although not so dramatic as those noted above, other cultural practices in New Guinea would be seen as abusive or neglectful by Western standards. Some of these are for the purpose of improving the child's health or beauty. In southern New Britain, for example, where a highly elongated skull is regarded as handsome, infants have their heads bound in bark cloth at birth; later the binding is renewed to ensure that the head will permanently have the desired shape (Chinnery 1925; Chowning 1972:158). The Kaluli people of the Great Papuan Plateau take day-old babies into the forest where they feed them crayfish and sago grubs; "the common concern is to 'make the child strong' and to please him and make him feel welcome so that he will not 'go back' to where he came from and die" (Schiefflin 1976:48). Sometimes children are malnourished as a result of certain food taboos even though the taboos are ostensibly for their protection (Lewis 1975). Sometimes they are forced to suckle against their will: "The only jarring note is some mothers' insistence on children suckling when sated. I have seen some savage conflicts when children of two or three years have protested against forced feeding. . . . conflicts over forced feeding are a child's first observable attempts at aggression towards others, and the outcome is variable" (Reay 1959:164). Asmat youths are made to sit with decapitated human heads between their outspread legs because it is believed the germinative power of the head (likened to a fruit) will be transferred to the genitals and thus make the boys able to reproduce (Zegwaard 1971:275). Again, we can only speculate as to the emotional or other consequences for the participants.

Still other practices, although they might have some conceivable educational value (as noted later), would be clearly unacceptable by American standards. Among the Bena Bena, young boys are sometimes given sticks and encouraged to chase and beat girls, the adults urging them to "stick it up her vagina" or "go and hit her hard." Both boys and girls are threatened "in fun" with axes and knives and they run crying in terror. Boys are sometimes told they will have their penes cut off (Langness 1972). Teasing of and threats to children are commonplace throughout much if not most of New Guinea, and even when done in play can reduce the youngsters to tears: "Sometimes boys or men sit facing each other and exchange endless numbers of these sexual or personal insults. This is usually carried off good-naturedly, but when young boys are involved, they are often reduced to tears by the end" (Heider 1970:191).

A widespread practice in New Guinea was the cutting off of small girls' finger joints during mourning ceremonies (Heider 1970; Langness 1972). In the Bena area the girls were rapped sharply on the elbow ("funny bone") and then the first joint of a finger was lopped off with a stone ax. In one case an infant's joint was actually bitten off by a man in mourning.

One could doubtless find many further instances of what western Europeans would regard as child abuse. Rather than attempting an inventory, however, let us examine one obvious, widespread, and relevant example, initiation ceremonies. Although there is considerable variation from area to area, and although such rites are absent in a few societies, the following description focussing on Bena Bena initiations contains several basic and fairly widely distributed elements.

Male initiations in the Bena and immediately adjacent area have three main stages. When boys are approximately five years of age they are dramatically removed from their mothers and their villages to participate in a daylong ceremony during which their earlobes are pierced. A sharp pig bone is driven through the lobe which is backed up with a piece of pork fat. The boys are feasted with pork, a relatively rare treat, and at the end of the day they are returned to their villages. Some idea of the experience can be gained from Read's account of similar rites among the neighboring Gahuku-Gama:

> Boys aged from five to seven years are removed from the care of their mothers during the course of the ceremony. They are not officially acquainted with the secret of the *nama*[3] yet, but the men compel them to bathe at dawn in a stream near the village and afterwards greet them with mock-triumphant shouts. They find the experience a shock, for they go to the stream in company with older boys and are surrounded by a throng of armed and decorated warriors whose continuous vigorous chanting is accompanied by the mass shrilling of the *nama* flutes. The children "go back to their mothers" at the end of the day, but their eventual separation from the women and their membership in the men's organization has been ceremonially foreshadowed. [Read 1952:11].

The experience is all the more traumatic because up until this time the boys have remained almost exclusively with their mothers and have spent only a little time with their fathers or other adult males. Barth's account for the Baktaman, which indicates clearly that the boys are badly terrorized, is similar (1975:51).

When they are about eight years old the boys go through a similar ritual in which the septum is pierced by the same means; by the age of ten or eleven they are permitted to sleep in the men's house, although they still do not know the secrets of the *nama* cult. Bena men say that before the boys are ten or eleven

---

[3] The *nama* is a mythical birdlike monster said to be with the men at this time. *Nama* is also the name of the bamboo flutes played at this time and regarded as sacred.

they do not have good sense and would not be able to escape from the men's house during the almost incessant raiding and warfare that occurred in the New Guinea Highlands prior to European contact.

The final initiation for most youths occurs when they are roughly between thirteen and seventeen or eighteen. At this time they are totally secluded from females for a period of at least a month or, probably more typically, for three or four months. During this period they live either in the men's house or in a special house prepared for them away from the village proper. At various intervals they are deprived of sleep. They are forced to stand uncomfortably near the fire and they are beaten with stinging nettles and with sticks. Sometimes they are actually held over the fire, especially if they have broken one of the many taboos they must observe. They may be denied water at times, and in some areas they are tricked into drinking contaminated water. The Keraki force their youths to swallow only partly slaked lime which severely blisters their mouths and throats (Williams 1936:201). The Iatmul of the Sepik River area practice painful scarifications of back and chest and submit their initiates to much bullying and humiliation (Bateson 1958). Among the Bena a small bow is used to shoot a miniature sharp-pointed arrow up the urethra until blood is drawn; the tongue is similarly shot until it bleeds. In some areas pieces of barbed grass are pushed up the urethra to achieve the same effect (Thurnwald 1916:265), and in still others the glans is cut with a piece of obsidian or, as among the Wogeo, with a crab or crayfish claw (Hogbin 1970). Finally, in the Bena and throughout much of the Eastern Highlands District, the youths are forced to swallow bent lengths of cane to induce vomiting. Bloodletting and vomiting are done in the river so that everything will be washed away, and the youths are enjoined not to allow blood or vomit to touch and thus contaminate any part of their bodies.

The initiation period ends with an enormous feast and exchange of pork at which the initiates are reintroduced into the community. They are dressed in new clothing, their faces are painted, and they wear beautiful headdresses of bird of paradise, cassowary, and parrot feathers. They also wear love magic to make themselves more attractive to females and usually other bits of magic to protect themselves from sorcery. As adult males they will practice bloodletting and cane swallowing for the rest of their lives when sick or, far more commonly, to rid themselves of the contamination of females after intercourse or even after prolonged contact with females.[4] Undoubtedly these rituals are exceedingly painful (Langness 1974).

---

[4]For far more detailed accounts of male initiation see Ian Hogbin's *The Island of Menstruating Men* (1970), K. E. Read's marvelously readable *The High Valley* (1965), and Gregory Bateson's classic account of the Naven ceremony (1958).

In some parts of New Guinea initiations of this general type are also characterized by male homosexuality. Among the Sambia, a remote Eastern Highlands group, young boys are made to live with older initiates and to practice fellatio. They spend several years as practicers of fellatio and then, when older, as the fellated. This practice is not accomplished without a great deal of coercion and fear but, interestingly, all males succumb and practice the acts and then, as married adults, rarely engage in them again (Herdt 1977). The Keraki of southwest Papua, with somewhat similar beliefs and rites, engaged in sodomy rather than fellatio (Williams 1936:194). Sodomy during male initiation was also practiced by the Marind-Anim farther to the west in what is now West Irian (Van Baal 1966:513). The Etoro of the Great Papuan Plateau engaged in oral intercourse; the nearby Kaluli practiced anal intercourse (Kelly 1977:16). The Onasbasulu, also nearby, produced the required semen by masturbation and then smeared it over the bodies of the initiates (Schiefflin 1972). It has been claimed that sodomy occurred in Tolai initiations (Parkinson 1907:544, cited by Errington 1974) and that the Karavaras engaged in fellatio at such times (Errington 1974). In any event, homosexual acts practiced on young boys were not uncommon in various parts of New Guinea, although bloodletting, beatings, humiliations, and tests of stamina were far more common. Before discussing the rationale for these initiation rites let us consider female initiations, which were in most respects quite different.

The initiation of New Guinea females usually occurs at first menstruation and, unlike male initiations, is an individual rather than a group rite. Although Bena Bena girls do at times have their noses bled with leaves just as the boys do, and Arapesh girls are reported to have stinging nettles rubbed on their bodies and thrust up their vulvas (Allen 1972:553), females in general rarely undergo the abusive treatment meted out to males.

Bena Bena girls are usually secluded for one complete phase of the moon. A special room is prepared for them inside the mother's or guardian's wife's house. The small room is decorated with colorful and magical leaves and a platform constructed for the initiate to sit on. She is not permitted to touch the ground during her seclusion and, in principle if not in fact, has to be carried outside by other women to perform her natural functions.[5] While she is in seclusion people prepare new clothing for her and gifts of string bags, tobacco, and other items. Often at night people from the villages, both male and female, come to sit outside the seclusion house and gossip and sing. Women and other girls of about the girl's same age visit her often and she is instructed in wifely

---

[5]The only explanation I have been given for this practice is that, if a girl sits on the ground, worms and/or snakes may get inside her and do her harm.

duties and skills. There is a certain amount of sexual banter, and often skits, mostly with sexual connotations and sometimes cross-dressing, are put on for the amusement of all. As far as I know there are no ordeals or painful rites associated with any part of this procedure.[6] The girl's "coming out" is a major daylong ceremony. Her legal guardian[7] slaughters pigs and gives gifts of pork and other foods to those who have given her gifts, come to sing to her, or otherwise participated in the ceremonies.

A Wogeo girl, at first menstruation, is unusually active for three or four days, during which time she ceremonially weeds the village gardens. She is not secluded from others. Her old skirt is ritually buried, she is anointed with red ochre, and there is much lewd jesting and sexual play. The men keep their distance and complain because the women so blatantly enjoy mimicking them and making remarks about their virility. At no time is the initiate harmed or humiliated (Hogbin 1970). In Manus a girl's menstruation occasions a great deal of ceremony and feasting, culminating in an exchange with her betrothed husband's family. Again, the girl being initiated is in no way badly treated or harmed (Mead 1968). Among Kapauku Papuans the girl is secluded for two nights and two days. She is kept company by a few older women, including her closer female relatives, who instruct her in wifely duties, bring her food, and advise her on the observance of taboos (Pospisil 1971:45). The Orokaiva ceremonies surrounding first menstruation were fairly elaborate, with seclusion sometimes lasting for several months but, as above, the girls were not mistreated in any way (Williams 1930:207).

In some New Guinea societies no rites at all are associated with first menstruation or female initiation; examples are the Kuma (Reay 1959:175) and the Mt. Hagen people (M. Strathern 1972:169).

At least three societies—Orokaiva, Koko, and Mundugumor—permit girls to participate in initiations with boys, but the girls' participation is always limited and they are exempted from most or all of the physical ordeals (Allen 1972:554).

That ritual defloration accompanying first menstruation was not completely unknown in New Guinea is indicated by the following early account:

> That same evening the orgies begin. When dusk breaks in, the men assemble on the streets of the village. The old men consult with each other, agreeing to

---

[6] Although I have witnessed at least half a dozen of these ceremonies it is impossible to be present at all times; thus I cannot say with absolute certainty that the girls undergo no painful experiences at all. It is my experience and my understanding that they do not.

[7] Every Bena girl has a legal guardian in the sense of a man who is responsible for arranging and accepting her bride-price and also for providing the pigs necessary to carry out her initiation ritual. The Bena explain their custom by saying simply that it is wrong for a man to accept pay for his own semen (Langness 1969).

distribute the . . . [newly pubescent girls] according to their custom. This custom was explained to me in the following way. The father of the chosen bridegroom really ought to take possession of the girl, but he is "ashamed" and asks his sib friend, his *mundu*, to initiate her into the mysteries of married life in his place. This man agrees to do so. The mother of the girl hands her over to the bridegroom's father, telling her that he will lead her to meet the goblin.

The bridegroom's father takes her to the goblin-hall and bids her enter. His *mundu* has already gone into the goblin-hall, and awaits her within. When she comes in, he, in the role of the goblin, takes her by the hand and leads her to the place where the big bamboo pipes (three to six meters long) are hidden. . . .

Before these hidden gods the couple unite. Afterwards the girl is led out of the goblin-hall, where her bridegroom's father awaits her and brings her back to her mother. The *mundu* returns home in a roundabout way, for he is "ashamed" to meet anybody on his way back.

The bridegroom's father goes back to the goblin-hall, and it is now his turn to perform the role of goblin, his *mundu* bringing him his son's bride.

After that, the same rite is performed with the other two girls.

The bridegrooms and the other boys, in the meantime, are confined in a house, set apart for this purpose, and watched by their mother's brother.

The fathers in their capacity of goblins are allowed to have intercourse with the brides on several subsequent occasions, but only in the goblin-hall.

The bridegroom is not allowed to touch her until she gives birth to a child. This child is called the goblin's child. [Thurnwald 1916:260–262]

It should be clear that male children especially, and females more rarely, are subjected to a variety of extremely abusive treatments when measured by Western standards. It is equally clear that by the local standards of New Guinea these practices were not regarded as abusive and, indeed, were believed to be absolutely necessary if children were to grow up to be healthy, normal adults.

Many of the practices I have mentioned, such as encouraging boys to be aggressive and attack girls, helping children to slay an enemy, forcing them to endure tests of stamina, and so on, can be understood as a result of the need to produce warriors. Traditional New Guinea societies were notorious for their almost incessant raiding and fighting[8] and for the value they placed on violence:

A characteristic of Highland cultures, and perhaps of Melanesia as a whole, is the high value placed on violence. The primitive states of Africa, and even the African stateless societies which we have been considering, are readily likened to the kingdoms and princedoms of medieval Europe, valuing peace but ready to go to war to defend their interests or to achieve likely economic rewards. Prowess in battle is highly rewarded but warfare is usually not undertaken lightly and most

---

[8]The best and most reasonable single account of New Guinea warfare is Mervyn Meggitt's recent book, *Blood Is Their Argument: Warfare among the Mae Enga Tribesmen of the New Guinea Highlands* (1977).

of the people most of the time want peace. In New Guinea a greater emphasis appears to be placed on killing for its own sake rather than as a continuation of group policy aimed at material ends. [Barnes 1962:9]

It is well known that the largest autonomous political groups in New Guinea were quite small and that most of these groups lived in almost constant danger from some or all of their neighbors (Berndt 1964; Gardner and Heider 1968; Meggitt 1977). To ensure survival a group needs many male children and each of them had no choice but to be a warrior. Socialization practices were designed to provide what was required.

Some of the customs can be understood as partly cosmetic, especially the piercing of the septum and the earlobes. In fact, the scarifications and piercings practiced on females might well be said to be primarily cosmetic. The cutting off of girls' finger joints is not so easy to understand, although it is done only in the context of mourning; adult women commonly cut off their fingers at such times as well. Philip Newman (personal communication) tells me that the finger joints are removed to placate ghosts. There is a widespread and intense fear of ghosts and children are particularly susceptible. The joint is removed so that the ghost will know that the child "will not forget his name." This would not, by itself, explain why only girls are mutilated, but boys probably escape because they have to become bowmen and warriors.

Perhaps the most complicated and most difficult to understand are the ritual bloodlettings and the homosexual practices associated with male initiations. First of all, one must realize that these rites are primarily religious in character (Read 1952). They are associated with the most fundamental beliefs about human nature, differences between male and female, and the relationship of people to their deceased ancestors and other supernatural beings. For the Sambia and others who engage in fellatio or sodomy, semen is believed to be the quintessential element for proper growth. Sambia boys are told that semen is the only means of attaining strength (Herdt 1977:237). If the youths are not inseminated regularly they cannot grow up to be strong men and successful warriors. Similarly, when a youth is later married his prepubescent wife should perform fellatio upon him to precipitate her growth (Herdt 1977:206). Much of the initiation has to do with ridding the initiates of any trace of feminine character or influence while at the same time maintaining power and control over females and the power of procreation:

> *Moku* initiation places an over-riding emphasis upon birth and sexuality. Men's concerns are to eliminate the "feminine" aspects of boys' being and, moreover, to simulate within him social and biological masculinity. This follows from a view of human biology in which feminity is believed to be an inherent process in maturation, whereas masculinity is not. Understandably, men over-emphasize masculinity at the expense of femininity. . . . Men harbour terrible anxieties

about the womb and menstrual blood, and they are concerned to eliminate these influences in a boy. But in addition men are blatantly envious of women's procreative powers, and they simulate them. These themes are interwoven throughout the beliefs and actions of all male ritual. [Herdt 1977:233]

Similar interpretations of male dominance and secret male cults have been made by others (Allen 1967; Hiatt 1971; Hogbin 1970; Langness 1967, 1974; Lindenbaum 1976; Meggitt 1964; Read 1952); the basic features are similar whether there is homosexuality or not. There is little point in pursuing this subject here beyond making the point that the elements involved, so obviously abusive in a western European frame of reference, are understandable in their own context. They are practices born of the ignorance of scientific biology and physiology and reinforced by the visible facts of female maturation, menstruation, and childbirth.

None of the practices I have mentioned would be seen by the practitioners as abusive. Strange as it may seem, child abuse in the sense that parents deliberately or even accidentally harm a child while punishing or disciplining it, as in Western groups, is virtually unknown.

With some rare exceptions, most New Guinea cultures seem to be extremely permissive. The following practice, although apparently acceptable among the Enga, would be unthinkable in the vast majority of other New Guinea groups:

A father early warns his children that the gardens are the mother's domain and must not be visited without her permission. A child who steals is lucky to escape with only a beating from the mother. Should she tell her husband, he is likely to punish the offender with great severity. He may slice the child's palm with a knife, chop off a fingertip, cut off an earlobe, cook it and make the child eat it, or smoke the culprit over a fire. At the least he will administer a sound thrashing. [Meggitt 1965:246]

In the Bena area farther to the east, and indeed in many groups geographically much closer to the Enga, children are virtually never punished, partly because children are believed to be irresponsible and even incapable of learning until they are approximately seven years old. As infants they are fondled and indulged almost incessantly, being picked up by someone whenever they cry and passed from person to person as a matter of course. The Bena almost without exception are fond of children and having children is the most important cultural goal (Langness 1965). This is true throughout New Guinea. The following description from the Keraki is fairly typical:

Parents show what is presumably a natural fondness for their young offspring. The show of care and affection is particularly noticeable between mothers and their young daughters. Whereas the small boys are running about in noisy troops at an early age, the little girl sticks by her mother's side, often finding her amusement in imitating her at her tasks, and as she grows in strength giving her some real help. . . .

The father will bestow his attentions impartially on his sons and daughters while they are infants. During his long hours of leisure he will often be seen sitting tailor-fashion before his house with the baby between his legs. He does not try to keep it amused but, perhaps more sensibly, leaves it to its own infantile devices while he gazes into space and just enjoys himself. But sometimes he will take it up and cuddle it, or stoop down to mumble its face in the full-lipped manner which is an acknowledged form of caress.

When the child is already running about and showing its independence, however, the father's interest seems to wane. In fact, now that the boy is amusing himself with his fellows, the father does not worry overmuch about him. He may remain fond and is always indulgent, but he gives small sign of that intense feeling of responsibility and solicitude which is relatively characteristic of the European parent. [Williams 1936:110−111]

Similarly, the following description of the Elema may be taken as representative of most of New Guinea:

Towards their children both fathers and mothers show a good deal of indulgence, especially in their early years. Of deliberate training there is obviously very little; of chastisement administered with a sorrowful hand with a view to moral correction, none at all. . . . One never sees a father using the metaphorical iron rod. He would hardly know how to do so. From childhood the boy begins to enjoy that peculiar private independence of will and action which seems to characterize the primitive society, however hidebound by custom. Fathers do not order their children about; and no full-grown native is ordered about by anyone. [Williams 1940:52]

Among Kapauku Papuans a mother may be reprimanded by her husband for even minor punishment of her children. Temper tantrums, which are common, are treated "through affection and through fondling" as they are believed to be out of a child's control (Pospisil 1971:39). Manus children, although taught some respect for property, are "allowed to give their emotions free play; they are taught to bridle neither their tongues nor their tempers" (Mead 1968:7). The Wogeo believe that as a child's vital spirit (*vanunu*) is free to return to where it came from at any time up to the talking stage, the "only hope of pleasing it . . . is to treat the child with indulgence." Thus infants "are fed even before they are hungry, comforted before they are hurt and reassured before they are frightened" (Hogbin 1971:182). Kwoma children are similarly indulged: " . . . all informants stated firmly that an infant is never punished" (Whiting 1941:29). Aside from occasionally being forced to nurse against his will, in a "somewhat haphazard but finally adequate way, a Kuma child is gradually prepared for life as a gregarious, extroverted adult, generous with things of little value and graspingly insistent on adequate return for things that matter" (Reay 1959:164). The Marind-Anim were "anxious to have children," and children were "welcome" and treated with "loving care" (Van Baal 1966: 138—140). The people on nearby Frederick-Hendrik Island[9] are so concerned to protect their children that they carefully wrap the children's feces in leaves and keep them in the house where they can be guarded against sorcery, since feces are one of the substances most commonly used by the ubiquitous New Guinea sorcerers. The Busama carry nurturance to such an extreme that new mothers postpone going back to their important agricultural tasks for four or five months[10] and when a toddler trips and falls, the ground itself is blamed (Hogbin 1963:60—62). These examples show that children, although painfully treated in the context of initiations or other institutionalized situations, are welcomed, indulged to an extreme, highly valued, and virtually never abused in the Western sense of that term.[11]

It could well be argued that the permissiveness of New Guinea child rearing actually results in neglect, but here, again, the perception of neglect is entirely relative. Certainly New Guineans do not perceive their behavior as neglectful. It is not at all unusual to see small children, even infants, playing with sharp bush knives, other dangerous objects, or fire (Hogbin 1963). Even from a most tender age, Bena children, especially boys, wander around together getting into all kinds of mischief, climbing tall trees, playing wherever they choose, with little attention from adults. Larger children sometimes attack smaller ones and, again, adults seldom intervene (Langness 1965, 1972). As children sleep more or less whenever and wherever they choose, they sometimes roll into the fire and can get badly burned. This is not to say that adults are not concerned, as they are, but given the kind of individuality and freedom they subscribe to, and given the facts of daily life, there is little they can do to regiment children's behavior. Indeed, they do not appear to wish to do so. Far from being "mere slaves of custom," most New Guineans are "rugged individualists" in the most meaningful sense of that term.

It is not that New Guineans do not perceive a category of child abuse. The Mt. Hagen people, for example, specifically recognize that parents,

---

[9]Apparently this island has been renamed Kolepon (Serpenti 1965:1).

[10]Four or five months is probably longer than average, but most New Guinea mothers apparently do stay away from their work for some period of time. Bena Bena women typically rest and stay with their newborn infants for at least a month.

[11]I have discussed the question of child abuse with six different New Guinea anthropologists who collectively have spent approximately 150 months in the field. With one minor exception, none of them reported anything that could reasonably be construed as child abuse and they all agree that child abuse, if it occurs, must be exceedingly rare.

though possessing the right of punishment, also have an obligation to protect the child from too severe punishment by the other parent (M. Strathern 1972:44). The Ilahita Arapesh understand clearly that although corporal punishment is well within the bounds of responsible parenthood it can at times get out of control and can be exercised for the satisfaction of the parent rather than for the good of the child (Tuzin 1976:161), precisely what seems to happen in many instances of child abuse in the United States. Similarly, the Bena recognize cruel or abusive treatment of children, perhaps partly because it happens so rarely. If such treatment does occur, a close relative usually intervenes, with the community sanctioning the intervention and shaming the culprit through gossip and avoidance. Although parents are universally perceived to have almost absolute authority over their children, the children are also regarded as belonging to the community.

That children are so rarely abused is all the more remarkable given that traditional New Guineans were known to be exceptionally violence-prone (Berndt 1962; Glasse 1968; Langness 1972; Meggitt 1977; Read 1955). In addition, parents, particularly fathers, had virtually unlimited authority over their own children and could, in principle, treat them any way they saw fit with little or no fear of outside interference other than gossip and shaming (Barth 1975:147; Reay 1959:75; Tuzin 1976:161; Williams 1930:91). Furthermore, in many areas of New Guinea there is a relatively high incidence of divorce (Glasse 1968; Glasse and Meggitt 1969), and there is almost ubiquitous hostility between husbands and wives (Brown and Buchbinder 1976; Langness 1967, 1969, 1974; Lindenbaum 1972; Meggitt 1964; Read 1952; M. Strathern 1972). All these factors are often linked to child abuse in the United States (Gil 1970; Kempe et al. 1962; Merrill 1962; Steele and Pollock 1968), but they do not seem to promote child abuse in New Guinea. How can it be, given the facts of New Guinea life, that there is so little child abuse? To understand why it is necessary to examine other dimensions of New Guinea culture and society.

First, given the existence and acceptance of both abortion and infanticide, there is no such thing as an unwanted child. As we have seen, children are desired and highly valued. Group strength depends upon having many children, especially sons, but female children are also valued. Both male and female children are economic assets and, of course, parents wanting to have the resources to provide wives for their sons must have daughters for whom they can get bride-prices from other groups.

After the first few days of infancy, the raising of children is in many respects a public activity. There is always an alternate caretaker available and the mother is never isolated with her child or left without help. Older female siblings are expected to look after the younger children, and they usually do so with a good deal of pleasure. Older experienced women ordinarily attend childbirth, especially first births, and they are always available to give advice if necessary. Adoptions of both male and female children are common, and so if someone does not take immediately to a child another parent can readily be found. Sociological parenthood is, practically speaking, more important than biological parenthood. Furthermore, even small children are free to change residences, at least temporarily, if they become angry or feel mistreated. As they always have relatives nearby, it is a simple matter to sleep with grand-mother, an uncle, or a cousin, and as the communities are small, the parents usually know where their children can be found. Thus a parent is never put into the situation of being the sole satisfier of a child's needs. Similarly, there is no such thing as an only child demanding constant attention from a parent. Children, especially male children, amuse themselves in gangs from a very early age, and even to see a lone child is a rarity. I have observed in the Bena, in fact, that boys resent it if a boy stays with his mother rather than joining them, and they openly express their disapproval. Adult males encourage them in such taunting and constantly remind them of the dangers of contact with females, who are universally believed to be polluting and potentially danger-ous to males.

In addition to these social factors, and equally or more important, are the values and beliefs of New Guinea cultures. Although physical punishment is by no means taboo in most New Guinea cultures, it is more or less randomly applied and seems to be more a result of frustration or disgust than an act of actual punishment. It is not uncommon for adults to strike children but the blows are seldom very hard. There is no such thing as a formal spanking. This leniency is related to the widespread belief that children under the age of seven or eight are basically unable to comprehend or reason and thus there is little point in trying to discipline them in any way. In a sense it is beneath an adult's dignity to attempt to discipline a child, so when children blatantly misbehave or refuse an adult's request they go unpunished and are simply ignored. For example, I have seen children on many occasions refuse to go for water when asked to, and I once observed some boys about six or seven years old stone a piglet to death and go unpunished.[12] But also related here are beliefs about the sanctity of the person. As indicated above, no one in New Guinea would presume to order anyone else about or assume that even if he did so the other would obey. New Guineans carry noninterference to the extreme of not even attempting to explain the behavior of others, simply shrugging it off as "their

---

[12]Actually, I have incident after incident of child misbehavior recorded in my field notes from January 1961 to May 1962, although they usually did not involve acts as serious as the killing of pigs.

way." This extreme individualism and tolerance are built into the socialization practices, and children quickly learn that they cannot be forced by others to do anything against their will. They are taught to dominate rather than submit. It is difficult to understand these traits and little has actually been written about them, but they are fundamental to New Guinea personality and culture and present a remarkable contrast to traditional Judeo-Christian beliefs about the rights and obligations of children. K. E. Read, one of the first anthropologists to visit the New Guinea Highlands, has written:

> Physical aggression, however, is not confined to intergroup hostility; it is the warp of the cultural pattern and is manifest alike in many day-to-day situations as well as many institutional contexts. Both men and women are volatile, prone to quarrelling and quick to take offense at a suspected slight or injury. They are jealous of their reputations, and an undercurrent of tension, even latent animosity, accompanies many inter-personal relationships. Dominance and submission, rivalry and coercion are constantly recurring themes, and although the people are not lacking in the gentler virtues, there is an unmistakeable aggressive tone to life. The majority of social rewards go to the physically strong and self-assertive, to the proud and flamboyant, to the extraverted warrior and orator who demands and usually obtains, the submission of his fellows. As a result, we find that people are markedly aware of themselves as individuals. They possess a strong feeling for or awareness of what I shall later refer to as the idiosyncratic "me," and the majority of social situations reveal a high degree of ego involvement. [Read 1955:254]

Obviously, to abuse a child would be entirely contrary to the type of character the culture both requires and values. "Strength" is a virtue in children just as it is in adults.

It is noteworthy that the one instance I observed of behavior that was clearly regarded as abusive and that outraged the entire village in which it occurred had to do with the unprecedented restraint of individual freedom. Two boys about six years old plucked the tail feathers from chickens that belonged to a "policeman" who had been appointed by the (then) Australian administration. Although the policeman was a member of the same village, and the act was not a particularly unusual one, for some reason he became angry and locked the boys in his house while he went away for the day. As the boys cried and screamed the angry villagers congregated in front of the house and stood for more than an hour, uncertain as to what they should do. They unanimously agreed that locking the boys in the house was a terrible thing for the policeman to have done. But as they had never had a policeman before and were frightened of the Australian administration that had appointed him, they were hesitant to act. Finally, they could stand no more. They broke open the door, released the boys, and threw a few shillings on the ground in front of the doorstep as recompense. The boys were not punished by their parents, either then or later. Not one single villager would defend the policeman's act and, in fact, people avoided him for several days thereafter. It was the physical restraint that was the issue, because traditionally such things did not happen.

One could also argue that another reason for the virtual absence of child abuse in New Guinea is that the daily stress and tension that often provoke parents into abusing their children are relatively absent in small-scale, face-to-face, slower-paced nonliterate cultures. Although there is no adequate way to measure the "quality of life," there is little question that members of such societies are not driven by the same motives to "succeed" or faced with the same choices and insecurities as those living in urban industrialized nations.

Finally, individual or idiosyncratic acts of child abuse may occur less frequently in New Guinea societies because of some of the customs I have mentioned. That is, whatever pent-up rage or hostility adults build up toward their children can be channeled into culturally constituted mechanisms that allow for its release. New Guineans, who are well aware of the painful and degrading character of their initiations, explicitly point out to initiates their past failures and inadequacies. "You didn't bring us food when we asked," or "You didn't help in the gardens and just ran around doing nothing," or "You didn't hear our talk when we told you so-and-so," are recurring themes when youths are being lectured during initiations. The hostility of adults toward children is manifest at these times, and elements of sadism and revenge, at least on the part of some parents, are obvious. The psychological components and the effects of initiation rituals are virtually unknown, but the evidence that is available points definitely toward this conclusion (Herdt 1977).

Yet to be "abused" by your own group acting collectively in accordance with all past tradition, and to hear that tradition and the necessity for it explained to you simultaneously, are quite different from being idiosyncratically abused by a disturbed and frustrated parent or stepparent. The social, psychological, and cultural consequences must be entirely different as well. The ability to endure the pain and degradation of abuse within the context of New Guinea initiations is a necessity if one is to become an accepted, knowledgeable, and valued member of the adult community. In the Western context, with which we are more familiar, such treatment appears to result in confusion and doubts about one's own self-worth, thus increasing the probability that the same confusion and doubt will be passed on to the following generation.

If it is true that initiation rites and other customs are institutionalized forms of abuse, and that this fact is recognized either implicitly or explicitly by the participants themselves, the question arises of whether certain behaviors may be considered as "abusive" irrespective of context. Abuse for the purpose of making strong warriors may still be seen as abuse. If we had a better grasp of the underlying psychodynamics of the participants, as well as of the various cultural contexts in which the different types of abuse occur, it might be possible to conceive of a more universal standard than we now possess. We might find in initiation rites, for example, that an older generation of men is (subconsciously) retaliating for the abuse they received as initiates, even though their behavior is rationalized as "for the good of the community." If the truth of this idea could be demonstrated, it would perhaps then be possible to argue that certain institutions are more "pathological" than others and that substitute means might be found for relieving such desires. It must certainly be true that male homosexual rites are motivated in part by desires for sexual gratification and dominance as well as for the stated purpose of making the youths grow faster. The fact that females are generally not "abused" during initiation rites and do not themselves abuse others in this way has suggestive importance in this context, yet little attention has as yet been given to it.

In addition to the commonplace principle that values and practices tend to be relative to the culture in which they are found, the materials I have discussed here lead to the inference that child abuse and neglect can be understood only in terms of the specific belief and value systems that either promote or inhibit them. It is not enough merely to assert that parents abuse their children because they themselves were abused, or that abusive parents are "psychotic," or that abuse is the result of poverty or retardation. We must also consider the value of children in a modern world where they are an economic liability, where poverty and affluence are two sides of the same coin, and where the generation gap stifles communication between parents and children. We also need to know what the psychological consequences of such changes may be. The Bena would be hard pressed indeed to understand how an infant could be allowed to cry because its hunger was not on schedule, or how children could be permitted to go hungry in a world of plenty. Although they would understand that a woman does not always want a child, they would not understand that some women would be systematically denied the means to abort them. They would be similarly perplexed that infants and children are made to sleep alone in private rooms and denied the breast in favor of sterilized bottles. Similarly, in 1962, when the first schools came to their area, the Bena were horrified to learn that children as young as six were required to attend. "How can they possibly be expected to sit still or learn anything?" was the immediate reaction, and more than one parent felt the ire of the European schoolmaster for failing to send their young children when requested. Had I tried to explain to Bena friends and informants in 1962 that some people in the United States beat small children until they are seriously damaged, lock them in closets, starve them, deliberately burn them, or whatever, I doubt seriously they would have believed me. That type of "savagery" would have been entirely beyond their comprehension.

REFERENCES

Allen, Michael
  1967 *Male cults and secret initiations in Melanesia.* Melbourne: Melbourne University Press.
  1972 Initiation. In *The encyclopedia of Papua New Guinea.* Melbourne: Melbourne University Press. Vol. I, pp. 552–558.

Barnes, John A.
  1962 African models in the New Guinea Highlands. *Man* 62:5–9.

Barth, Fredrik
  1975 *Ritual and knowledge among the Baktaman of New Guinea.* New Haven: Yale University Press.

Bateson, Gregory
  1958 *Naven.* Stanford: Stanford University Press.

Berndt, Ronald M.
  1962 *Excess and restraint.* Chicago: University of Chicago Press.
  1964 Warfare in the New Guinea Highlands. *American Anthropologist* 66, pt. 2(4): 183–203.

Brown, Paula, and Georgeda Buchbinder
  1976 *Man and woman in the New Guinea Highlands.* Special Publication of the American Anthropological Association, no. 8.

Chinnery, E. W. Pearson
  1925 *Anthropological reports nos. 1 and 2.* Territory of New Guinea. Melbourne: H. J. Green, Government Printer.

Chowning, Ann
  1972 Child rearing and socialization. In *The encyclopedia of Papua New Guinea.* Melbourne: Melbourne University Press. Vol. I, pp. 156–164.

Errington, Frederick Karl
  1974 *Karavar: masks and power in a Melanesian ritual.* Ithaca: Cornell University Press.

Gardner, Robert, and Karl Heider
  1968 *Gardens of war.* New York: Random House.

Gewertz, Deborah
  1977 From sago suppliers to entrepreneurs: marketing and migration in the Middle Sepik. *Oceania* 48(2):126–140.

Gil, David
  1970 *Violence against children: physical child abuse in the United States.* Cambridge: Harvard University Press.

Glasse, Robert M.
  1968 *Huli of Papua.* Paris: Mouton.

Glasse, Robert M., and Mervyn J. Meggitt, eds.
  1969 *Pigs, pearlshells and women: marriage in the New Guinea Highlands.* Englewood Cliffs, NJ: Prentice-Hall.

Heider, Karl
  1970 *The Dugum Dani.* Chicago: Aldine.

Helfer, Ray E., and C. Henry Kempe, eds.
  1968 *The battered child.* Chicago: University of Chicago Press.

1976 *Child abuse and neglect: the family and the community.* Cambridge: Ballinger.

Herdt, Gilbert
1977 The individual in Sambia male initiation. Ph.D. dissertation, Australian National University, Canberra.

Hiatt, Les
1971 Secret pseudo-procreation rites among the Australian aborigines. In *Anthropology in Oceania*, ed. L. R. Hiatt and Chandra Jayawardena. San Francisco: Chandler Publishing. Pp. 77–88.

Hogbin, Ian
1963 *Kinship and marriage in a New Guinea village.* London: Athlone Press.

1970 *The island of menstruating men.* San Francisco: Chandler Publishing.

1971 A New Guinea childhood from conception to the eighth year. In *Melanesia: readings on a culture area*, ed. L. L. Langness and John Weschler. San Francisco: Chandler Publishing. Pp. 173–213.

Kelly, Raymond C.
1977 *Etoro social structure: a study in structural contradiction.* Ann Arbor: University of Michigan Press.

Kempe, C. Henry, Frederic W. Silverman, Brandt F. Steele, William Droegmueller, and Henry K. Silver
1962 The battered child syndrome. *Journal of the American Medical Association* 181:17–24.

Langness, L. L.
1965 Hysterical psychosis in the New Guinea Highlands: a Bena Bena example. *Psychiatry* 28(3):258–277.

1967 Sexual antagonism in the New Guinea Highlands. *Oceania* 37(3):161–177.

1969 Marriage in Bena Bena. In *Pigs, pearlshells and women*, ed. R. M. Glasse and M. J. Meggitt. Englewood Cliffs, NJ: Prentice-Hall. Pp. 38–55.

1972 Violence in the New Guinea Highlands. In *Collective Violence*, ed. James F. Short, Jr., and Marvin E. Wolfgang. Chicago: Aldine. Pp. 171–185.

1974 Ritual, power and male dominance in the New Guinea Highlands, *Ethos* 2(3):189–212.

Lewis, Gilbert
1975 *Knowledge of illness in a Sepik society: a study of the Gnau, New Guinea.* London: Athlone Press.

Light, Richard J.
1973 Abused and neglected children in America: a study of alternative policies. *Harvard Educational Review* 43:556–598.

Lindenbaum, Shirley
1972 Sorcerers, ghosts, and polluting women: an analysis of religious belief and population control. *Ethnology* 11(3):241–253.

1976 A wife is the hand of man. In *Man and woman in the New Guinea Highlands*, ed. Paula Brown and Georgeda Buchbinder. Special Publication of the American Anthropological Association, no. 8. Pp. 54–62.

Martin, Harold P., ed.
1976 *The abused child: a multidisciplinary approach to developmental issues and treatment.* Cambridge: Ballinger.

Mead, Margaret
  1963 *Sex and temperament in three primitive societies*. New York: William Morrow.
  1968 *Growing up in New Guinea*. New York: William Morrow.
  1977 *Letters from the field, 1925–1975*. New York: Harper and Row.
Meggitt, Mervyn J.
  1964 Male-female relationships in the Highlands of Australian New Guinea. *American Anthropologist* 66:204–224.
  1965 *The lineage system of the Mae Enga of New Guinea*. New York: Barnes and Noble.
  1977 *Blood is their argument: warfare among the Mae Enga tribesmen of the New Guinea Highlands*. Palo Alto: Mayfield.
Merrill, E. J.
  1962 Physical abuse of children: an agency study. In *Protecting the battered child*, ed. V. DeFrancis. Denver: American Humane Association.
Parkinson, Richard
  1907 *Thirty years in the Southseas*. Trans. from German by N. C. Barry. In collection of Australian National University Library, Canberra.
Pospisil, Leopold
  1971 Kapauku Papuans and their law. In *Yale University Publications in Anthropology*, no. 54. New Haven: HRAF Press.
Radbill, Samuel X.
  1974 A history of child abuse and infanticide. In *The battered child*, ed. Ray E. Helfer and C. Henry Kempe. 2d ed. Chicago: University of Chicago Press. Pp. 3–21.
Read, K. E.
  1952 *Nama* cult of the Central Highlands, New Guinea. *Oceania* 23(1):1–25.
  1955 Morality and the concept of the person among the Gahuku-Gama. *Oceania* 25:234–282.
  1965 *The high valley*. New York: Scribners.
Reay, Marie
  1959 *The Kuma*. Melbourne: Melbourne University Press.
Schieffelin, Edward L.
  1972 The Gisaro: ceremonialism and reciprocity in a New Guinea tribe. Ph.D. dissertation, University of Chicago.
  1976 *The sorrow of the lonely and the burning of the dancers*. New York: St. Martin's Press.
Serpenti, L. M.
  1965 *Cultivators in the swamps*. Assen: Van Gorcum.
Steele, Brandt F., and Carl B. Pollock
  1968 A psychiatric study of parents who abuse infants and small children. In *The battered child*, ed. Ray E. Helfer and C. Henry Kempe. Chicago: University of Chicago Press. Pp. 103-147.
Strathern, Andrew
  1972 *One father, one blood*. Canberra: Australian National University Press.
Strathern, Marilyn
  1972 *Women in between*. New York: Seminar Press.
Thurnwald, Richard
  1916 Banaro society. In *Memoirs of the American Anthropological Society*, Vol. III, no. 4.

Tuzin, Donald F.
> 1976 *The Ilahita Arapesh: dimensions of unity*. Berkeley, Los Angeles, London: University of California Press.

Van Baal, J.
> 1966 *Dema: description and analysis of Marind-Anim culture (South New Guinea)*. The Hague: Martinus Nieshoff.

Whiting, John W. M.
> 1941 *Becoming a Kwoma: teaching and learning in a New Guinea tribe*. New Haven: Yale University Press.

Williams, F. E.
> 1930 *Orokaiva society*. Oxford: Clarendon Press.

> 1936 *Papuans of the Trans-Fly*. Oxford: Clarendon Press.

> 1940 *Drama of Orokolo: the social and ceremonial life of the Elema*. Oxford: Clarendon Press.

Zegwaard, Gerald A.
> 1971 Headhunting practices of the Asmat of West New Guinea. In *Melanesia: readings on a culture area*, ed. L. L. Langness and John Weschler. San Francisco: Chandler Publishing. Pp. 254–278.

CHILD ABUSE AND NEGLECT IN SUB-SAHARAN AFRICA 3

Sarah LeVine and Robert LeVine

In Africa south of the Sahara children remain the most highly valued possessions of their parents: they represent the continuation of religious and moral life as well as economic hope for the future. Africa is home to the heaviest concentration of preindustrial people, many of whom are still largely unaffected in their outlook and values by the principles of any one of the great world religions. Outsiders tend to view Africans as exotic, if not barbaric, especially in terms of traditional practices related to child rearing and initiation. They tend to evaluate these practices in negative terms, without regard to the purposes they might be fulfilling within a particular cultural context. Though Leontine Young may insist that child abuse and neglect are an integral part of the modern world (Young 1964), even in our own society we have difficulty in defining these terms satisfactorily. Definition, then, is likely to be all the more problematic in an exotic culture.

Any attempt to generalize about Africa must take into account its size and scope. It is the second largest land area in the world, with more than a quarter of a billion people divided by language and custom into 800 or more groupings and a wide range of habitats, institutions, and life-styles. Sub-Saharan Africa alone contains enormous socioeconomic and cultural variations, documented in an extensive anthropological literature. By contrast, however, documentation on childhood in Africa is sparse: a handful of monographs, a larger number of ethnographic articles and chapters, and a small but growing number of psychological studies. It would probably be correct to state that there is no published information concerning child care among the majority of African peoples; we are left to assume that their beliefs and practices in that domain resemble those of their neighbors living under similar conditions on whom there is some fragment of description.

Given this state of affairs, a genuine survey of child abuse and neglect in sub-Saharan Africa is not yet feasible. In its place, we present material from our own research and observations in Kenya and Nigeria, supplemented when possible by data from published sources. In order to facilitate comparison with other parts of the world, we generalize beyond cited sources when our experience leads us to believe it is justifiable. The evidence, however, is thin, and other observers might interpret it differently.

Child abuse and child neglect are properly seen from an anthropological perspective as categories indigenous to the West which arouse public condemnation here and have recently become matters of grave public concern. The use of these terms presumes our culture's contemporary standards of care for children. Since the standards of Africans differ from ours in some respects, we may expect to encounter the usual problems inherent in using one culture's criteria to classify behavior in a different cultural context. For example, in the 1950s and early 1960s we found the force-feeding of infants to be a common practice in certain parts of Kenya and Nigeria; it was also reported in Ghana (Kaye 1962). In this process the baby's nostrils are blocked in order to induce the intake of gruel, which often causes a good deal of coughing and is risky for the child's health and survival. Western observers using their own standards might classify force-feeding as a form of child abuse. The anthropologist, however, seeking to understand indigenous standards, comes to view it as part of African folk pediatrics, resulting from a cultural definition of infancy as a chronic medical emergency in which the continuous intake of liquids is required to prevent a dehydration that might be fatal (see LeVine 1977). If this interpretation is correct, force-feeding is intended to contribute to the child's survival. Whether it does so in fact is an empirical question concerning the efficacy of a folk medical system, not a moral question centered on parental attitudes toward the health and welfare of their children.

Similar problems arise in regard to ceremonial circumcision and clitoridectomy and the arranged marriage of young girls. By Western criteria these practices may be seen as abusive and coercive, but an ethnographic account of their institutional and ideological contexts shows how they conform to local ideals and how parents believe they are acting in the best interests of their children. To judge such customs without considering both their indigenous meanings and the parental attitudes that accompany their enactment would be worthless.

In approaching this subject for Africa, then, nothing is more important than clarity as to whose standards are being invoked when issues of abuse and neglect are discussed. We shall be as clear as possible on this point, by organizing our presentation around it. We begin with the question of what types of treatment are considered abusive or neglectful by African standards and proceed to consideration of practices tolerated in Africa which might be considered abusive or neglectful by external or transcultural standards. Last we offer some comments on the nature of the child who is the product of these practices.

CHILD ABUSE AND NEGLECT AS SEEN BY AFRICANS

Since problems related to child care have not yet become matters of continuous public discourse in Africa, the task of describing and explaining indigenous parental attitudes and behavior falls to anthropologists who have worked with parents in African communities. What African rural parents want for their children is not substantially different from what parents elsewhere in the world want: health and physical survival, the development of economic and social competence. Their ideas about how to achieve these goals reflect the environmental conditions in which they are raising children, including a generally high level of infant mortality, domestically organized agriculture and animal husbandry, and an age stratified structure of authority. They define infancy as a period of intensive physical care, with an emphasis on feeding, health care, rapid response to crying, and constant availability of mother or other caretaker. Goals of physical growth and development, including motoric maturation, are paramount during this time. This does not mean that behavioral development during infancy is of no consequence for rural Africans—there are many individual and cultural variations in this domain— but the primacy of physical nurturance seems to be universal among them. Indeed, African parents often speak of it as related to one of their most fundamental values, fertility. Everywhere in Africa, the positive value of reproduction is given an emphasis, in collective as well as personal expressive forms, which can hardly be overestimated. The nurturing of healthy and strong infants is the realization of this value. After infancy, parents tend to emphasize obedience in both its pragmatic (child labor) and moral (respect for authority) aspects. They assume that the young child will be largely socialized by his older siblings and other children as the mother turns her primary attention to the next child. This context, briefly stated, is the one in which most rural Africans think about the care of children and from which discussions of child abuse and neglect in Africa must start.

In the traditional period in Africa it would seem that, as in Western agricultural society before the industrial revolution, life was hard and often very short, but it was lived within the multiple constraints of a tight social system which clearly spelled out its demands and expectations. It is when that social system starts to fall apart that we begin to come upon instances of abuse and neglect which the old order largely prohibited. Contemporary African parents, however, might yet be hard put to identify instances of abuse per se: child rearing is the exclusive province of the family into which outsiders of any sort, whether neighbors or representatives of governmental agencies, are not licensed to intrude. Parents believe that they should be at liberty to handle their offspring as they think fit, the assumption being that their behavior will be in accordance with the socialization goals of their particular culture. Thus Africans would have difficulty in agreeing on what kinds of behavior constitute abuse; sexual molestation or excessive physical punishment of children by an adult might be two rather rare examples of consensus. Excessive physical punishment, as seen in the "battered child syndrome" in the United States, is, in our experience, extremely rare. Corporal punishment was widely prescribed in traditional Africa for disobedient children and the methods included caning and, in some areas, painful punishments such as rubbing hot pepper into the anogenital regions. Our experience in East and West Africa suggests that corporal punishment occurred everywhere, was more talked about than practiced, and was reserved by most parents for serious infractions of family rules. We have not seen cases of children injured by parental punishment. Our general impression is that the kind of rage that results in the battering of children in the West tends to result instead in wife beating (for men) and in other hostile activities directed toward women (for women).

Sexual molestation of girls is a known phenomenon in tropical Africa. Among the Gusii we have encountered cases, for example, of rape of prepubescent girls by adult men who in many instances are the classificatory fathers of their victims (i.e., they are closely related members of their victims' parents' generation). We have also come across actual father-daughter incest. In addition, the seduction of pubescent girls by male schoolteachers is the occasion for recurrent scandals in Nigeria and Kenya. Intrafamily incest is often treated as a religious offense rather than a civil crime, but the seduction of schoolgirls arouses public ire and regularly results in teachers losing their jobs. It is our impression, moreover, that both battering and sexual molestation are more common where the impact of social change is conspicuous.

It would seem that Africans have less difficulty in reaching agreement on what kinds of behavior constitute child neglect. In the contemporary period, social and economic pressures have eroded traditional structures all over the continent and there is widespread awareness that the welfare of children has suffered accordingly. In many areas the population has doubled in little more than a generation, placing intolerable burdens on natural resources. Whereas in the past a subsistence economy may have provided a more than adequate nutritional level, the depletion of the soil and the continual division of land into ever smaller parcels has resulted in dietary deficiencies for the local population; in areas where conditions were already marginal at best, the reduction of resources and yields has been proportionate. Except in instances where inadequacies of diet can be rectified by major food purchases, nutritional intake tends to be increasingly marginal. Furthermore, having gone through pregnancy on a poor diet, mothers give birth to infants whose prospects for healthy development are already impaired, even before they are assaulted by a host of endemic physical hazards. Those who survive early childhood are often chronically anemic with low resistance to infection. Overpopulation tends also to have certain serious psychological consequences. The concept of "limited good" pertains to the African peasant as much as to any agricultural people the world over. When the "good" is viewed as not only limited but swiftly diminishing, it is likely that both as group affiliates and as individuals people will become more protective of their property and more suspicious of and competitive with others. In such circumstances a child tends to grow up with a heightened sense of precariousness and a tendency to be suspicious of others at very slight provocation; trust, while not easily established, is too easily forfeited.

Although these may be some of the more subtle effects of contemporary demographic trends, ordinary Africans recognize and deplore the consequences to children of grosser social and economic changes. They realize that out-of-wedlock pregnancies, the abandonment of the form and constraints of customary marriage, as well as the increase, in many areas, of divorce, result in large numbers of children whose physical care and socialization are likely to be less than optimal for the ultimate production of mature adults as defined by the standards of those societies.

Infanticide, as formerly practiced for religious purposes in certain African societies (for example, the ritual murder of twins among the Kikuyu), would seem to have been eliminated in the contemporary period. Nowadays, however, it appears in a rather different form involving illegitimate offspring, that is, of a woman who has never lived in a conjugal relationship with the child's father. More usually, at least in Gusiiland, the victim is male rather than female, for in a patrilineal society a baby boy compromises his young mother more than does a baby girl. On the other hand, the ultimate solution of infanticide is probably very rarely employed. Meanwhile most "marginal" children, whether they are the residue of casual unions or of marital breakup, constitute a rapidly increasing high-risk population. Cared for by older women of the grandparental generation who, with their childbearing days over, may be disappointed at being deprived of leisure, by stepmothers, or by young mothers whose primary preoccupation is with finding a husband, these children are likely to bear the brunt of their caretakers' ambivalence. Thus in the course of our research among the Gusii, we discovered that those children who were born out of wedlock or who came from marriages terminated by divorce or by the death of one parent, while constituting only 2.5 percent of the study population, amounted to 25 percent of the malnourished children in the area. Marginal children tend to receive inferior care, in effect because they are dispensable (Dixon et al. 1976). The Gusii have a saying, "Another woman's child is like cold mucus," that is, something most unattractive which clings. Other proverbs graphically illustrate the thanklessness of rearing a child to whom one has not oneself given birth; when the immediate biological tie is absent one has little chance of receiving any future return for one's efforts. In the present generation, in which even biological parents often have their expectations of economic support from adult offspring disappointed, the rewards of stepparenting are all the more uncertain. Meanwhile, at a time when domestic resources are diminishing, the financial investment required in child rearing is, with the spread of Western education, escalating rapidly. It was hardly surprising then to discover that, in our research community of 2,100 people located in a fertile area, enjoying a relatively healthy climate, five of the eight children under five years of age who died in a two-year period were either illegitimate, that is, born of a casual union in the maternal home, or were being reared by grandmothers. In a society that values children above all else, we found nevertheless that some children were valued more highly than others.

An additional stress on family life in some parts of Africa is alcoholism. This phenomenon, which has long been a feature of both reservation and urban life in central and southern Africa, has in the last generation had a marked impact on domestic affairs in East Africa as well. Why alcoholism should be a major social problem on the eastern but not the western side of the continent is a complicated question, and one that we can here touch on only briefly. It seems that the fact that beer drinking played a less vital part in the cultural life of West as opposed to East and southern African societies has some bearing on this issue, although the impact on East and southern African self-esteem of having to accept inferior status to a European settler population must also be of relevance. In addition, while West Africans tended tradition-ally to live in towns and villages that could continue to provide social supports even after those societies began to experience the impact of modernization, the Bantu people of East, central, and southern Africa lived in scattered settle-ments, each lineage head occupying his own homestead at a distance from his neighbor, to whom he might or might not be closely related. This arrangement offered fewer social supports to its adherents than did the clustered settlements of West Africa. The line between a sense of well-being and one of loss and anomie may perhaps be rather easily crossed in a setting in which interdependence between one family or lineage and another is relatively uninstitutionalized. Thus we find that whereas in the past in many East African groups drinking was a feature of ritual events, or was used as wages after group work projects, participated in by senior men and women past menopause, it is now available to people of both sexes and all ages, including children. Thus the capacity of parents who are heavy drinkers to make the economic and disciplinary inputs, considered essentials of parenting in traditional times, is reduced, and the process of social disintegration is accelerated as problematic families, in both rural and urban areas, release their poorly equipped offspring into a stressful environment. The rate at which parents under the influence of alcohol are actually abusive to their children is difficult to determine. During our fieldwork in Gusiiland we frequently heard of drunken men beating their wives, or vice versa; rarely did instances of inebriated parents inflicting undue physical harm upon their children come to our attention. On those few occasions it was most often the father who was the offender; rather than abusing young children, in each case he had beaten an adolescent son who, having retaliated in kind, escaped. Much more frequently we came across evidence of the ongoing daily social and economic deterioration that occurs when parents spend a large proportion of their time and financial resources on alcohol. Our data show that if only the father drinks, the repercussions on the family's welfare are considerable. But the consequences are much more severe if the mother is a "serious" drinker, whether or not her husband is also of that persuasion. In an era in which farms are frequently no more than, and often less than, two acres, women may have more free time now than in the past; thus, if they confine their drinking to the latter part of the day, they may not in fact be neglecting their agricultural tasks to any marked degree. However, the quality of family life is inevitably impaired. For example, in our survey of drinking mothers, many stated that they could not afford to drink as much as they in fact did. We observed, moreover, that these mothers, regardless of whether they drank a little or to excess, spent more time out of the home than did nondrinkers: not only were they occupied in the fields for many hours in the earlier part of the day, but, having finished those tasks, several times a week they went off to "find beer" and did not return until dark. Their young children were left alone for many hours, often without adult supervision. Only rarely did we find a drinking mother who consistently went to the trouble, even when food was abundant, of providing her family with a hot meal in the middle of the day, whereas this practice was common among nondrinkers. In addition, older children of drinking mothers were less likely to be attending school than were children of teetotalers, in some instances because of parental poverty. Sometimes, even when the building fees had been paid and uniforms bought, children were truant, since their mothers, whose husbands were often working out of the district, were unable or unmotivated to enforce school attendance. Even in those families whose children did not seem to be economically or educationally deprived, the domestic climate was affected: marital discord seemed to be a more prominent factor as husbands accused wives of adulterous behavior while drunk, and late afternoons in the homestead were routinely turbulent when mothers returned from beer parties or the neighborhood club. In some instances children were habitually left alone after dark. When an older sibling was in charge, firewood could be gathered and the evening meal prepared in the mother's absence, but children who were all still small might be forced to go hungry until very late. In homesteads where beer was brewed and sold, children were subjected to more insidious forms of neglect. In an inflationary period many women risk imprisonment to brew and sell beer and corn liquor at home in order to generate an income to supplement meager cash returns from agricultural products. In such cases children are exposed from infancy to drunken strangers, as well as to alcohol itself. We frequently saw babies drinking millet beer and sometimes corn liquor. It was our impression that such children often grow up addicted to alcohol, and their need for it leads them to various kinds of delinquent behavior from an early age.

Whereas in the past beer drinking in Gusiiland was an institutionalized activity, to be pursued under restricted circumstances, in the current period it is the most widely manifested expression of personal depression and discontent. Moreover, our data suggest that the single most important indicator for sustained success in the modern sector is whether or not a person drinks at all: under stress someone who hitherto drank rarely may suddenly begin to drink to excess, a tendency the community has no resources to rectify.

Although parents may themselves be only marginally involved in the modern sector, their children face great pressure to achieve in nontraditional ways, since to fail is to accept consignment to an anomic vacuum. Gusii children, like all children growing up today in a situation of rapid and disorganized social change, need a reassuring familial environment, quite as much as, if not more than, their parents did. That those whose needs for such reassurance are not met are at risk is evident to many Africans today. They regret the effects on children of certain social problems, much as in the preindustrial West our ancestors might have regretted the effect on family life of similar problems in their own times.

AFRICAN PRACTICES CLASSIFIED AS ABUSIVE OR NEGLECTFUL BY EXTERNAL STANDARDS

In this section we review practices that have a basis in African norms of social behavior but would be deemed abusive or neglectful by Western standards.

In agricultural societies throughout history the familial domestic economy was of primary concern, and both the methods and objectives of child rearing closely reflected this priority. Like our own ancestors, African parents today are also concerned with input and output: rather brief periods of intensive nurturing should rapidly produce rewards in terms of the child's capacity to contribute to the economic life of the family. Parents are often dependent on their children's labor, which is regarded not as exploitation but as the universal obligation of the young to those who nurture them as well as valuable preparation for the child's future role in society. The use of child labor, like many other aspects of African child-rearing practices which have evolved in response to the exigencies of an agricultural economy, might seem harsh or neglectful by Western standards. Such practices should thus be carefully examined for their adaptive value before any negative judgment is made. Outsiders are often struck, for example, by the apparent lack of concern Africans have for the emotional—as opposed to the social, economic, or religious—consequences of their child-rearing techniques. As noted earlier, their objective is to produce an obedient and respectful toddler whose compliance with familial authority will be automatic. The period, then, of maternal indulgence tends to be short; even though a mother may nurse her child until the end of the second year of life, her role is one of pacifier and physical nurturer rather than of stimulator. Our Gusii data show that after infants are three months old the amount of eye contact permitted by their mothers declines rapidly and after seven months is rare; when it does occur, it is fleeting. While infants sometimes continue well past their first birthdays to attempt to engage their mothers in reciprocal play, particularly while nursing, their mothers tend to ignore these efforts. That they remain aloof must be the result of a number of factors: for example, a reluctance to spend valuable time in play when so many domestic tasks await their attention, and a perception that playful behavior, in and of itself, is not appropriate to the maternal role. In addition, never having been played with by their own mothers, these Gusii women might be uncomfortable with any activity directed toward pleasure rather than some specific utilitarian goal. For a mother to engage a small child, let alone an infant, in "conversation" would, to these women, seem eccentric behavior indeed, since, to a traditional African, a child is not a valid human being until he reaches the age of "sense," that is, until he is six or seven years old. Conversely, the practice of speaking to a child only to give him a command, far from constituting emotional neglect or even cruelty, seems to be entirely appropriate behavior.

The starkly functional nature—by Western standards—of the mother-child relationship which we noted in Gusiiland might be observed in many African societies. But if babies in Africa today may infrequently experience the kind of emotional reciprocity with their mothers considered essential to the future well-being of children in our own society, we would be mistaken in assuming that they do not establish relationships of trust and mutuality with other family members, particularly with older siblings and grandmothers.

In societies in which there is institutionalized avoidance between successive generations, the process by which children learn to differentiate between those individuals whom they should treat with respect and those with whom they may be intimate is initiated at a very early age. A Gusii mother, for example, uses the word "baba," which means "mother," as a term of endearment to her child; but since she herself has *chinsoni*, respect, for her own mother and must not engage in any sexual talk with her, the very word she uses as an endearment signifies her ambivalence. It is as if she is saying, even as she nuzzles her infant, "you and I are irrevocably separate." Gusii children receive both subtle clues and overt directives as to what is or is not appropriate kinship behavior. While the transgressions of a toddler may be tolerated, by the time he is four years old any failure to approximate the code would result in castigation for the offender who is seen to be, while yet a preschooler, *tari amasekane*, without respect. In much the same way, a Hausa child who ignores the *kunya*, or avoidance rules, between himself and his parents would be subject to chastisement. To an outsider such structures might seem gratuitous if not downright cruel, but a child growing up in these societies is generally assured of alternative sources of empathy.

If in infancy a Gusii baby's efforts to initiate play are largely ignored by his mother, very often a sibling will respond to his attempts by taking him from their mother's lap for an extended period of play, interspersed with soothing behavior. By the end of the first year, if not long before, babies have learned to direct their social behavior away from their mothers to alternative and more responsive partners. Although grandmothers may be reluctant to assume exclusive care of their grandchildren, they are often eager, provided they are physically fit, to engage a young child in the kind of playful behavior for which his own mother has neither time nor, in some societies, permission. Thus in a stable domestic situation children may find multiple sources of emotional nurturance and support, even though their mothers tend to be much less available to them, particularly after they have been weaned from the breast, than Western mothers would be. It is when these alternative relationships are less than adequate or unavailable that we find children who might, with justification, be termed deprived.

Although Africans themselves might recognize the physical deprivation resulting to young children from social isolation, it is unlikely that they would be aware of the emotional consequences. While in the Western world today we have become acutely concerned with factors that have a bearing on emotional development, some historians of the European and American family are of the opinion not only that this concern is a recent phenomenon (Stone 1977), but that our ancestors' methods of child rearing were at best harshly pragmatic, at worst sadistic; before the industrial revolution childhood was an unhappy period to be hurried through as quickly as possible. This may be an overly severe interpretation of the data available, but our preindustrial ancestors did seem to be motivated, of necessity, by survival factors. Upon them, as upon contemporary Africans, certain priorities were imposed, obligating them to function within a set of compelling constraints which allowed parents little leeway for maneuver. Thus, though children were highly prized as future security, their well-being may have had to be compromised on occasion in favor of immediate concerns. We are told, for example, that French Alpine mothers left their infants alone for many hours during harvest time, a practice that Shorter (1975) takes as evidence of neglect. But before accepting his evaluation we should first determine the age of the babies, the number of hours the mothers were away, and the distance from home at which they were working. Were there really no substitute caretakers like grandmothers or older children in the vicinity? Given the fact that to eighteenth-century French parents, just as to Africans today, children were highly valued, it seems unlikely that mothers would deliberately behave in a way that might endanger their children's well-being. Thus, if economic survival demanded that they leave their children on a routine basis for long periods, it should be assumed that, except in emergency situations, they made reasonable arrangements for children during their absence. What constitutes reasonable arrangements is of course open to debate. A French peasant of two hundred years ago and an African peasant of today might more easily reach agreement with each other regarding this issue than would a modern American with either of them. An American might perceive, for example, the practice of committing a baby to the care of a six-year-old nurse for a large part of the day as a hardship to both charge and caretaker, and he might find support for his views among educated Africans. Joseph Lijembe, a Luya from western Kenya, remembers that when he was four years old his baby sister, in the absence of any suitable female caretaker in the family, was committed to his care during the daytime: "As soon as my mother left for the farm in the morning, the loneliness would set in. I was in charge of a huge house and it was very dark and extremely untidy and even filthy" (1967:5). Outside were wildcats and thieves, and at first the little boy was frightened. He had to feed porridge to the infant, and when his charge was asleep he spent the time trying to comfort himself by imitating as best he could the domestic tasks he had seen his mother perform. In most African societies women, not men, are primarily responsible for routine agricultural tasks such as plowing, planting, weeding, and harvesting. If their role is triple-faceted, the role of farmer is next in importance to that of mother and stands before that of wife. A woman may not devote herself to childbearing and child rearing at the expense of her economic activities. Although, as in the instance described above, boys are sometimes engaged, child nurses tend more frequently to be girls, who, while freeing their mothers for agricultural work, are performing an essential task and at the same time learning by doing the fundamentals of the role of nurturer. Not yet strong enough to work in the fields, a preschooler can nevertheless contribute in a vital way to the family economy. Furthermore, it seems unlikely that these child nurses are often left entirely on their own. Lijembe (1967) tells us that, on becoming more at ease with his responsibilities, he began to venture outside the home and discovered other children similarly employed in the immediate neighborhood with whom he could play. It was certainly our experience in our work among both the Hausa and the Gusii that having responsibility for an infant sibling impinged rather little upon a preschooler's social life. Gusii boys, especially those approaching circumcisional age, would complain at being corralled into performing what they regarded as a feminine task, whereas girls, just as among the Ngoni (Read 1960), seemed to derive considerable satisfaction from taking care of a younger sibling. They were free to play in the meadow with other children but were rarely out of earshot of an adult; either a grandmother would be available in an emergency or else the mother herself would be working a few hundred yards away. Provided they were in good health, both baby and caretaker, more likely than not, seemed to find the arrangement mutually beneficial. Each found in the other a vital source of stimulation and affection. Even if the caretaker's attention to her charge tended to be sporadic—to be fitted in between other excitements—nevertheless an adult woman would often say that in childhood her closest relationship had been with that older sister who had acted as her *omoreri*, or child nurse.

In his autobiographical account Joseph Lijembe lists, in addition to caring for his sister, the many other duties for which, as a young child, he was responsible. These included gathering firewood, building and watching fires, fetching water, sweeping, and cooking. Only later, after circumcision, would he learn masculine tasks, such as house building and clearing the bush

(Lijembe 1967). By the time he entered school, at age seven, he was already fully integrated into the economic life of his family, having become competent in a number of areas which Western children today are not required to master.

Not only are African preschoolers of both sexes expected to contribute to the maintenance of the household, but in many societies children over the age of six are often sent elsewhere to perform menial tasks for other families. Such fostering arrangements or "child exchanges," found commonly in preindustrial Europe as well, separate young children from their mothers and might be assumed by the contemporary Western observer to have all manner of traumatic consequences for the children. For example, 50 percent of a sample of Gonja adults of both sexes had spent part of their formative years outside their families of origin, and 18 percent of a sample of children were currently being fostered (Goody 1973). But if fostering plays a prominent part in African domestic life today, it was even more pronounced in seventeenth-century England, according to Peter Laslett (1971). He estimates that two-thirds of all children at that time were either fostered out or sent as servants to other families for some part of their childhoods. The emotional consequences of these arrangements are difficult to determine, as our ancestors were disinclined to speculate on them. The upper classes then were far more concerned to obtain lifelong patronage or to strengthen ties of kinship; and the lower classes, to provide a child with an opportunity to learn an occupation.

In a largely preliterate society, fostering could be and can still be a form of apprenticeship which provides for the personal and economic advancement of the young person and at the same time enhances his usefulness to his family of origin. Just as parents in preindustrial Europe and America sent their children to live with—and be useful to—people whose social and economic status they perceived as being somewhat superior to their own, in the same way African parents ask an influential kinsman to take in a son or a daughter. In return for his or her labor and companionship, the child will acquire a formal education or some traditional skill such as weaving, dyeing, or smithing. The Gonja may prefer to use fostering as a way of consolidating maternal kinship ties, but in practice they send their children to kin with whom they are connected in a wide variety of ways. The Dinka, like the Gonja, prefer that their children be raised after weaning by the mother's family, returning only at about age six (Deng 1972). Among the Hausa, a woman's first child is born in the maternal home where mother and infant remain for some months. The mother returns to the father's house for the latter part of the nursing period. At weaning, the child, whose relationship with both parents is subject to strong avoidance constraints, is frequently sent back to his maternal grandmother with whom he will live until puberty (Smith 1954). In a patrilineal and patrilocal society, as an adult he will live in his father's place, but his emotional ties may be with his mother's family and his first marriage will most probably be with his mother's brother's daughter. Moreover, in societies, of which the Hausa is one among many, where life expectancy is low and the divorce rate is high, the need to maintain ties with the maternal kin is of great importance; at any moment a woman may require consanguineal support and, by entrusting one or several of her children after weaning to the charge of her own relatives, she is able to maintain an ongoing and reciprocal relationship.

In preindustrial Europe and colonial America the premature death of a parent, rather than divorce, was the primary cause of family dissolution; parental death signaled the dispersal of the older children into "service" and of the younger children to relatives (Thompson 1966). Our ancestors, like contemporary Africans, assumed that they could draw on their kinsmen in essential life-sustaining ways which are rarely available to us today. Often in times of severe need we must turn to public institutions to care for our children. Africans, in contrast, assume that fostering is beneficial to children, whether it is intended to provide the child with training for a short period, with a disciplinary experience following misbehavior (Colson 1958), or with a permanent home after familial dissolution. Furthermore, in many African societies children are regarded as the property not only of their own biological parents but of the extended kin group or lineage. In areas where, for example, infertility is a major problem, a childless woman can demand that her sister allow her to take and bring up one of the latter's children, usually a daughter. Mothers are obliged to respond to such requests, regardless of their personal feelings; the biological mother can reclaim her child only if cruelty on the part of the foster mother is proven (Smith 1954).

In traditional Africa people value group solidarity highly, and those who refuse the demands of relatives do so at great personal risk. Until recently children were fostered almost entirely by relatives, whose claims upon one another's resources could scarcely be denied. Nowadays, as African societies become more diversified along economic lines, poorer parents, like poorer parents in Europe and America only a hundred years ago, are increasingly willing to send their children as servants to economically advantaged but unrelated people. While children often receive payment for their services in money, clothing, or schooling, they are at the same time in the charge of strangers whose behavior is unconstrained by considerations of clientage or kinship. The dangers inherent in such arrangements are exemplified by an incident that occurred in Kisii District in the mid-1960s. Several dozen boys were recruited by a timber company in neighboring Tanzania. The father of each boy was given a sum of money in return for which it was understood that he terminated his parental rights and ceded them to the company, which then took its "slaves" (as they were called locally) off to the forests of Tanzania.

After Kenyan government officials discovered what had transpired, the children in question were repatriated and returned to their parents.

The incident was especially noteworthy because, unlike among the Ibo of West Africa, for example, where child slavery was known, it occurred in an area where no such tradition existed and no previous instance of the alienation of parental legal rights had been known. Indeed, even today parents virtually never surrender their infants for adoption to strangers, despite the increasing economic hardship incurred by raising large families. This incident suggests that mounting economic pressure might cause Gusii parents to consider selling their circumcised sons as a way, perhaps, of disinheriting them; unlike those of an infant, whose childhood still stretches before him, the claims of a circumcised boy on dwindling land resources must be acknowledged, unless, that is, they can be conclusively repudiated.

Economic pressures, then, have brought about profound alterations in the institution of fostering or child exchange in some areas, alterations about which African parents have mixed feelings. They are keenly aware of the differences between a voluntary and a commercial arrangement and of the risks inherent in the latter; in the absence of any other solution, they will send their children as hired help to strangers, with some regret. Indeed, at least in East Africa, as Western education becomes more widespread the practice of fostering children, whether by relatives or strangers, is viewed with increasing ambivalence by all parties concerned: parents, fearing mistreatment, are reluctant to send their offspring; would-be employers are skeptical about the staying powers of foster children (whether or not they receive remuneration for their services); and the children themselves are quick to exploit this ambivalence, either by exacting better conditions or by quitting the job.

We find, in addition, widespread ambivalence with regard to genital operations, particularly clitoridectomy, in groups that traditionally accepted them as rites of passage to full membership in the tribe. Early European travelers in Africa, especially missionaries, were horrified by these practices, and not knowing their cultural significance, began a crusade against them, with some success. Among the Kamba and Kikuyu of Kenya, for example, who have been subjected to missionary pressure for three-quarters of a century, the performance of female circumcision is declining and adolescent boys are likely today to be circumcised in a medical setting. Among the Gusii, however, whose traditionalism may be partly explained by their remoteness from the capital and by the fact that theirs was an area of Catholic rather than more revolutionizing Protestant missionary activity, circumcision for both boys and girls remains universal. At the beginning of the colonial period initiation rites were being performed in late adolescence, but nowadays they take place at an earlier age: girls are circumcised between the ages of eight and ten; boys, a year or two later. If children in the lower age range express reluctance, their parents wait until the children voluntarily request inclusion in that year's rites; without exception, children do indeed volunteer before they reach the upper age limit. Gusii initiation ceremonies take place at harvest time. The initiates in a neighborhood are separated according to sex, from before dawn of the circumcision day until midday, when they go into seclusion. They are subjected both to severe physical pain and to merciless hazing by older women in particular, who on this occasion are at liberty to unleash their anger at being displaced sexually. The initiates are admitted to "adulthood" only after they have unflinchingly endured physical and emotional humiliation. While certain adults speak freely of the traumatic nature of their own initiations, they do not view these procedures with the horror long exhibited by Westerners. On the other hand, some Gusii parents may recall their sufferings less with pride than with doubt that they were justified. They surrender their own children to the ordeal, but they may privately hope that their grandchildren will be spared, provided their status as AbaGusii, adult members of the tribe, is assured. Other practices such as scarification as treatment for illness, removal of the uvula in infants, and the application of tribal markings are being abandoned, depending on the degree of Western contact, in parts of Africa where they were traditionally performed.

Yet another African traditional practice to which Westerners have long taken exception is child marriage, which occurred mainly in Muslim areas. In the northern Nigerian town where we worked it was not uncommon to find women who had been married at age ten to men three or four times older than themselves. The articulated rationale for this practice was to ensure that girls were married before they reached puberty in order to avoid the risk of out-of-wedlock pregnancy. In the upper reaches of Hausa society there were often important political considerations as well. Our informants recalled the fear and unhappiness they had felt as the most junior, often the fourth, wife of men old enough to be their grandfathers, but they were not compelled to remain in their marriages.

Indeed, in our sample of 500 women more than half had been divorced and more than half again had been divorced more than twice. They were licensed then to flee the arranged marriage of childhood and take husbands of their own choosing, without incurring any stigma. Moreover, Cohen's data from the neighboring Kanuri reflect a similar flexible social situation (Cohen 1971). Although the practice of arranging marriages between young girls and older men continues in Muslim areas, the sharp rise in primary school attendance, at least in Nigeria in the past few years, suggests that many girls, particularly those of the feudal aristocracy who tend to be the first to gain access to education, are now waiting until they complete primary school to be married. The experience of an arranged marriage to a much older man may not be wholly palatable, but it may be less traumatic for a literate fourteen-year-old than it was for her illiterate prepubescent mother.

While, as noted earlier, there is little evidence of the use of excessive corporal punishment, African parents employ other forms of discipline to which Westerners might take exception. Among many East African groups, for example, a child is threatened by his elders from toddlerhood with supernatural punishment and attack by wild animals. Joseph Lijembe (1967:17) recalls that fear played a large part in growing up: "Whenever my sister refused to suckle, my mother always forced her to do so by slapping her. If she continued to cry for a long time she would be thrown out in the dark and my mother would invite wild beasts to come and eat her. As I grew older and had to sleep [after circumcision, which excluded him from the parental quarters] outside our home, I found it frightening to move about at night. I had to be given escort by my mother or father. I was afraid of the existence of night runners [witches], wild beasts and even ghosts, which my parents used to say haunted our home area". Like their Luya age-mates, Gusii children are threatened by their mothers with being eaten by wild animals, particularly hyenas, which, in those densely populated areas, have not in fact been seen in many years (LeVine and LeVine 1966). One is reminded of nineteenth-century English mothers who warned their fretting children, "Bogey [Napoleon Bonaparte] will get you," generations after Waterloo. Parents who even as adults are themselves terrified of both wild animals and evil spirits deliberately transmit such terrors to their own children. Again, having been similarly mocked in childhood, they ridicule the dependency wishes of the newly replaced child who is foolhardy enough to express his anguish. When a Tonga toddler wants his mother's attention, after she has given birth again, he is told, "I'll beat you if you try to sit on my lap again! You're no longer a baby!" After a time, when he has been punished enough for his tantrums, he will emerge from a period of depression and be absorbed into a play group of siblings and cousins (Colson 1958).

Discipline seems to reflect parental goals in much the same way as do other features of African child rearing. Americans look for ongoing emotional gratification from their children during childhood with uncertain prospects for financial return thereafter: they are concerned with emotional reciprocity and do their best to protect and promote this kind of relationship with their children. Thus, ideally, parental discipline involves, even with very young children, discussion and the temporary withdrawal of love. If physical punishment is imposed, Americans tend to experience regret and guilt afterward. In contrast, Africans regard their children as economic investments which, while they should begin to generate a return as soon as possible, offer maximum rewards during the parents' old age. Given the very different value they attach to the parent-child relationship, Africans are at liberty to assert their authority more directly than Americans. They also know, however, when they are overstepping the bounds of severity. Raum (1940) reports, for example, that a Chaga father, after beating his delinquent child, rubs salt and fat into the weal marks on his buttocks and then puts him into a bag filled with nettles. Yet we are also told that these punishments, though found among the Chaga and surrounding tribes, are rarely employed and then only by parents who have completely lost control of themselves. Furthermore, Raum adds, after such extreme behavior a parent always attempts to make recompense and to reestablish harmony: with younger children, by physical affection; with older ones, in some ritualistic manner. In the same way Gusii parents who curse their circumcised children are required to perform *ogosansorana*, reconciliation rituals of various kinds, without which they believe their children or their children's children will die or go mad. Without descendants to fulfill the requisite ritual obligations, parents would endanger their own moral and spiritual survival after death. A Gusii child, then, like children in many Bantu groups, is protected from parental violence by religious beliefs which dictate that transgressions of normative behavior necessitate ritual restitution.

Having different expectations of the parent-child relationship, an African parent feels less culpable when problems arise. Nor are onlookers quick to apportion blame; parents who fail to approximate proper standards of child care do not seem to be harshly judged. Mistreatment of children, though regrettable, is thought to be the result of a number of factors, of which the nature of the times, the fear of neighborly malevolence, and the possibility of ancestral retribution are just a few. In effect, abuse or neglect of children is not regarded as premeditated behavior, perpetrated with malice aforethought by a particular parent against a particular child. In Africa, where parental expectations are different, parental disappointments and frustrations are correspondingly different from those of a Western parent. Furthermore, those disappointments and frustrations, such as they are, are less likely, at least within a traditional supportive setting, to engender the kind of explosive rage and cruelty which we see occurring with ever increasing frequency in our own society.

THE NATURE OF THE AFRICAN CHILD

Despite the enormous changes taking place in Africa, the extended kin group has still not given way to the isolated nuclear family. With the possible exception of children of elite or single-parent families in an urban environment, most children spend their early years in a setting approximating the traditional situation. Women, then, can usually rely upon a female support group to provide for their own needs and also for those of their children; the latter are free to seek alternative sources of stimulation and affection in the larger circle of kin. When the burden of nurturing can be shared the consequences of parental omissions may be minimized. Children, meanwhile, continue to be regarded by their parents as economic capital. The primary maternal objective is still to ensure that the infant becomes a quiescent child ready to be put to work as soon as possible. Indeed, by Western standards the African toddler is a passive creature; he rarely looks for stimulation from his parents and rarely receives it, unless it is a directive of some sort. Our research into behavior disorders of young Gusii children revealed that hyperactivity, resistance to separation from the mother, and refusal to share food and playthings, to name just a few examples, are all known, but they are rare and are dealt with by punishment in varying degrees of severity and ingenuity. Bed-wetting, a common occurrence, is usually ignored in the preschooler, but a five-year-old might be told to climb a tree, to urinate at the top, and to climb down again, both ascent and descent to be accomplished with the eyes shut. Such an experience is expected to cure the problem. The Luyas, a people closely related to the Gusii, cure bed-wetting by tying a dead snake around the waist of the offender. Whereas the most frequently invoked method of coping with misbehavior of any sort is physical punishment, considered throughout the continent to be the right of the parent to inflict and the obligation of the child to receive, nevertheless, given the quiescent nature of most children, beatings are rarer than one might assume. A Sukuma mother is less and less indulgent of her baby as he grows older, resenting being distracted from her duties; she becomes annoyed if the child cries for any reason other than hunger or illness. He soon learns, then, to avoid incurring maternal displeasure. Meanwhile the frequency of positive responses a Sukuma mother shows to her baby is also diminishing (Varkevisser 1974). Gusii infants, whose early experience seems very like that of Sukuma infants, may do their utmost to draw their mothers into reciprocal play, but they soon meet with resistance. Their efforts at engaging their mothers are either ignored or perceived as an unwelcome intrusion. These babies soon learn that requests for maternal attention, other than for purely physical needs, generally provoke a negative response; as a result, from a very early age they protect themselves by adopting a "low profile." Thus only a minority of replaced children protest when their mothers set off to the fields with their new babies. Indeed, for most African toddlers the separation between mother and child is effected at the point when the mother realizes she is pregnant again. Weaning, which may follow that realization, is handled in Africa in various ways, ranging from abruptly, as among the Hausa, to very gradually in other groups. The primary physical connection is then severed, but even before that the toddler may already be closer to his grandmother, to an older sister, or to his nurse than to his mother. He has already begun to learn that dependency behavior, while permissible within some other relationships, is largely unacceptable to his mother, who expects him to be compliant, respectful, and unproblematic in her presence.

CONCLUSION

In a traditional African setting the mistreatment of children is rare. As a result, however, of increasing social disorganization, parents tend to be less protected than in the past from emotional and physical stress, and instances of mistreatment, particularly of neglect, seem to be rising. Why some parents care adequately for their children while others do not is a complex question; some issues, such as the impact of the breakdown of social and economic systems, are more readily open to investigation than are psychological determinants. It may appear, for example, that a father behaves punitively toward one of his sons while enjoying normal relationships with the others; but it is not known whether this kind of behavior, which in our own society is thought to be caused by a combination of certain psychological factors, has the same meaning in an exotic context. Indeed, the variables that have bearing upon the mistreatment of children in Africa remain largely unexplored.

REFERENCES

Cohen, Ronald
    1971 *Dominance and defiance: a study of marital instability in an Islamic African society.* Washington: American Anthropological Society.
Colson, Elizabeth
    1958 *Marriage and the family amongst the plateau Tonga.* Manchester: Manchester University Press.
Deng, Francis Mading
    1972 *The Dinka of the Sudan.* New York: Holt, Rinehart and Winston.
Dixon, Suzanne, Robert LeVine, and Sarah LeVine
    1976 High fertility in Africa: some considerations and consequences. Paper presented at meeting of the American Studies Association.
Goody, E.
    1973 *Contexts of kinship: an essay on the family sociology of the Gonja of northern Ghana.* Cambridge: Cambridge University Press.
Kaye, S.
    1962 *Bringing up children in Ghana.* London: Allen and Unwin.

Laslett, Peter
    1971 *The world we have lost: England before the industrial revolution.* 2d ed. New York: Charles Scribner and Sons.
LeVine, R. A.
    1977 A cross-cultural perspective on parenting. Unpublished paper.
LeVine, R. A., and B. B. LeVine
    1966 *Nyansongo: a Gusii community in Africa.* New York: Wiley and Sons.
Lijembe, Joseph
    1967 The valley between: a Muluyia's story. In *East African childhood*, ed. Lorene Fox. Nairobi: Oxford University Press. Pp. 4–7.
Raum, O. F.
    1940 *Chaga childhood.* Oxford: International Institute of African Language and Culture.
Read, Margaret
    1960 *Children of their fathers: growing up among the Ngoni of Nyasaland.* New Haven: Yale University Press.
Shorter, Edward
    1975 *The making of the modern family.* New York: Basic Books.
Smith, Mary
    1954 *Baba of Karo.* London: Faber and Faber.
Stone, Lawrence
    1977 *The family, sex and marriage in England, 1500–1800.* New York: Harper and Row.
Thompson, E. P.
    1966 *The making of the English working class.* New York: Vintage Books.
Varkevisser, C. M.
    1974 *Socialization in a changing society.* The Hague: Royal Tropical Institute.
Young, Leontine
    1964 *Wednesday's children: a study of child neglect and abuse.* New York: McGraw-Hill.

THE SOCIOECONOMIC CONTEXT OF CHILD ABUSE AND NEGLECT IN NATIVE SOUTH AMERICA[1]

4

Orna R. Johnson

There has been considerable interest in identifying the conditions that contribute to child abuse and neglect in Western urban settings. Research based largely on clinical populations has identified some of the psychological characteristics of abusive parents and the qualities of abused children which are likely to predict high risk (Helfer 1973; Helfer and Kempe 1972; Kempe et al. 1962; Martin 1976). In addition, environmental and social factors in child abuse have been identified, including poverty, social isolation (Martin 1976), lack of adequate support networks (Garbarino and Crouter 1978), and a pervasive atmosphere of violence in the community which breeds more violence (Steele 1977:5). From a universal standpoint, anthropology, through cross-cultural comparison, helps identify the kinds of social and economic systems, personality traits, and ideological features that are associated with parental indifference and neglect (Rohner 1975).

The forms of abuse most commonly described in the Western literature are idiosyncratically motivated, involving physical battering of children. In most cases the abuse is impulsive, out-of-control punishment for minor infractions which impedes, rather than promotes, the development of competence in the child. This form of abuse is highly uncommon in traditional band and

[1]I would like to thank Barbara Herr, Lorraine Kaufman, Jill Korbin, and Susan Scrimshaw for their helpful comments on an earlier draft on this paper. Research among the Machiguenga was supported by NSF grants GS 33012 and BNS 76-12167.

village level societies. Nevertheless a wide range of parental behavior in these societies can be seen as abusive by Western standards.

In general, I would define child abuse as any child-rearing technique that results in physical harm or death or emotionally deprives the child of self-esteem and a sense of competence. Within each category it is necessary to take contextual factors into account (cf. Korbin 1977:11), to distinguish among (1) culturally acceptable patterns such as infanticide or relative indifference to children's emotional needs, (2) socially sanctioned painful rites of passage or punitive actions that motivate the child to behave according to cultural standards, and (3) idiosyncratic, aberrant forms of abuse that seriously damage the child and erode his or her sense of self-worth.

In this paper, with three objectives in mind, I discuss the range of caretaking behaviors in native lowland South America. First, I describe some of the variation in the treatment of children among Amazonian cultures in relation to differences in social and economic institutions. Second, I show how child fostering and the control of family size preselect against unwanted or disobedient children, thereby reducing the likelihood of idiosyncratic forms of abuse. Third, I look at intracultural variation in order to identify some of the social variables that have been suggested as influencing individual parents' behavior toward their children.

CULTURAL VARIATION IN CHILD CARE

Native South America is of special interest because it consists of numerous relatively isolated and unacculturated groups. In addition, although similar in environment (tropical rain forest) and technology (horticulture with hunting and/or fishing), these groups show important differences in the quality of their interpersonal relationships, including behavior and attitudes toward children. While many ethnographic descriptions touch briefly on matters relating to childhood, few provide enough detail on parental attitudes and behavior to give a comprehensive overview of socialization in Amazonia. Fortunately, the societies for which information is available cover a wide range in terms of aggression, including societies that are actively warlike, those that have been pacified yet display strong feelings of hostility between villages, and those that are traditionally peaceful and emphasize the need to restrain anger and aggression.

The most brutal behavior toward children is reported for the Yano-mamo, a relatively large and isolated group located in Venezuela and Brazil which still actively practices warfare against neighboring villages. From the account by Helena Valero, a Brazilian girl who was kidnapped by the Yanomamo, we learn of the treacherous killing of children by raiders. "The men began to kill the children; little ones, bigger ones, they killed many of them. They tried to run away, but they caught them, and threw them on the ground, and stuck them with bows. . . . taking the smallest by the feet, they beat them against the trees and the rocks. The children's eyes trembled" (Biocca 1971:35).

The brutality, however, is directed outside the group, for the Yanomamo make a clear distinction between their own children and those belonging to other groups of Yanomamo, defined as enemies. Although the Yanomamo studied by Chagnon are unusually violent and reputed commonly to beat their wives, even for minor offenses (1968:83), they do not physically abuse their own children. In fact, according to Chagnon, "boys are treated with considerable indulgence. . . . They are encouraged to be 'fierce.' . . . [A man], for example lets [his son] beat him on the face and head to express his anger and temper, laughing and commenting on his ferocity" (1968:84). It does not follow that the Yanomamo are particularly warm and affectionate toward their children, but that in training children to be fierce, they use positive reinforcement for physical aggression. This suggests that in socializing for warriors, parents do not abuse their own children. Rather, they single out their male children for special attention and encourage aggressive behavior through self-assertion. As Rohner (1975:115–117) argues, the negative consequences of severe emotional rejection would be maladaptive in environments that are hazardous and demanding.

Yanomamo displacement of aggression outward, away from consanguineal kinsmen, reflects a pervasive pattern related to the we/they distinction found throughout Amazonia. Although the boundary between kin and nonkin varies in relation to specific contexts, it nevertheless provides the basis for identifying an external target for blame and an outlet for aggression, either in the form of accusations or physical confrontations. People feel obligated to protect those they define as being within the orbit of their responsibilities and are either openly hostile or indifferent to all others.

In the second type of society—pacified but still experiencing hostility between neighboring villages—mothers initially provide infants with warmth and constant attention but then gradually withdraw their affection, starting about the eighth month when the mother returns to work. For example, among the Jivaro, who are located along the border between Peru and Ecuador, mothers leave their infants for several hours at a time without supplementary feeding. Mothers seem to be short-tempered; on being awakened by a baby's crying, a mother may "scold and strike it in anger" (Harner 1973:87). For older children, nettle spanking is common. Harsher punishment consists of "dropping a large quantity of peppers into a fire and forcing the child to remain over the fire under a large cloth until he becomes unconscious—or giving a child a particularly strong hallucinogenic drug that will put him into a trance state" (Harner 1973:89—90).

A similar pattern of initial warmth, followed by abandonment when the mother returns to work, is found among the Pilaga of Argentina. According to Henry and Henry (1974), the period of most severe suffering for the Pilaga child begins when it starts to walk. "During the period when the baby is investigating the outer world it is almost continuously in tears. Not only is it frightened by contact with strangers, but its mother leaves it more and more alone as she goes about her work. Formerly she had left the baby for hours; now she leaves him alone for a whole day" (1974:16). Not only is the Pilaga mother preoccupied, but other adult kinsmen, including the father, are largely indifferent to children. The result, as seen in the Henrys' doll-play observations, is that children are hungry for attention, extremely violent, and quarrelsome.[2] The Henrys attribute the general indifference to children to an overall lack of solidarity within the household, repressed hostility between husbands and wives, and the reluctance to share food in times of scarcity which in turn leads to more tension and hostility.

The resentment that Jivaro and Pilaga women show toward toddlers is associated with a number of factors, including general hostility and suspicion, relatively low female status, and a lack of solidarity between husbands and wives. These conditions isolate women, making it difficult for them to provide emotional security for themselves or their children.

The exception is found in societies where, despite past warfare and sex antagonism, women are able to experience solidarity with one another. Among the Brazilian Mundurucú, women are preoccupied with processing manioc and are ideologically considered inferior to men, yet their behavior toward children is more nurturant. The showing of care for children is attributed to matrilocal residence, which generates close-knit ties among female kinsmen, and to emotional support that enables women to share domestic responsibilities (Murphy and Murphy 1974:169—171). Although Murphy and Murphy (1974:170) note that infants tend to cry much more when left in someone else's care, the constant presence of female relatives enables

---

[2]The Henrys' data raise an interesting problem that goes beyond the scope of this paper. They suggest that while Pilaga children show certain types of behavior, such as quarreling and hysterical clinging to the mother, which would be considered pathological in our own society, these behaviors do not seem to have the same effect on the child as they do in our culture. Pilaga parents consider these behaviors as temporary phases which should therefore not be punished. The Henrys note that even the most disturbed children do not have night terrors, never suck their thumbs, or show as much sibling rivalry in their doll play as do American children.

children to seek help and comfort from people other than the preoccupied mother. The Mundurucú try to fulfill their children's wishes and needs and never administer corporal punishment.

In the third group of societies, characterized as peaceful and nonviolent, behavior toward children is more consistently affectionate during early childhood than in societies that demonstrate hostility. It is instructive in this respect to compare the Pilaga with the Siriono of Bolivia, who also suffer periodic food scarcity. Unlike the Pilaga, however, the Siriono find that their economic insecurity reinforces kin group solidarity rather than hostility. Although people complain and quarrel about the distribution of food, they make sure that younger children receive preferential treatment (Holmberg 1969:243). As the child gets older, the periods of food deprivation become more frequent and more intense, but the child never experiences emotional rejection. In fact, according to Holmberg, the opposite seems to happen. "Children [are] shown greater love when they are suffering from hunger, fatigue, or pain than at other times. . . . Among the Siriono, love frequently serves as a compensation for hunger" (1969:256).

In addition to group solidarity, nonviolent societies have more egalitarian relationships between husbands and wives and closer relations between children and parents. Among the Machiguenga of southeastern Peru, where I did my own fieldwork, mothers make every effort to take children with them when working in gardens and even nurse their infants and toddlers while planting crops. Husbands and wives form a close conjugal unit and children spend between 35 and 43 percent of the daylight hours in the company of both parents (Johnson 1978:185). Children learn to perform tasks by observing adults. From early on, they are asked to perform simple tasks like fetching or passing household items to family members. The child's actions are closely monitored; requests are repeated several times until the child gets it right. The child is thus encouraged to be obedient and to show a high degree of compliance. Owing to close supervision, mischievousness is constrained and there is little opportunity for children to express hostility toward siblings.

Among the Kalapalo, located in the Xingu area of Brazil, the bond between the mother and her infant is ritually established through a period of postpartum seclusion lasting up to a year after the first child and a shorter time after each subsequent birth; during this time the mother devotes herself completely to the child (Basso 1973:81). As the child grows, it is fed on demand not only to keep it strong but also to prevent it from becoming dissatisfied with its parents. It is believed that a dissatisfied child is capable of suicidal revenge by wandering off into the forest and attracting jaguars that would devour it (Basso 1973:82).

The neighboring Mehinaku practice the couvade: after the birth of a child the father goes into seclusion, where he is restricted in his behavior. The restrictions, which include food taboos and prohibitions on strenuous activities, are related to the child's well-being and directly implicate both parents in the welfare of their children (Gregor 1977:270–273).

Unpleasant practices are nevertheless used in these nonviolent societies as educational measures to promote personal strength and proper behavior in children. Among the Machiguenga, children, starting at birth, are periodically given ritualized scalding baths. Such baths, which are literally translated as "to burn with water," do not damage the child but are regarded as unpleasant experiences intended to teach children to endure pain and to help them become diligent workers. Similar rituals for self-improvement are characteristic of the Mehinaku and the Kalapalo. During puberty seclusion, children submit to scraping with dogfish teeth to make their bodies fat and strong and to teach them to bear pain with dignity (Basso 1973:71; Gregor 1977:228). In both societies severe scraping may be used on rare occasions as a form of punishment by angry parents, leaving children with lifelong scars on their bodies.

Physical sanctions are also administered against children who cry excessively. Because of the close proximity engendered by living arrangements, excessive crying is difficult to tolerate, especially when more than one family is living in the confines of a single room. Mothers are therefore especially concerned about keeping their children quiet. In some cultures, however, the exception is transitory age-appropriate temper tantrums among toddlers while they are being weaned from their symbiotic tie with the mother. This is the only time when crying is tolerated. Otherwise, active steps are taken. If a child cries because it is hungry or frightened, the mother immediately tries to comfort the child by giving it the breast either as a source of nourishment or as a pacifier. Or, if the child is sick, the mother prepares an herbal remedy to cure the ailment. If the crying persists, it is then believed that the child must be angry and more drastic steps are taken. Among the Machiguenga, scalding baths are administered as punishment to drive out the child's anger and enforce restraint. The peaceful Warao of Venezuela similarly see excessive crying as deviant. According to Wilbert (n.d.), the Warao believe that excessive crying reflects badly on the child's mother, who must have been promiscuous during her pregnancy, and that the child is unruly because it cannot cope with the different kinds of semen that mixed with the mother's blood in utero. To avoid such accusations, the Warao mother makes special efforts to keep her children quiet. When all else fails, she takes the child to the river and dips it into the water several times. As the child gasps for air, the crying immediately stops.

These examples show that even in nonaggressive societies which demonstrate marked solicitude for children, children are subjected to some degree of physical pain intended to build strength and regulate impulses. It is noteworthy that these practices are ritually administered and are aimed at benefiting the child. The same practices are also used as culturally accepted disciplinary devices to overcome the child's reluctance to conform. Although some parents may be more severe than others, disciplinary actions almost never take on a sadistic quality, nor do they seriously damage the child. The endurance of pain is not perceived by the society as a rejection or a condemnation, but as a constructive device designed to build strength and enforce compliance.

The only type of sadistic behavior I witnessed among the Machiguenga was the torture of animals. Adults and children alike would take keen pleasure in shooting arrows into animals that had been trapped in a snare. On one occasion, when a wild bird was brought back alive, people stood around laughing hilariously while others took turns poking and kicking it. Such treatment would never be accorded to pets; people in fact refused to kill or eat parrots or baby monkeys that were kept in the house. Wild animals, however, are perceived as different from humans and serve as appropriate targets for sadistic impulses. Since the Machiguenga are extremely careful to avoid expressing anger and aggression in their interpersonal relations, the cruelty toward animals is evidence that there is restraint on aggression and not merely absence of it.

CULTURAL SOLUTIONS FOR UNWANTED CHILDREN

A number of conditions account for the lack of aberrant child abuse in native South America. First is the practice of infanticide. Although infanticide may be considered cruel and inhuman by Westerners (cf. Radbill 1974), human populations have long been regulated in accordance with environmental resources and expectations concerning the quality of life, with infanticide as the most widely used method of population control (Cowgill 1975; Dickman 1975; Dumond 1975; Polgar 1972). In this respect, infant mortality may be a covert or an implicit way of attaining a given family size, and infanticide an extension of induced abortion. The psychological impact of killing infants can be dulled by "culturally defining them as nonpersons, just as modern pro-abortionists define fetuses as non-infants" (Harris 1977:5).

Since an unwanted child may be a source of stress in the family, infanticide reduces the risk of overburdening parents who may misdirect their anger toward the child. The ability to determine family size in turn increases the likelihood that those children who do survive will be wanted by their parents and will be in a position to receive adequate caretaking.

Institutionalized infanticide is found among the Tapirape of the Brazilian Amazon whose social structure prevents them from splitting and forming new villages when the community becomes too large for the subsistence base. As a result, there is an ironclad rule that no woman should have more than three living children and no more than two should be of the same sex (Wagley 1977:135). On one occasion when a fourth child was born, Wagley witnessed the husband dig a hole inside the house. The umbilical cord was not cut and the child was buried alive with the afterbirth almost immediately. There was no sign of grief and no mention of a child being born (1977:137).

Elsewhere, decisions regarding family size are left to the individual mother. It is likely to be an unmarried woman or a woman recently abandoned by her husband who turns to infanticide. Women say the reason they kill an infant is because there will be no one to hunt and provide food for it.

Among the Machiguenga, a mother shows a certain degree of indifference to her baby immediately after birth. After the umbilical cord is tied and cut with a bamboo knife, the newborn is put aside while the midwife attends to the mother. The mother is bathed with scalding water to deaden the pain and the mat upon which she gave birth is discarded so that all traces of blood are carefully washed away. Then the midwife turns to the baby; she bathes it with scalding water, swaddles it in an old garment, and lays it next to the mother to await her recovery. It is at this time that the child is at greatest risk of being killed. The Machiguenga say it is only after the mother nurses the child, which may not be for several hours or until the next day, that she develops an attachment to it and becomes concerned for its well-being (Johnson 1978:161). As Devereux (1948:127) notes for the Mohave Indians of North America, a child that lives long enough to be put to the breast is no longer likely to be killed. Hence maternal bonding does not necessarily take place immediately after birth. The mother goes through a recovery period before she is pleased with or interested in the infant. Her own physical and emotional well-being appears to be a precondition for bonding (cf. Brazelton 1976:47).

It is difficult to judge just how the Machiguenga feel about infanticide, a subject upon which they do not care to elaborate. Some insights, however, can be drawn from an incident of attempted infanticide I witnessed in 1973. A pregnant woman from another settlement, whose husband had abandoned her for a younger woman, came to the community to visit her daughter. She gave birth during the middle of the night and then, feeling especially alone and abandoned, tried to kill the baby by cutting its head with a safety pin, apparently the only device that was available. The baby did not die. The next morning I was summoned to treat the wound and my husband and I sewed up the baby's head. Surprisingly it lived. The next day, when it looked as if the baby would survive, the mother nursed it. Although reluctant at first, she soon accepted the child and became a good mother to it. When we visited the community in 1975, the woman came to see us, bringing her two-year-old daughter with her. The child seemed healthy and well adjusted, and the mother was pleased that she had survived.

Other circumstances occasionally warranting infanticide are malformation of the baby, a difficult pregnancy and/or delivery causing the mother pain and hence anger, and fretfulness of the infant which the mother comes to find an intolerable annoyance (see Cowlishaw 1978:266-267 for similar examples from Australia). Any of these factors may endanger the life of a child perceived as unacceptable. The Machiguenga believe that excessive crying without reason (e.g., if the child is not ill, hungry, or frightened) is an expression of anger. Since anger carries a strong antisocial connotation, a mother is more likely to reject an infant that cannot be comforted.

Deliberate infanticide is not the only process that selects against unwanted children. Infant death owing to health problems is a common enough occurrence, yet it is apparent that some infant deaths are in part caused by poor maternal care, a sort of "underinvestment" in, or "benign neglect" of, some children. Cross-cultural evidence shows that infant mortality rates may be an unconscious or even an overt way of attaining a given family size and that the most vulnerable children are those who have a high birth order, who form a closely spaced pair, or who are unattractive or otherwise not acceptable (Scrimshaw 1978). Although public ideology encourages fertility, unconscious underinvestment or benign neglect selects against those children for whom the parent is not willing to provide. Benign neglect is best reflected in cases of sick children. There is considerable variation in the attention a mother gives a sick child: whether or not she seeks medical assistance or how early in the course of the illness she treats the child. An example is seen in the following description of the difficulties of a young Amahuaca mother in the Peruvian Amazon who had a toddler and four-month-old twins: "One of the twins was unusually small, being awakened by constant diarrhea for several months. . . . [The mother] often appeared not to want the sickly baby to live. She frequently ignored its crying or shoved it impatiently away from her breast" (Dole 1974:31). It is apparent that, though such a child is allowed to live, the mother's reluctance to nurse and to provide adequate care sharply reduces its chances for survival. In other instances the selective process may be much more subtle. A mother who is emotionally unprepared to care for a child is less likely to lactate effectively (Raphael 1973). Supplementation may be provided but may indirectly cause infant mortality through intestinal or nutritional disorders. It should be pointed out, however, that although benign neglect helps to control family size, it nevertheless compromises those neglected children that do survive. Surviving children may eventually be accepted by their parents but they are likely to suffer from nutritional and emotional deficits inconsistent with full physical and mental development (cf. Neel 1970).

A third practice that reduces the likelihood of abusive behavior toward children who have been weaned is fostering. In Western societies abuse is often attributed to problems that parents have with a specific child (Helfer and Kempe 1972; Martin 1976; Lynch 1976). In native South America, the flexibility of the social structure enables parents to transfer responsibility for children of various ages for indefinite periods of time. In fact, the removal of a child, to be brought up elsewhere, is often a convenient solution to domestic difficulties.

Among the Machiguenga foster children are welcome additions to the household. It is recognized that children provide social and economic advantages in the form of companionship and service. In fact, kinsmen may claim rights to children, whom they "borrow" for specific purposes such as child care, water fetching, and garden assistance.

Children who are orphaned are gladly taken in as helpers by other families, but often such adopted children are at a disadvantage if they lack close kin. Although ideally adopted children are equal to one's own children, it is admitted that they are expected to work longer hours and to be highly obedient, lest they be sent away to strangers. In this respect, an adopted child is more vulnerable. The child is valued for its labor but adoptive parents are less tolerant if the child misbehaves. If domestic problems arise, an adopted child is more likely to be the target of blame. Unlike a fostered child who may be able to return home, the orphan does not have the same alternative if he or she faces problems of adjustment.

INDIVIDUAL DIFFERENCES IN CARETAKING

Cross-cultural research has shown that individual differences in child-training behavior are largely determined by intrasociety variability and that situational factors like household composition and economic status have powerful effects on socialization practices (cf. Minturn and Lambert 1964:54). Although ethnographies on native South America occasionally comment on unusual incidents that are regarded as deviant by the culture as a whole, they do not elaborate on the conditions associated with such cases.

Recent research among the Shipibo of the Peruvian Amazon suggests that the social life of the mother may be crucial in determining the mother's relationship with her infant (Abelove 1978). Abelove found that a mother who interacts more frequently with people in the community will have a more sociable infant. She argues that the mother's positive interactions are communicated empathically to her infant through her mood and her attitudes toward other people. On the other hand, a mother who is socially isolated is more likely to communicate her antipathy toward others to her infant. This type of preverbal communication influences the infant's own attitude toward others (besides the mother), and the infant will have fewer positive social interactions with its own peers. Although the communication of antisocial attitudes to a child does not constitute child abuse, the example nevertheless shows the indirect effect of the mother's social life on her child's development.

More directly, social relationships have a pragmatic function in providing the mother with alternate caretakers. Caretaking is an essential resource in relieving an overburdened mother who would not only impose her bad mood on the child but would also be more verbally and/or physically aggressive toward the child (cf. Minturn and Lambert 1964). Among the Machiguenga, some women are constantly surrounded with visitors from other households who socialize with the mother and also help with domestic activities, including child care. Besides providing care for the child, such ties give the mother an important sense of emotional support upon which she can rely, especially if she encounters domestic problems with her husband. The most common response to domestic tension among the Machiguenga is social disengagement. An offended wife customarily takes off to stay with her kinsmen until feelings get sorted out (Johnson 1978:202). Women who are socially isolated, having no one to turn to, take their bad feelings out on their children. Afraid to confront their husbands directly, they vent their anger on their children. Such mothers not only berate and threaten their children but are much more likely to hit them for no good reason, when no one is watching (see Abelove 1978:7 for a Shipibo example).

Support networks also play an important role in caring for the sick. As noted earlier, mothers vary in their response to sick children. Since it is usually the sole responsibility of the nearest of kin to help in caring for the sick, kin ties are crucial in helping the mother gain access to special herbal remedies or Western medicine. Among the Machiguenga, only kinsmen can be relied upon in time of need, as is clearly illustrated by Wayne Snell (1964:138), who has worked as a missionary with the Machiguenga for many years:

> We saw a young lad stricken with chicken pox who was allowed to lie all day with no food because he had no near kin in the vicinity. When he asked that something be brought to him, he was served a banana and a small piece of fish, both of which were only half cooked and unedible. Yet he was well liked and highly respected in the village.

Here is a clear example of the indifference of people toward nonkin, discussed earlier. Since rights and obligations are always defined in kinship terms, a lack of established kin ties places the stranger outside the realm of community responsibility.

In our own experience in dispensing medicine among the Machiguenga we found that parents with whom we had established ties were more likely to ask for medical help early in the course of a child's illness, while those with whom we did not have ties were more hesitant. They usually waited until the child was seriously ill and then would send word, by way of a messenger, that their child was "nearly dying." This left it up to us to offer help, which was always gladly accepted. Although no one died during the time we were with the Machiguenga, the embarrassment and fear of rejection associated with asking a stranger for assistance clearly compromise the child's health and well-being. In this situation the availability of extended kin ties is directly related to the prognosis for recovery and survival.

SUMMARY AND CONCLUSION

Despite the wide range of caretaking practices found throughout lowland South America, certain patterns have emerged to help account for different types of child abuse and neglect. It is widely acknowledged that throughout Amazonia mothers attend to infants with scrupulous care, nursing them on demand and providing close physical contact. It is only when a child reaches the crawling or walking stage that parents in some cultures become indifferent to the child's needs. Children are left for long periods of time without food and are denied emotional reassurance.

The social and economic conditions associated with such neglect are similar to those that have been suggested as contributing to child abuse and neglect in Western cultures: insecure resources, social isolation, lack of support, and general feelings of hostility in the community. In comparing Amazonian cultures with one another, several additional points have emerged. As we have seen, people in even the most violent society do not taunt or physically abuse their own children. This restraint suggests that societal violence is not in itself a sufficient cause for child abuse. Nor is food scarcity, for that matter. The Siriono do their best to protect the very young from hunger and pain despite periodic hunger frustration.

The most important variable associated with positive caretaking is social solidarity. The availability of supportive kin ties in the community accounts for both intercultural variation and individual differences in caretaking behavior. Mothers lacking support from their husbands and/or extended kinsmen are more likely to find their children frustrating, are less inclined to consider their needs, and are more harsh and punitive.

An important element in the lack of aberrant forms of child abuse is the number of alternatives that are culturally available for solving the problem of unwanted children. Although infanticide and benign neglect may be viewed as cruel and inhumane, it is evident that these practices have long been used as regulatory devices. These cultural practices not only promote biological adaptation, but also increase the likelihood of emotional well-being by ensuring that those children who do survive will receive favorable parenting. The potential for abuse is further reduced through the flexibility of adoption practices that help allocate children where they are wanted and can be useful, thus increasing the likelihood that children will be spared the damaging emotional effects of rejection and/or physical abuse.

REFERENCES

Abelove, Joan
 1978 Infant sociability among the Shipibo: pre-verbal cultural learning. Paper presented at meeting of the American Anthropological Association, Los Angeles.
Basso, Ellen B.
 1973 *The Kalapolo Indians of central Brazil*. New York: Holt, Rinehart and Winston.
Biocca, Ettore
 1971 *Yanomamo: The narrative of a white girl kidnapped by Amazonian Indians*. New York: Sutton.
Brazelton, T. B.
 1976 Comment. In *Maternal-infant bonding*, ed. Marshall Klaus and John Kennel. St. Louis: C. V. Mosby. P. 47.
Chagnon, Napoleon
 1968 *Yanomamo: the fierce people*. New York: Holt, Rinehart and Winston.
Cowgill, George
 1975 On causes and consequences of ancient and modern population changes. *American Anthropologist* 77(3):505-525.
Cowlishaw, Gillian
 1978 Infanticide in aboriginal Australia. *Oceania* 48(4):262–283.
Devereux, George
 1948 Mohave Indian infanticide. *Psychoanalytic Review* 35:126–139.
Dickman, Mildred
 1975 Demographic consequences of infanticide in man. *Annual Review of Ecology and Systematics* 6:100-139.
Dole, Gertrude
 1974 The marriages of Pacho: a woman's life among the Amahuaca. In *Many sisters: women in cross-cultural perspective*, ed. Carolyn Matthiasson. New York: Free Press. Pp. 3–35.
Dumond, Don E.
 1975 The limitation of human population: a natural history. *Science* 187:713-721.

Garbarino, James, and Ann Crouter
1978 Defining the community context for parent-child relations: the correlates of child maltreatment. *Child Development* 49:604–616.

Gelles, Richard J.
1973 Child abuse as psychopathology: a sociological critique and reformulation. *American Journal of Orthopsychiatry* 43(4):611–621.

Gil, David
1970 *Violence against children: physical child abuse in the United States.* Cambridge: Harvard University Press.

Gregor, Thomas
1977 *Mehinaku.* Chicago: University of Chicago Press.

Harner, Michael
1973 *The Jivaro.* New York: Anchor Books.

Harris, Marvin
1977 *Cannibals and kings.* New York: Random House.

Helfer, Ray E.
1973 The etiology of child abuse. *Pediatrics* 51(4):777–779.

Helfer, Ray E., and C. Henry Kempe
1972 *Helping the battered child and his family.* Philadelphia: Lippincott.

Henry, Jules, and Zunia Henry
1974 *Doll play of Pilaga Indian children.* New York: Vintage Books. 1st ed., 1944.

Holmberg, Allan
1969 *Nomads of the long bow: the Siriono of eastern Bolivia.* New York: American Museum of Natural History.

Johnson, Orna R.
1978 Interpersonal relations and domestic authority among the Machiguenga of the Peruvian Amazon. Ph.D. dissertation, Columbia University.

Kempe, C. Henry, Fredric N. Silverman, Brandt F. Steele, William Droegmueller, and Henry K. Silver
1962 The battered child syndrome. *Journal of the American Medical Association* 181: 17-24.

Korbin, Jill E.
1977 Anthropological contributions to the study of child abuse. *Child Abuse and Neglect: The International Journal* 1(1):7–24.

Lynch, Margaret
1976 Risk factors in the abused child: a study of abused children and their siblings. In *The abused child: a multidisciplinary approach to developmental issues and treatment,* ed. Harold P. Martin. Cambridge: Ballinger. Pp. 43–56.

Martin, Harold P.
1976 The environment of the abused child. In *The abused child: a multidisciplinary approach to developmental issues and treatment,* ed. Harold P. Martin. Cambridge: Ballinger. Pp. 11–25.

Minturn, Leigh, and William W. Lambert
1964 *Mothers of six cultures: antecedents of child rearing.* New York: John Wiley and Sons.

Murphy, Yolanda, and Robert F. Murphy
  1974 *Women of the forest*. New York: Columbia University Press.

Neel, James V.
  1970 Lessons from a "primitive people." *Science* 170:815—822.

Polgar, Steven
  1972 Population history and population policies from an anthropological perspective. *Current Anthropology* 13(2):203—211.

Radbill, Samuel X.
  1974 A history of child abuse and infanticide. In *The battered child*, ed. Ray E. Helfer and C. Henry Kempe. 2d ed. Chicago: University of Chicago Press. Pp. 3—17.

Raphael, Dana
  1973 *The tender gift: breastfeeding*. Englewood Cliffs, NJ: Prentice-Hall.

Rohner, Ronald P.
  1975 *They love me, they love me not: a worldwide study of the effects of parental acceptance and rejection*. New Haven: HRAF Press.

Scrimshaw, Susan
  1978 Infant mortality and behavior in the regulation of family size. *Population and Development Review* 4(3):383—403.

Snell, Wayne
  1964 Kinship relations in Machiguenga, M.A. thesis, Hartford Seminary Foundation, Hartford, CT.

Steele, Brandt F.
  1977 Child abuse and society. *Child Abuse and Neglect: The International Journal* 1(1):1—6.

Wagley, Charles
  1977 *Welcome of tears*. New York: Oxford University Press.

Wilbert, Johannes
  N.d. Warao enculturation. University of California, Los Angeles. Unpublished manuscript.

CHILD REARING AND SOCIAL STRUCTURE IN RURAL INDIA: Toward a Cross-Cultural Definition of Child Abuse and Neglect[1]

Thomas Poffenberger

5

1. INTRODUCTION

The way children are treated, and thus child abuse and neglect, are rooted in the unique social structure and norms held in any society at a given point in time. This chapter draws upon a study of child-rearing practices in a village in India. The Indian material is compared with past and present Western views on the proper treatment of children. The objective is to contribute to a better understanding of child abuse and neglect in a cross-cultural perspective.

There are, to date, no international criteria for defining child abuse and neglect. In this context, the moral difficulties of judging other people's child-rearing practices are clear. Still, when children are hurt, can we not label "abusive" those who are responsible for their care? Steele (1977:1) writes:

> Next to making sure of its own individual survival, the prime task of any organism is to reproduce and provide offspring to insure the survival of its species. In child abuse we see a seriously distorted form of this biological process. The offspring are treated in ways which damage them rather than ways which assure their optimal growth and development so as to form the healthiest possible generation.

[1] I wish to express my appreciation to Karen Blumenfeld for assistance given in the preparation of this paper. Not only was she a significant help in editing and organizing the paper, but she was also a perceptive critic of the concepts as they developed.

Yet every society has its own norms for acceptable child-rearing practices, norms that grow out of the society's requirements for adult behavior and prepare children to adopt that behavior. In the framework of a society's expectations, the optimal growth and development of the individual may, in fact, be anathema to the survival of society at large. In peasant societies such as rural India, for example, group solidarity is valued. In a sense, such societies require a curtailment of individual development in order to maintain conformity and group cohesion. Research has indicated that authoritarian-restrictive discipline results in passive and obedient behavior (Becker 1964:191). We would therefore expect to find authoritarian treatment of children as a normative feature of child-rearing practices in societies that value group norms and adult conformity.

In India, what might be considered child abuse by Western standards may often fulfill a normative function in child-rearing practices. Such treatment is motivated, for the most part, by the parents' belief that a particular form of harsh treatment will best prepare the child to function in a group-oriented society, and it is therefore generally considered to be in the best interest of the child.

Abusive parental behaviors that deviate from the norm and result from adults' emotional disturbances, on the other hand, may not find widespread expression in India. Although a peasant society such as rural India may dictate child treatment that would be considered abusive in the United States, there is probably less of the kind of extreme, irrational abuse that is common in the West. This is because of the stronger family support system available to Indian parents and the restraining influence of extended family members when parental tempers get out of control.

Neglect or deprivation, as well as abuse, may also serve a normative function in India, albeit less explicitly. Tube-Becker (1977) states that in the West it is usually infants who are the victims of negligence; and negligence generally takes the form of food deprivation. In India, infants may also suffer deprivation of food, usually because there is simply not enough of it to go around. As we shall see, however, in traditional Hindu society negligence has been associated with females. This differential treatment of male and female infants is said to be largely responsible for the higher death rate among the latter. In the West today, neglect of a female deviates from societal norms. Among some peasant groups in India, however, such behavior still seems to find at least passive support.

Child Abuse and Social Change

It is clear that child-rearing practices not only differ among societies but that they vary over time within societies. The comments in this chapter relate only to traditional peasant India. It should be pointed out, however, that changes are taking place throughout the country in rural as well as urban areas. It was evident at the time of our study that the child-rearing practices we observed were changing. While we cannot predict the exact direction or full nature of this change, it may be useful to keep in mind the gradual modification of values regarding the treatment of children in the West, as rural European peasantry gave way to secular urban trends.

In an article on the history of child abuse, Solomon (1973) points out that in seventeenth-century Europe infanticide and child neglect were common. In preindustrial Europe the child had no inherent rights. Children were taught to obey their elders, and deviations from expected behavior at home, in school, or at work could result in severe physical punishment. Children as young as six were expected to serve their families, as they are in village India today. A good parent was one who was firm in discipline. Kagan (1978) writes that in the Europe of the 1600s children were beaten regularly to control "in-born evil tendencies." It was not until the industrial revolution, and the resulting exploitation of children for economic gain, that the question of the child's rights was seriously considered by a significant portion of society.

In America, until the late nineteenth century, the child was viewed as innately sinful but potentially redeemable through the constant and determined efforts of his parents (Takanishki 1978), presumably by discipline that today would be regarded as abusive. That belief was highly resistant to change because it was rooted in the traditional right of the family to control its internal affairs. As a result, other institutions were reluctant to interfere with family activities. According to Solomon (1973), until the last half of the nineteenth century the only agency willing and able to intervene in clear cases of child mistreatment was the American Society for the Prevention of Cruelty to Animals.

Kagan (1978) believes that the gradual change from a functional view of the child to one of love-orientation may have been the result of urbanization. Before the sixteenth century children in rural Europe were viewed primarily in economic terms. But as people began to migrate from the rural areas to the cities in the late sixteenth and early seventeenth centuries, children lost much of their economic value as farm helpers. The decline in family size in urban areas is usually attributed to the decreasing economic utility of children. According to Kagan (1978:58),

> The middle class father, feeling economically more secure than the 16th century rural parent, was probably less concerned about becoming emotionally dependent on his grown sons when he was too old to work. It is likely, then, that the child's role gradually changed from an object of utility to one of sentiment. Although the child could not contribute to the family's economic position, he could enhance the family's status by mastering academic skills and attaining prestige and position in the larger community. Now more parents would begin to identify with their children because of the latter's potential accomplishments.

This change in the child's function in the family could have produced an enhancement of the attitude we call parental love.

Concern with the effect of early childhood experiences on later adult personality grew in the early part of the twentieth century. This trend began with Freud in Europe and spread to America. In recent years solicitude for the child's welfare has increased. Today, proponents of self-determination for children believe not only that children must be physically and emotionally protected, but that their rights must be safeguarded as well (Farson 1974; Holt 1974). Their assumption is that every child has the right to self-determination: the right to exercise control over his own environment and to make decisions about what he wants in various facets of his life.

As Baumrind (1978) suggests, however, to grant children the rights of adults contradicts propositions that have generally been held as valid in the United States. Maturity has been regarded as the result of growth and children have been assumed to require protection while passing through stages leading to adult competence. To assert that children must be both protected and granted the rights of adults is a contradiction. In fact, it may be predicted that the cost to society of its emphasis on individualism may be a return to a more conservative position.

In the West, then, history would indicate a movement in values from a point where the child had no rights, except as a member of the extended family, to a point where the child is elevated to a position of nearly total self-determination. In the former position the child was subject to whatever sanctions his family deemed necessary in order to exact conformity. In the latter position the child finds strong social and legal sanctions in his favor, intended to inhibit societal control. Ironically, the importance placed on the child may contribute to parental frustration and child abuse.

At least some resemblance between the position of children in modern rural India and that of children in the preindustrial West is discernible. That physical punishment may be as much a part of Indian life today as it was in seventeenth-century Europe should not be surprising in view of the commonalities in peasant societies. In view of the course of Western history, it is likely that normative child-rearing practices in India will change as industrialization and urbanization begin to erode the traditions of peasant society and the value of the group over the individual. In this chapter, however, there is no attempt to deal with the complex problem of cultural change; rural India is considered only in a traditional context.

In the next section the cultural roots of Indian child-rearing practices are examined in terms of how they may be anchored in Hindu tradition. Section 3 will cover aspects of Hindu social structure which may result in neglect and/or death of female infants, as well as abuse and death of young females in the homes of their in-laws. Section 4 is a report on the child-rearing practices in an Indian village we studied as they may relate to the issue of child neglect and abuse.

2. THE CULTURAL BASIS FOR CHILD-REARING PRACTICES

A feature of Indian socialization practices which has far-reaching implications for our understanding of child abuse and neglect is variation according to gender. We are therefore particularly interested in those traditional values that may help to predict and explain the differential treatment.

The Great and Little Traditions

European peasant societies have been referred to by Kroeber as part-societies with part-cultures (Foster 1967). Redfield (1967) asserts that European peasants hold "Little Traditions" in their villages, but that these traditions are in constant interaction with, and largely determined by, the "Great Traditions" of the main society. He suggests that the Great Tradition/Little Tradition formula characterizes other indigenous civilizations of the world as well, such as those in Indonesia, China, and India. In India, Hinduism is the Great Tradition which underlies all village behavior. Village behavior patterns can, in fact, be understood only in terms of the larger civilization of which they are a part.

Of the complex elements that compose the Great Tradition of Hinduism (Panchanadikar and Panchanadikar 1970:60–66), this section will deal only with those factors that relate to differences in the treatment of boys and girls: the patrilineal nature of Hindu society and the tradition of the extended family. The male's important role both in the society in general and in the extended family in particular suggests that the treatment of boys is related to preparing them for their adult roles in their families of orientation. Conversely, it seems that the treatment of girls has evolved out of the need to prepare them for their future roles in their families of procreation, as well as from other societal, economic, and religious realities of having a daughter.

Preference for Sons

In India, the patrilineal nature of society has led to strong preferences for having sons and, concomitantly, significant costs of having daughters. In a patrilineal society the oldest male stood as the authority figure of the family. All property was passed on to sons; it was the sons who remained part of the extended family, while the daughters left to join the families of their husbands.

Sons were important not only because they continued the family line, but also because they were the parents' sole form of social security. Sons were therefore highly valued, especially by mothers, who would probably be widowed and rely on their sons for support. A son was important from a religious standpoint as well. Only a son could carry out the *shradda* ceremony at his father's death, giving the latter spiritual salvation. The traditional value of sons was so high that the woman's primary function was to bear them.

Traditionally, sons were too important to society to be left to their own devices. The value of their loyalty to the extended family and caste required strict sanctions in order to exact compliance with group norms.

Costs of Daughters

Whereas having a son in traditional Hindu society was thought to be an unmitigated blessing, having a daughter imposed certain costs. A daughter was a potential liability from three points of view: spiritual, social, and economic.

For the male, religious rites (*samskara*) providing salvation were performed from the time of conception to the time of death. For the female, however, marriage was the only rite (Kapadia 1966:141). Since a girl's salvation depended on marriage—without it she was no better than a low-caste untouchable—the family of a daughter was under pressure to ensure her marriage.

The marriage of a daughter was regarded as more important than that of a son, because through her marriage a daughter could elevate her family's status within caste. Caste, a central feature of Hinduism, determined not only the role and status one would hold throughout life, but also one's occupation. A good marriage was defined in terms of the caste standing of the prospective bridegroom and the degree to which it would increase the status of the bride's family. The choice of marriage partners rested with the families rather than with the couple, since the stakes were far too high to allow individual choice.

Since the parents of the girl had the most to gain by the marriage, the parents of the boy were in the best bargaining position. In addition, in order to marry a girl into a family of higher status, a dowry was usually required. The combination of hypergamy (marriage of a daughter into a higher-status family) and dowry, together with the fact that a girl would contribute her labor to her family of orientation for only a very few years, resulted in daughters being a distinct disadvantage from an economic standpoint. In each stage of life she was under the direct control of a male: her father, her husband, and, if she outlived her husband, her son. Marriage was a transference of the father's dominion to the husband. According to Kapadia (1966:142), the ideal of wifehood required the negation of a woman's personality. She was to worship her husband as a god, regardless of his personal characteristics or his treatment of her. A wife, in order to give unqualified attention to her husband, was expected to have had little contact with other men, and upon her husband's death she could not remarry.

Early marriage for girls was the logical outcome of these customs. A father was regarded as committing a sin if he failed to marry off his daughter before she reached puberty (Goode 1963:208). His sin was probably related to her potential sin of premarital intercourse. Parents accepted the existence of their daughters' sexuality and also viewed daughters as tempting to men. Consequently, parents had to guard their girls carefully and marry them off at an early age if premarital sexual relations were to be avoided. The belief that if a girl was married at an early age she would not be set in her ways and would adapt more easily to the family of her in-laws also made early marriage more desirable.

In rural areas a girl traditionally married within her caste but outside her village of birth. Early marriage of a boy and a girl from different villages, who often had not seen each other before and had no resources of their own, had the additional advantage of making them completely dependent upon the extended family.

According to Kapadia (1966:143), child marriage probably did not become prevalent until the twelfth century. But once it was adopted by high-caste Brahmins, it became a norm for the Hindu community as a whole. Although early marriage was the custom, consummation was not to take place until the girl reached puberty. Still, there was evidently enough concern during the period of British rule that the Indian Penal Code of 1860 was passed to declare consummation below ten years of age to be rape. Concerning the law, Kapadia (1966:147) writes:

> It may be contended that the Hindu wife, trained since childhood by solemn precepts and overt examples to revere her husband, to obey him meekly and to stand by him always, could hardly conceive of availing herself of this law even if such cruelty had been perpetrated on her. The legislation would thus appear to have been ineffectual; nevertheless, it did pave the way for fixing the age of marriage at a later date. The law of rape posed for the first time the problem of infant marriages in its grim reality.

3. SEX PREFERENCES AND DIFFERENTIAL TREATMENT OF BOYS AND GIRLS

The fact that there is a preference for sons in India has long been noted. But the same preference has been noted in other societies, both in the developing and in the industrialized world. What is unique about the subcontinent is the sex ratio.

Sex Ratio in India

In most of the world the expectation of survival at birth is almost universally higher, and infant mortality universally lower, for females than for males. These facts obtain both in industrialized countries with low overall mortality and in developing countries with higher overall mortality levels. Sri Lanka, Pakistan, and India appear to be the only exceptions to this predominant pattern, according to a United Nations report.

The underreporting of females, and the statistic that more than 105 males to 100 females are usually found in cross-national studies, have been offered as explanations for the unusual sex ratio, but these explanations have been examined and repudiated (Jain 1975:98–99; Wyon and Gordon 1971: 144). The U.N. report states that excessive female mortality in the reproductive ages explains part of the difference, but it adds that high reproductive mortality is also found in other developing countries (United Nations 1973:155).

Indian census reports over the years, noting the unbalanced sex ratio, consistently suggest the possibility that neglect of female infants is in part responsible for it. The report of 1931 says, "The female infant is definitely better equipped by nature for survival than the male but in India the advantage she has at birth is probably neutralized in infancy by comparative neglect and in adolescence by the strain of bearing children early and too often" (Census of India 1931:138).

Other studies also attribute the unusual sex ratio to "benign neglect" of daughters by their parents. Minturn and Hitchcock (1963:284) report that of some ninety children in a Rajput village they studied in the Punjab, almost two-thirds were boys. Owing to their interest in this difference, they questioned thirty-six mothers regarding the sex of children who had died, not including those who died in miscarriages and stillbirths. The mothers reported that nearly twice as many girls as boys had died in childhood. Although infanticide was practiced in the past among high-caste Rajputs, the authors attribute the shortage of girls in the village to better medical treatment for boys.

In an earlier study in the Punjab, Lewis (1958:16) reported finding a preponderance of males over females. He also discounted infanticide, despite historical reports that it was common among the Jats whom he studied. In another study in the Punjab, Wyon and Gordon (1971:193-195) found that the rates of death from all causes were higher among females than males, except that at least three times as many males as females died from tetanus. Girls under two years of age were found to have a substantially smaller chance of survival than boys of the same age. Wyon and Gordon concluded that the reasons for the disparity were higher-quality medical care and possibly more supplementary food for boys. Only after the age of fifty did the male mortality rate exceed the female.

Female Infanticide

Sex ratios differ from one part of India to another. The 1971 census records a low of 87 females per 100 males in the Punjab and a high of 102 females to 100 males in Kerala (Census of India 1971:76—78). When fewer females survived in the past, infanticide has been cited as part of the cause, particularly in sections of Gujarat, Punjab, Rajasthan, and the United Provinces (Mehta 1966).

Different methods of infanticide have been reported in various parts of India. In the Punjab, infants were drowned in water, while in Kacch they were drowned in milk. In Kathiawad, opium was placed on the mother's breast until the child died of an overdose. In much of Gujarat, infants were reported to have died from starvation as a result of not having been permitted to breast-feed (Mehta 1966). The outstanding example of female infanticide in Gujarat was practiced by the Jhareja Rajputs of Kathiwar and Kacch, where a census taken by British administrators in 1805 found almost no daughters (Pakrasi 1970). During the 1800s the administration in Gujarat also became concerned about the low sex ratios among the Kanbi-Patidars (Clark 1976). The evident failure of the British administration in India to stop female infanticide resulted in the passage of an act in 1870 which authorized close examination of the causes of deaths in castes suspected of the practice.

The actual extent of female infanticide has always been a matter of debate because of the difficulty in establishing the exact causes of infant deaths. Goode (1963:237—238) quotes a 1911 census report by E. A. Gait, who believed that while deliberate infanticide continued long after the act was passed, the majority of female deaths were more likely to have been owing to neglect, either unconscious or deliberate. Neglect, the report said, was "due partly to habit and partly to the parents' great solicitude for their sons. The boys are better clad, and when ill are more carefully tended. They are allowed to eat their fill before anything is given to the girl. In poor families, when there is not enough for all, it is invariably the girls who suffer."

Hypergamy and Dowry

A considerable literature during the British period speculated on possible causes of female neglect and infanticide among the Patidars in Gujarat.

These practices were generally attributed to the tradition of hypergamy and to the dowry system.

As noted earlier, family status was enhanced by the marriage of a daughter to a family of higher position than its own. With the growth of castes and endogamy within castes, hypergamy became the primary method of establishing prestige in social hierarchy. The hypergamous system resulted in competition among wealthy families from lower-status villages for sons in higher-status villages. As a result, dowries for such marriages became increasingly large, and the attendant costs of having a daughter also increased.

While having many sons was a distinct advantage, having many daughters could be a disaster. The fewer the daughters, the larger share of the family resources could be concentrated on each one, resulting in the ability to pay larger dowries. The high cost of dowries became firmly institutionalized among the higher castes, and it was in these castes that the fewest women were found. Indeed, an excessive number of daughters was said to bring economic hardship to families at every economic level, even when a bride-price was paid. Thus arose a motive for behavior which limited the number of daughters in the extended family.

Deaths of Young Brides

The social structure that yields higher mortality rates for female infants and children also takes its toll among young girls after marriage. The fact that these girls have often barely reached puberty justifies a brief comment in a chapter on child abuse and neglect. The higher death rate for females in their late teens and twenties is partly attributable to childbearing. But it is also attributable to deaths that result from adjustment difficulties in the extended families of young girls' in-laws.

A regional Indian report for Gujarat state found that the rate of suicide for women was twice as high as for men (Government of Gujarat 1966). In contrast, the suicide rate in western Europe and the United States is three or four times higher for men than for women. The Gujarat study also discovered that, of suicides occurring among women for reasons other than physical illness or psychosis, 55 percent were of women below twenty-five years of age, and nearly three-quarters took place in joint families.

The police reports used in the government study indicate that in many cases of alleged suicide the victim had actually been poisoned, beaten, drowned, burned, or hanged. The study states that women who did commit suicide did so "because of the unbearable and harsh treatment at the hands of a husband or mother-in-law. . . . persistent and calculated physical and mental torture was employed in some castes to deliberately do away with the daughter-in-law" (Government of Gujarat 1966:75).

4. CHILD-REARING PRACTICES IN RAJPUR VILLAGE

The research on which this section is based began while the author was with the Department of Child Development, University of Baroda. A series of related studies were carried out in the rural section of Baroda Tuluka between 1962 and 1967, and again from 1969 to 1971. Most of the work focused on fertility behavior, although the original study of village families was oriented toward child-rearing practices.[2] A major focus of the study was on parental attitudes and behavior regarding oral, anal, sex, dependency, and aggression training and the techniques of control used in such training.

In late 1962 Rajpur village,[3] located several miles from the city of Baroda, was selected for the study. Because of its location Rajpur was becoming, even as early as 1962, a suburban village with industry springing up between the city limits and the village. Some villagers had already sold farmland for factories. Many of the men had long since given up traditional occupations to work either in the city, which they could reach by bicycle or bus on a paved road, or in factories that were within walking distance. Rajpur was therefore a village undergoing rapid change. For this reason we had the advantage of being able to examine traditional behavior while at the same time getting some measure of the influence of urbanization. Furthermore, in spite of the village's long contact with the urban area (the road was paved in 1920), its structure and culture at the time of the study remained basically the same as in more remote villages.

The village at the time of the study had a population of 1,690 with 333 households. There were 18 castes and 33 subcastes, but four major castes and

[2]Although the interviews and observations focused on the five-year-old, all the families had other children whom we observed and inquired about. Particular attention was paid to ten-year-olds, on whom extensive data were collected regarding school as well as home activities. Interviews and observations were carried out by a team of three women and two men, all of whom had earned advanced degrees at the university and had had previous village field experience. Interview data were collected over a period of two years, 1963 and 1964, from 66 mothers and 60 fathers. Six Baria fathers were so resistant to interviewing that they were omitted. Twenty-four families, six from each of the major castes, were selected for more intensive study, and return visits were made to these families until 1967. Much of the latter data had to do with studies of social change and fertility behavior (see Poffenberger 1975; Poffenberger and Poffenberger 1973). A later survey (Poffenberger 1976) of students between 16 and 19 years of age, in the eleventh standard of a village secondary school in the same locality but farther from the city, supports the material presented in this chapter.

[3]The name of the village is fictitious. Baroda is the second-largest city in Gujarat State, about 240 miles north of Bombay, near the west coast of India. The author is grateful to Amita Verma, Bihari Pandya, Rupa Patel, Smita Patel, Taru Parikh, Katy Mohta, Manubhai Patel, Haribhai G. Patel and Shirley B. Poffenberger for their invaluable help in conducting the study.

communities comprised 76 percent of the population. These groups were Patidars, traditional landowning farmers; Barias, largely tenant farmers; Bhils, a tribal group; and Vankers, one of three groups of former untouchables.

The Sex Ratio and the Value of Sons and Daughters

Our data from Rajpur, as in much of north India, indicated a clear sex differential favoring males: the census of all households in the village showed 89 females to 100 males. The breakdown by age revealed that the widest differences were in the early years. From birth to six months there were 59 females to 100 males. This ratio increased to 77 for ages seven months to 14 years, and to 94 from 15 years to 54 years. After the age of 54 the ratio was 147 females to 100 males. Apparently, if a woman survived her early years, the chances were good she would outlive her husband.

A record was kept of infant deaths in the village for a 28-month period. The infant mortality rate per thousand for this period was 93 for females and 63 for males. We also found that the sex ratio differed according to the age of the mother. On the average, mothers under 25 years of age reported 85 daughters to 100 sons. Mothers 25 to 34 years of age reported 79 daughters to 100 sons, whereas mothers 35 to 44 reported only 67 daughters to 100 sons. It seems likely that, since one daughter is usually considered desirable, first-born girls have a better chance of survival than those who are born later.

The average age of the mothers in the sample of 66 families was 35.4 years. The mothers had an average of 4.4 living children, 2.5 of whom were boys and 1.9 of whom were girls. While the census clearly indicated a higher female mortality rate, mothers reported that an average of 0.9 boys and 0.9 girls had died. They had forgotten or did not want to report some of the female deaths. We also asked how many boys and girls were regarded as ideal for a family to have. Mothers said that they wanted an average of 2.5 sons (the average number they actually had), but only 1.4 daughters. Fathers on the average reported an ideal of 1.9 sons and 1.2 daughters.

Mothers and fathers consistently stated that the advantages of having sons were for support in old age, continuing the family lineage, and assistance in farming or other work. Fewer than one-third of the mothers and fathers mentioned a single disadvantage of a son. When a disadvantage was stated, it was in terms of fear that a son would not fulfill his obligations to his parents.

In contrast, 67 percent of the fathers and 54 percent of the mothers said there was no benefit at all in having a daughter. Most comments stressed the economic costs. One father said, "There is no benefit in having a daughter. She goes to another family when she is 15 or 16 years old." Another said, "She will take away whatever we have. A daughter is a demanding person. We may have to dispose of our property for her wedding expenses." Nevertheless, 29 percent of the fathers and 13 percent of the mothers said an advantage of daughters was assistance given to mothers. Nearly 30 percent of the mothers resisted giving any direct answer to the question, indicating perhaps that they felt some ambivalence about the topic. One mother revealed a feeling that many evidently shared: "A daughter is helpful and loves her parents more than a son. A daughter is like a cow. She is mild in nature and she obeys her parents' orders so daughters do not make any disturbances as sons do." But the emotional closeness with daughters is offset by their economic costs. Another mother said: "I am satisfied with all three of my children but I am most satisfied with my daughter. But I don't want too many because we have to spend money on their marriage."

Case histories in Rajpur show no evidence of deliberate female infanticide. There were, however, cases of relative neglect. More important, perhaps, was the fact that boys were regarded as needing special attention and care while girls were regarded as being more hardy. One mother said, "A girl is like a stone and nothing can hurt her but a boy is like a flower and must be treated with care."

Beliefs Regarding the Use of Praise

One way to assess the culturally desired end result of the child-rearing process is to examine commonly held attitudes toward the use of praise with children. Praise as a positive, love-oriented technique of child rearing is widely regarded as important for boosting feelings of self-worth and self-esteem, which enhance independence.

It was assumed that village parents would be concerned about the use of praise, since the development of ego strength would tend to weaken the control of the family over the individual. In the Khalapur study of child rearing in the Punjab, Minturn and Hitchcock (1973:325) found general agreement that a child should not be given praise because it would make him disobedient. A similar attitude was expressed by villagers in a study in south India (Mencher 1963). The Rajpur findings were consistent with the Minturn and Hitchcock and Mencher studies.

The implication, as Mandelbaum (1970:121) points out, is clear. The village child must be trained to be obedient, and obedience might not develop if a child is praised too much or "loved too much" and comes to feel a sense of his own importance. Such a child might not easily accept subordinate status. The Rajpur interviews with parents clearly highlighted the widely held beliefs that praise would produce a child who was proud and difficult to control and that if praise was to be given it must not be done in front of the child. The attitudes expressed on the use and withholding of praise were consistent with the findings, discussed in the next section, of general indulgence in infancy and increasing severity of training as the child grows older.

Early Socialization

Although both daughters and sons are socialized to be obedient, there are differences in the severity and the outcome of socialization practices. Sons are expected to remain in their families of orientation, but daughters must be prepared to adjust to a new family, often under extremely difficult circumstances, as the mortality rate for young wives indicates. Child rearing cannot be so severe as to destroy a girl's feelings of adequacy and self-worth. Indeed, a strong personality is required for her survival. It should also be pointed out that the submissive young girl who enters the home of her in-laws is the same person who, having established her status through her sons, becomes the strong-willed, dominating, and controlling mother-in-law in her later years.

We can only guess regarding the differences in socialization which result in relatively weaker dependency needs for girls than for boys. Sons are clearly preferred and are treated better than daughters in a physical sense. If, however, daughters do survive infancy and early childhood, mothers seem to be less hostile and less emotionally cold to them than to sons. One may speculate that having been dominated by males all her life, a mother finds it more difficult to be warm to a son, whom she is expected to treat like a king, than to a daughter who is regarded by the extended family as being insignificant, but with whom she identifies. In addition, a daughter is helpful around the house and responsive to a mother's needs, so a close companionship often develops between mother and daughter which is seen less often in mother-son relationships.

Although the mother-son relationship may not be one of companionship, the importance of the bond between mother and son, as Mandelbaum (1970:62) explains, "is celebrated in the sacred writings, romanticized in popular tale, and upheld in family life." The mother must prepare a daughter to leave her family, but she must condition a son so that he feels guilt and shame at the very thought of leaving. Studies have found that this conditioning is usually successful. Husbands report that they are closer to their mothers than to their wives (Gore 1961), and one of the fathers in Rajpur said, "Of course I beat my wife. When she disagrees with my mother, what else am I to do?"

The initial foundation for the attachment of sons to their mothers seems to evolve out of a long period of maternal closeness, followed often by a sudden termination of the relationship. We might assume that for girls, if regarded less important at birth, the early mothering may not be as intense and the separation less dramatic.

The bond between mother and child is established in the earliest stages of a child's life. Infants in the village are breast-fed for prolonged periods of 18 months or more. During breast-feeding the baby is fondled, and the experience of continued tactile sensations is highly rewarding (Harlow 1962). During the period of breast-feeding the infant sleeps with his mother and is in almost constant physical contact. Bowlby (1960, 1969) points out the intense attachment of the child to a mother figure in the first, second, and third years of life, and the effects of termination of this attachment. In a study of children between 15 and 30 months of age, Bowlby found what he called "primary anxiety" in those children for whom the maternal attachment had been ruptured.

While physical separation from its mother does not often occur for the village child, weaning is frequently reported to be swiftly accomplished by putting the juice of the bitter neem leaf on the breast. It is arguable that so abrupt a termination, after a long-established relationship with the mother, can be significant in personality formation. If village child-rearing practices are intended to produce dependence and subordination to adult authority, perhaps the process is begun in the first few years.

Even if weaning itself was not traumatic, what might follow for the child was. Observation over a period of time of a mother and her two-year-old son illustrates the point. After the birth of the next child, the mother was occupied with the new infant and had no time for the older child. The mother would breast-feed the new infant while the older child attempted to continue the responsive relationship he had had with his mother in the past. But this conduct was bothersome for the mother, and the child was usually pushed away. The physical rejection resulted in hostility on the part of the child, who often struck at the mother with his fists. The mother responded with statements of rejection and threats. This description of initial indulgence followed by withdrawal of gratification was characteristic of the treatment of both sons and daughters, but mothers seemed to be somewhat harsher with sons.

Carstairs (1961:150) suggests that there is a gentle prelude to socialization in rural India, since children are not scolded or forced until weaning. He asserts that Hindu children begin life with an abundantly rewarding experience. It is said in India that a young child is equal to a king and that a "good mother will pick the child up at once and let it have her breast whenever it complains" (Carstairs 1961:64). At the time of the weaning, however, the child suddenly finds his mother withholding love, while increasing the pressure for him to show respect and obedience to elders (Carstairs 1961:146). He is expected to be more controlled in his behavior, while at the same time experiencing increasing frustration and anger. Lois Murphy (1953:48) points out the end result of this change in expectations: "A gloom settles down on adolescents like a fog and the warmth goes out of their faces." Carstairs (1961:161) explains: ". . . it is in the seeming 'betrayal' by a child's mother that we must seek the explanation for the change from spontaneity in infancy to relative unresponsiveness and lack of initiative in later childhood."

Indulgence withdrawal, which begins sometime during the second year, is probably related to the time at which the child begins to walk. The mother, who may be concerned with a new infant, has no time for the toddler. When the child attempts to climb up on the mother's arm, she rebuffs him with angry words and hostile facial expressions. He slowly becomes aware of the meaning of the words and finds that they are threats of personal destruction.

A common remark in Rajpur was: "You are not my child, go away." Although it was difficult to determine the effect on the child of such remarks, in some cases it was clear. An interviewer who heard a mother make such a comment, recorded the child as responding in fear, "No, no, mother—I am your child, I am your child, don't make me go away!" A wide range of threats were made to children in Rajpur, all of them designed to create fear. A common threat was to invoke ghosts, evil spirits, and goblins who were asked to take the child away. When the child stopped crying, the mother would often reward him by saying, "Do not come, my child is now silent."

The mothers sometimes used the interviewers to threaten the child with separation. We observed that even the possibility of separation aroused fear in the child. In one case the female interviewers made their first contact with a family when the baby was about five months old. During the next few visits they played with the baby and the child showed no fear. When the child reached one year of age, the interviewers began to notice that he would become fearful whenever they arrived. The cause was soon evident. The mother would cover him with her sari and say, "Don't cry, my child, the bens [sisters] will not take you away." Then she spoke to the interviewers: "Don't take my baby away, he will be good." When they returned at one and a half years, the child screamed in terror.

Threats of death were also common. A mother reported: "I say to him, 'I will put you on the road and the State Transport truck will run over you and you will die.' " Such comments as "Why don't you die, it would be better for me," were made. Another mother reportedly told her son that she would cut off his legs when he disobeyed her by following her out of the compound.

The threats were so common and were repeated so often that older children came to ignore them. On very young children, however, such threats had an obvious and perhaps lasting effect.

In summary, a possible explanation of the process by which a mother binds her son to herself begins with providing an early sense of trust. The prolonged nature of that close relationship makes it all the more important when it is withdrawn. The frustration felt by the child results in hostility and aggression directed toward his mother. The mother, however, who has been the source of love and protection for so long, not only rejects the child but threatens abandonment and destruction. Either through identification with the mother, or through repression of any feelings of hostility, the end result seems to be a compulsive attachment to the mother on the part of the son.

As noted earlier, mothers were probably warmer toward daughters than toward sons. Punishment was also less severe for girls, as will be seen in the following discussion on punishment for masturbation and on the most severe form of punishment we found, hanging children by the hands.

Threats of Punishment for Masturbation

Ford and Beach (1951:156) in their survey of sexual behavior among 190 societies, found that some social pressure is leveled against masturbation in nearly all the societies for which they had such information. The village research found, as did Carstairs for the Rajputs (1961:72), that as children grew older, increased sanctions were imposed for such behavior. In our interviews concerning five-year-olds, the mothers and some of the fathers were asked about punishment for masturbation. Some parents denied that their child engaged in genital play at all, but most of them admitted that it was a problem for children other than their own. A few stated that it was not worthwhile to control such activity until the child was six or seven years old, but other parents indicated that they used some form of sanction at an earlier age.

While fathers seemed to be more permissive than mothers about most kinds of behavior, they were particularly concerned about masturbation by the time the child was five years of age. A Patidar father offered three years as the age after which a child must be punished for masturbation: "A child should not play with his penis after three years of age. His mother tells him that she will jab his penis with a burning stick." Such threats seem to have been made often and sometimes were carried out. One Patidar father did so: "Once I put a burning stick to Nevin's penis and this frightened him very much." The father added that he found the threat of cutting off the penis to be even more effective. One Baria father said that if he saw neighbor children masturbating he would attempt to get them to stop by threatening to hang them by the hands. A Baria mother believed it "very important to prevent it [masturbation] in a child even when he is eight months old. If we notice him playing with himself we try to stop it by giving him a slap. If we don't stop it in the child, he might form a habit. If he does it later we have to give him the fear of branding with fire and beating severely so that he will never do it again."

From the comments of parents, as well as from our observation of the reactions of children, it was clear that threats were often effective with young children. As they grew older, however, children, particularly boys, found that threats were seldom carried out. They therefore became increasingly difficult to control. With older children, threats had to be plausible and at least occasionally implemented. One such threat was to inflict what villagers called "hanging by the hands."

Hanging by the Hands as Punishment

Hanging by the hands was a dramatic and feared experience used to reinforce the early socialization of boys in order to maintain obedience and submission. Children as young as five or six and into the later teens might be so punished. The method was used particularly by the upper-caste Patidars, but also by other village castes. Younger children were threatened with hanging to suppress masturbation, for talking back to parents, and for general disobedience. For older boys, it was used to reinforce prohibitions against sex, smoking, gambling, eating nonvegetarian food, and mixing with lower castes. The procedure was to tie the youth's wrists together with one end of a long rope and throw the other end over a rafter. The child was then pulled up until his feet were hanging above the ground.

Hanging by the hands, regarded as a rather extreme disciplinary technique, was not generally admitted to. Fathers especially seemed opposed to its use. Hanging, however, was a common enough practice so that many children reacted in fear when its use was threatened. Although it was not asked about specifically in the Rajpur interviews with ten-year-olds, one boy said that his mother had hung him by the hands. A number of mothers admitted that they had inflicted this severe punishment. In general, although there were cases of young girls who had been so punished, there were no recorded cases of older girls being treated this way. Boys, however, were evidently hung well into the adolescent years. Clearly, hanging was relied upon only when very severe punishment was deemed necessary.

Of particular interest was the reaction of children to such punishment, since any discussion of child abuse must consider the effect on the child. In a cultural analysis, the psychological costs may depend in part upon the way harsh treatment is perceived. If the child regards the treatment he receives as similar to the treatment accorded his peers, his view of it may be different from his response if he feels he alone is the object of unusually harsh punishment. Obviously, there were variations, but in general the reaction may be best described as panic. One indication of the possible long-term consequences was given by a medical doctor at the university. In a personal discussion the author asked him if he knew of this form of punishment. The doctor was quiet for a time and then said it was something that no one talked about; however, he continued, it had happened to him when he was about six years old. His mother died and his aunt had taken over his care. He did not remember what he had done to displease her, but he recalled that she had tied his wrists together, hung him on a large hook from the ceiling, and threatened to start a fire under his feet. He was so terrified that he had never forgotten the experience. He believed that his fear and awe of authority could be traced to that event.

Several examples of hanging in Rajpur may be given. It was reported that the sixteen-year-old son of a Patidar family was asked by his mother to go to the store and purchase peanut oil. He met some boys on the road who urged him to play cards. He lost the money and then borrowed enough to buy the oil. The person from whom he borrowed the money, however, told the boy's uncle. As punishment, the uncle and the grandfather hung the boy from the rafters. He was beaten with a stick by the grandfather during the hanging—an added practice more common with older boys.

A Baria mother told the interviewer that she had recently hung her seven-year-old daughter for five to ten minutes (the interviewer thought it was unlikely that it was that long). The daughter was reported by the neighbors to be difficult to control, and she often called her mother names. In this instance, the child apparently called the mother a prostitute, probably having heard neighbor women refer to her that way since the mother was evidently having extramarital relations. While the interviewer was talking to the mother the child walked into the house. The mother looked at her and said, "Mind you, I don't care if Ben [Sister] is here; I'll get the rope if you don't behave." When the child ran from the house in fear, the mother smiled at the interviewer. She was obviously pleased that she had finally discovered a way to control the girl.

Variations in Child-Rearing Practices

The traditions which seem to form the basis for normative behavior in regard to child rearing in a village setting have been presented. As in every society, however, a range of beliefs were expressed as to how children should be treated. We found that parents were quite willing to discuss which practices they considered acceptable and which they deemed abusive. It was clear from parents' accounts of their actions, as well as from our own observations, that physical punishment was used by almost all mothers and fathers and at all ages from the time of weaning into the teen years. The comments of parents and our observations also revealed that some parents were more lenient and some were harsher than the accepted norm.

Strict parents were critical of those whom they regarded as too lenient and thus as not doing an adequate job of child rearing. A Baria mother said:

"My children are afraid of me as I am very strict. I tell them I will give them a severe beating or that I will hang them upside down with a rope. In this village some mothers do not take proper care of their children." In another interview, however, the same mother admitted that others considered her too harsh: "My neighbor tells me that I beat my children more severely than other mothers. My children are very naughty compared to other children and I am short-tempered. I do beat them more."

There was also an indication that some parents felt guilty about punishing their children and that others thought harsh punishment was counterproductive to the child's growth and to the parent-child relationship. A Patidar mother said: "Sometimes I beat them, but then I feel bad about it for the rest of the day because I feel that it was not necessary. I try not to hit them. I beat the five-year-old only when I get angry." She also said that she never told her son he was unwanted: "I never say that. How can we say that to him? He is my child." The father in this family seemed to reject harsh treatment for fear a son might leave him when older: "I am afraid that he might run away from the family." Another father said: "Giving them slaps is not good because it creates a bad impression for the child and because the child soon forgets it anyway. I don't use physical punishment but my wife does."

Although mothers, particularly, made constant threats, there was often either no follow-up or just a slight slap on the face or back of the head, called a *tapli*. As a mother commented, "I say to her, I'll beat you, but then afterwards I don't feel like beating her."

There was also fear among parents that the child might suffer physically. One mother said: "I don't beat them because they might die from such punishment." And another commented: "Why should we beat our children when we give them precious food to eat? Only at times I slap her when she doesn't listen to me." A Vanker father of a ten-year-old boy, when queried about punishment, said: "See, Ben [Sister], I don't believe in spanking children. When we work hard to provide food for children to become strong, should we beat them and make them weak? Even if their mother beats them sometimes, I never do."

While fathers were generally regarded as more lenient, one mother thought her husband was too strict. She reported that her eleven-year-old son was severely beaten with a stick by his father because the teacher complained that the boy was not attending class regularly. He was also beaten by his father for not doing his lessons. The mother told the interviewer: "I tried to tell his father not to beat him so much but he said if I interfered he would beat me. So I could do nothing. But you know, Sister, it is for their own good. It is not us that will be helped by his [our son's] study."

V. CONCLUSION

The lack of information on child abuse and neglect in India, and indeed on socialization practices, makes obvious the preliminary nature of what is here presented. In addition, the vastness of the country and the diverse cultural and linguistic groups represented in India make any generalizations speculative. Despite these limitations, India offers an opportunity to contrast Western concepts of child abuse with those of a traditional and functioning peasant society.

In rural India, the structure of the extended family and the roles that are a part of that structure, together with the cultural values assigned to such roles, provide limits within which parents may make choices in child rearing. In addition, the situational forces presented in this chapter, such as hypergamy, dowry, and the lack of any long-term security other than living sons, make the practices we observed rational in the Indian context.

Young girls must be obedient and must learn to conform both in their own homes and in the homes of their in-laws. The difficulty in adjusting to a new family requires strength of personality, and so the kind of emotional dependence on the mother desirable in sons is not encouraged in daughters. This concept may account for a qualitative difference between mother-daughter and mother-son relationships. Although a daughter may be un-wanted at birth, if she survives she is more likely than a son to be treated warmly; and as she grows up, she tends to develop a closer relationship with the mother. This is particularly true as the daughter nears the time she must leave for the family of her in-laws.

A son must be socialized to remain with the extended family and support his parents, particularly his mother when she is widowed. Sons must therefore be not only obedient, but emotionally dependent. These characteristics may be socialized through a prolonged period of infant gratification followed by indulgence-withdrawal and threats of abandonment and destruction. This early conditioning may be followed in later childhood by rather severe physical punishment.

Neglect that results in death, and severe child-rearing practices that seem contrary to Western ideals for the optimal growth and development of the individual, may occur with some frequency among peasant groups in India. Such communities, although concerned with the welfare of children, place major emphasis on the needs of the group rather than on those of individuals.

Harsh treatment of children, unrelated to purposeful socialization and unsupported by cultural norms, must be labeled neglect and abuse in any society.[4] There is, however, a second category of harsh treatment, more difficult to label as either neglect or abuse: that is, adult behavior believed necessary by a society to limit the number of children or to prepare children for their adult roles. In rural India, the submission of individuality to family and caste is obligatory. Consequently, socialization practices cannot encourage individual expression. Rather, they focus on restraining individual desires and producing an obedient, submissive personality which will be accepting of a rigid social structure with assigned roles and duties.

The child-rearing practices recorded in this chapter are normative and traditional and are regarded as necessary to the continuation of rural society and the values held. It can be argued that to produce a personality that would strongly resist such restrictions would be irresponsible on the part of parents. Because parents may treat their children harshly, they do not consider it desirable or good to do so. Indeed, village parents would prefer not to hurt their children. They believe, however, that harsh treatment is necessary in order to maintain discipline.

Discipline may be common in India, but the kind of battering abuse and neglect found in the United States is not common. In India, the very social structure that requires conformity provides parents with a support system of other adults and older children. The presence of others in the household offers restraint to parental tempers and reduces the likelihood that frustration will lead to uncontrolled violence.

Child abuse in America may, on the other hand, partly reflect family dysfunction and current values. It is nonnormative, in that those who abuse and neglect children are regarded as deviating from approved child-rearing practices. In the United States, importance is placed on individual self-realization not only for children but for each individual parent. Since the needs of different family members are often in conflict, frustration and aggression may result.

The objective in this chapter has been to examine child-rearing practices in rural India in an attempt to better understand the nature of child neglect and abuse in a cross-cultural context. Debates on neglect and abuse, thus far largely clinical in nature, have generally been concerned with the welfare and potential development of the individual. Parental behavior can be viewed on a

---

[4]Various kinds of extreme maltreatment of children in India are sometimes taken by Westerners as common: for example, the practice of maiming children for the purpose of begging. While such cases may be found, there is no evidence that they occur frequently. In fact, in a large random sample of beggars in Delhi, only 10 percent were younger than ten years old and of the total sample fewer than 8 percent reported that their parents had initiated them into begging. No cases of child maiming were reported in the study (Gore 1959:262–263).

continuum from socialization practices that totally subjugate the child to society's demands to practices that virtually demand individualism and imbue little sense of responsibility to the group. In attempts at a cross-cultural definition of child abuse and neglect, it is suggested that the child-rearing practices of a people and the resulting behavior patterns be considered within the balance of individual and group needs.

REFERENCES

Baumrind, D.
 1978 Reciprocal rights and responsibilities in parent-child relations. *Journal of Social Issues* 34(2):179–196.
Becker, W. C.
 1964 Consequences of different kinds of parental discipline. In *Review of Child Development Research*, ed. M. L. Hoffman and L. W. Hoffman. Vol. I. New York: Russell Sage.
Bowlby, J.
 1960 Separation anxiety. *International Journal of Psychoanalysis* 41:89–113.
 1969 *Attachment and loss*. New York: Basic Books.
Carstairs, G. M.
 1961 *The twice-born*. London: Hogarth Press.
Census of India
 1931 *Report*. Pt. I. Government of Baroda: Baroda State Press.
 1971 *Series I. Provisional population totals*. Paper 1 of 1971 Supplements. New Delhi.
Clark, A.
 1976 Female infanticide as a means of maintaining caste dominance. Paper presented at Fifth Wisconsin Conference on South Asia, Madison.
Farson, R.
 1974 *Birthrights*. New York: Macmillan.
Ford, C. S., and F. A. Beach
 1951 *Patterns of sexual behavior*. New York: Harper.
Foster, G. M.
 1967 Introduction: what is a peasant? In *Peasant society*, ed. J. M. Potter et al. Boston: Little, Brown. Part I, pp. 2–14.
Goode, W. J.
 1963 *World revolution and family patterns*. New York: Free Press.
Gore, M. S.
 1959 *The beggar problem in metropolitan Delhi*. Delhi: School of Social Work.
 1961 The husband-wife and the mother-son relationship. *Sociological Bulletin* 11:71–102.
Government of Gujarat
 1966 *Report of the Suicide Inquiry Committee, May 1960–April 1964*. Ahmedabad: Government Central Press.

Harlow, H. F.
  1962 The nature of love. *American Psychologist* 13:673−685.
Holt, J.
  1974 *Escape from childhood*. New York: Dutton.
Jain, S. P.
  1975 *Demography: a status study on population research in India*. Vol. II. New Delhi: Tata
       McGraw-Hill.
Kagan, J.
  1978 The parental love trap. *Psychology Today* 12(3):54−61.
Kapadia, K. M.
  1966 *Marriage and family in India*. Calcutta: Oxford University Press.
Lewis, O.
  1958 *Village life in northern India*. Urbana: University of Illinois Press.
Mandelbaum, D. G.
  1970 *Society in India*. Berkeley, Los Angeles, London: University of California Press.
Mehta, M. H.
  1966 A study of the practice of female infanticide among the Kanbis of Gujarat.
       Journal of the Gujarat Research Society 28:57−66.
Mencher, J.
  1963 Growing up in south Malabar. *Human Organization* 22:54−65.
Minturn, L., and J. T. Hitchcock
  1963 The Rajputs of Khalapur India. In *Six cultures: studies in child-rearing*, ed. B. B.
       Whiting, New York: John Wiley. Pp. 203−361.
Murphy, L. B.
  1953 Roots of tolerance and tensions in Indian child development. In G. Murphy, *In
       the minds of man*. New York: Basic Books. Pp. 46−58.
Pakrasi, K. B.
  1970 *Female infanticide in India*. Calcutta: Editions India.
Panchanadikar, K. C., and J. Panchanadikar
  1970 *Determinants of social structure and social change in India*. Bombay: Popular
       Prakashan.
Poffenberger, T.
  1975 *Fertility and family life in an Indian village*. Michigan Papers on South and
       Southeast Asia, no. 10. Ann Arbor: University of Michigan Center for South
       and Southeast Asia.

  1976 *The socialization of family size values: youth and family planning in an Indian village*
       Michigan Papers on South and Southeast Asia, no. 12. Ann Arbor: University
       of Michigan Center for South and Southeast Asia.
Poffenberger, T., and S. Poffenberger
  1973 The social psychology of fertility in a village in India. In *Psychological perspectives
       on population*, ed. J. T. Fawcett. New York: Basic Books. Part II, pp. 135−162.
Redfield R.
  1967 The social organization of tradition. In *Peasant society*, ed. J. M. Potter et al.
       Boston: Little, Brown. Part I, pp. 25−34.
Solomon, Theo
  1973 History and demography of child abuse. *Pediatrics* 51(4): 773−776.

Steele, B. F.
1977 Child abuse and society. *Child Abuse and Neglect: The International Journal* 1(1)1–6.

Takanishki, R.
1978 Childhood as a social issue: historical roots of contemporary child advocacy movements. *Journal of Social Issues* 34(2):8–28.

Tube-Becker, E.
1977 The death of children following negligence. *Child Abuse and Neglect: The International Journal* 1(1):25–30.

United Nations
1973 *The determinants and consequences of population trends.* Department of Economic and Social Affairs, Population Studies, no. 50. New York.

Wyon, J. B., and J. E. Gordon
1971 *The Khanna study: population problems in the rural Punjab.* Cambridge: Harvard University Press.

SOCIOECONOMIC AND PSYCHO-CULTURAL CONTEXTS OF CHILD ABUSE AND NEGLECT IN TURKEY[1]

6

Emelie A. Olson

An examination of child-rearing practices and potential abuse in Turkey provides an opportunity to explore some of the explanations of child abuse in Western literature. Although statistical data on the epidemiology of child abuse in Turkey are scanty, there appears to be relatively little of the kind of punitive child abuse vis-à-vis infants and "preschoolers"[2] in Turkey which was the central concern of such reseachers as Davoren (1968), Steele and Pollock (1968), and Gil (1970). This complex which I am going to term "classic" child abuse, refers to the highly punitive, extremely exacting, and overly controlling behaviors by parents which lead to mistreatment of the child. In its more extreme forms, this type of abuse results in what is called the "battered child syndrome" (Helfer and Kempe 1968).

A precise description of child rearing and child abuse in Turkey is made difficult by the fact that the ethnography not only is spotty and somewhat sparse but has generally focused on topics other than child rearing. Nearly all the ethnographies now available, however, have appeared within the last ten years, thus giving us a relatively recent picture of several regions in contempo-

---

[1] I would like to thank Barbara B. Helling, Ciğdem Kağıtçıbaşı, Jill Korbin, Orhan M. Öztürk, and Atalay Yörükoğlu for their comments and criticisms of earlier drafts of this manuscript. The final responsibility for its contents remains, of course, with me.

[2] Today, most Turkish children begin primary school at the age of seven. To my knowledge, however, there is no common Turkish term that is the equivalent of "preschooler."

rary Turkey. Further, this ethnographic literature is supplemented both by more extensive scholarly publications in medicine, sociology, history, and political science, and by a copious nonscientific literature including plays, poetry, fiction, and accounts by travelers and foreign students. As a result, there is in some ways a wealth of material available which has a bearing on the issue of child abuse and neglect in Turkey. I have drawn on material from very different sources for this paper, utilizing what Munroe and Munroe (1976:2) call the "strong inference" approach which is heavily interpretive of the data available.

General statements about child rearing and child abuse in Turkey may be unusually subject to error because of Turkey's complex history and ecology. Turkish society and culture are heterogeneous because of the country's geographical location as an ancient crossroad between Europe and Asia, as well as because of its diverse topography and ecology, complex political history, rich ethnic and religious heritage, and the rapid social change it has been undergoing in the twentieth century.

For simplicity, I will work with an ideal model of Turkish society and culture, one that I will call "traditional" Turkish culture. An intentionally generalized ideal type, traditional Turkish culture refers to behavior patterns and rules judged to be of long duration and commonly found in the nonelite sectors of the population in rural and urban areas both at present and in the recent past. In the final section I discuss the more recent changes occurring in many sectors of Turkish society and their implications for child abuse and neglect in the future.

A review of the *Turkish Journal of Pediatrics* from 1958 to the present yielded no references to the possibility of classic child abuse. Because this journal tends to technical discussions of etiology, diagnosis, and treatment of individual pathology rather than to considerations of its psycho-socio-cultural context, the absence of such references cannot be regarded as conclusive evidence for a low incidence of child abuse. Dr. Atalay Yörükoğlu, a psychiatrist at a large university hospital in the capital city of Ankara, writes: "Our hospital records do not show any cases of child abuse or battered child syndrome. I am sure some such cases have been hospitalized and treated. But they were either overlooked or listed under the general category of 'traumas.' As you know Hacettepe Children's Hospital is a big center drawing patients from all over the country. And almost all of the senior staff, having had their training in the States, are aware of this particular syndrome. Therefore it is safe to assume that classic child abuse is rather rare in Turkey" (personal communication, 1978).

The relatively low incidence of child abuse in Turkey should not be viewed as an indication of the overall mental health of the traditional society, but only as evidence that stress in traditional Turkish society seems to be expressed in symptoms other than classic child abuse. Dr. Orhan M. Öztürk, chairman of psychiatry at Hacettepe University School of Medicine, cautions against a tendency to romanticize non-Western cultures: "We know that mental health problems, in severe or in mild forms, are not any less in traditional societies, but the forms of handling these problems may be quite different from those of modern societies. In other words, if we consider 'child abuse' as a symptom, this symptom may not be so prevalent in the Turkish traditional child-rearing system, but other symptoms may be present"[3] (personal communication, November 1978).

One of the cultural factors accounting for the apparently low incidence of this classic complex of child abuse may be Turkish beliefs about causation and, more specifically, the concept of locus of control and responsibility. In traditional Turkish etiology, the pervasive view seems to be that the ultimate cause of everything in this world is transcendent of human will. Although phrased in Muslim terms, attributing the ultimate cause to God, this view is probably less a reflection of dogmatic Muslim theology than part of the general Turkish world view, and it may well predate Islam in Turkey. A statement of the villager's version of this view is provided by a Turkish psychiatrist: "The Koran states that all evil and good come from God, and God is therefore the literal provider of health and sickness in the eyes of the villager. . . . God is the foremost etiological agent" (Öztürk 1965b:168). Within this ultimate etiology there are lesser causal agents that are also beyond the control of the village Turk. These include the natural environment, supernatural beings and powers like jinns (supernatural beings in human or animal form), and the evil eye: "Human life, instead of being well regulated and subject to secure human care, is generally more exposed to chance and to the mercies of the natural and the supernatural" (Öztürk 1965b:174).

As a result, ultimate control and responsibility are neither the privilege nor the burden of humans, who are thereby relieved of guilt: "Human will and responsibility have nothing to do with the anxieties and fears" (Öztürk 1965b:177); "There is little or no awareness of guilt associated with one's own impulses or responsibilities as long as one complies with the rules and rituals of these forces" (Öztürk 1965b:178).

The traditional Turk's response to life is not, however, always one of passive acquiescence, as is so often alleged (cf. Karpat 1960:153). Rather, this viewpoint frees some of his energies to act; he need not be anxious about the

---

[3]Professor Öztürk reports his investigations of some of these symptoms in his recent publications (Öztürk 1973, 1978; Öztürk and Öztürk 1977).

outcome of his actions—the Omnipotent will not permit anything to happen against His will. This paradox is expressed by a professor of theology at Ankara University who argues that Muslims should not hesitate to use contraception because "God is so great, His will cannot be thwarted by birth control if He wants a child to be born" (Ateş 1968). It is also reflected in the birth control behavior of a village woman who told me that she had twice tried to abort her current pregnancy by injections. When neither injection succeeded, her husband suggested that it was God's will that this child be born and she made no further attempts to abort the fetus (Olson-Prather 1976:354-355).

This general theory of causation is reflected in at least two ways in child-rearing behavior. First, babies and small children are viewed as part of the natural and social environment which is largely beyond the control of the actor. In contrast, then, with the classic child abuser's definition of parental disciplinary goals as total control of the children (Davoren 1968:155), the traditional Turkish parent probably cannot even conceive of such control vis-à-vis infants and small children. The Turkish parent is thus unlikely to feel indicted as a failure by less than instant obedience from his tiny offspring and, as a result, to abuse the child for proving parental incompetence.

Second, this general theory of causation seems to be reflected in an overall pattern of unsystematic, largely nonpurposive child rearing which places the locus of control elsewhere than in the individual himself (Helling 1960:194; Kağıtçıbaşı 1977:64). The fact that child-rearing techniques are traditional and that knowledge of them is acquired incidentally also contributes to this unselfconscious, spontaneous approach to child rearing. The Turkish adult has few doubts about what he should do or how he should go about it when dealing with children (Helling 1960:194). The interaction between beliefs about causation and traditional learning fosters a tendency for discipline of infants and small children to be "directed toward controlling the immediate situation rather than toward developing a particular character in the child" (Helling 1960:196). The primary criterion for discipline appears to be whether the child is irritating the adults present at that moment in time, so that the rules are arbitrary, the result of adult whims rather than reflections of absolute standards of behavior (Helling 1960:20; Kağıtçıbaşı 1977:64). "Direct social control" predominates rather than "inner personal control" (Kağıtçıbaşı 1977:64). Unlike the classic child abuser, who tends to measure his own worth by his success in molding his child's character and thus punishes the child who "shows him up," the Turkish parent tends to treat his very young offspring so as to provide for his own immediate comfort rather than for either his or the child's ego.

The role of beliefs about causation in reducing child abuse is complemented by another cognitive factor: the definition of children in terms of their needs, wants, and capabilities. In Davoren's formulation, child-abusing parents suffered from both unrealistically high expectations of the very young child's physical and emotional capabilities and an insensitivity to the child's own needs and wants (Davoren 1968:155). The data available suggest such attitudes are highly unlikely in the traditional Turkish setting. Rather, the Turkish infant is regarded from birth as a very limited human being who will grow up at his own pace. The general response of the parent is one of warmth and acceptance to a degree that some observers have regarded as indulgent. "Especially during preschool years parents spoil their children a great deal thus fostering and prolonging their dependency. As a result most of the misbehaviors children show are not punished but simply tolerated as childish naughtiness" (Yörükoğlu, personal communication, December 1978).

This view of children is also reflected in such traditional practices as swaddling babies for much of the first year and having them ride on someone's back most of the time until they are three or four years old. Further, there is very little pressure on children to control their bowels and bladders, control that seems to be achieved without stress by about three years of age. This is facilitated by the fact that village children out of the cradle wear only dresses or shirts, so it is easy to respond to their "signs." They are taken out of doors whenever they give a sign, intentional or not, or immediately following involuntary elimination. A child is not punished for an "involuntary," but an adult may be held responsible for not taking appropriate measures. "Accidents" are quickly and matter-of-factly cleaned up by the mother or another female relative (Helling 1960:195-196).

Further, it is assumed that a child's needs and wants reflect his limitations and that his demands should be met insofar as possible.

> His impulses and demands, from his first cries for food, are regarded as legitimate and to be satisfied if possible rather than regulated or thwarted. This is reflected in the nursing practices, in the general absence of routine in the child's activities, and in the fact that techniques of control involve *persuading* the child . . . by distraction, threats, or deception rather than by force. [Helling 1960:199]

For example, in the village of Zek, Helling noted that a baby was nursed every time it cried and only when it cried. It was never wakened for nursing to suit the mother's convenience, nor was it fed automatically upon wakening. Preschool and primary school-age children were also fed on demand rather than on schedule, except for breakfast, the one real meal of the day. There was also little regulation of sleeping times: both infants and children were expected to fall asleep whenever they became tired, in whatever corner was convenient, in the same room where the adults were talking or involved in other activities. If an overly tired child annoyed the adults present, a mother would sometimes lie on the floor or mat beside the child until he fell asleep.

This accepting, pragmatic, spontaneous style of traditional child rearing also facilitates the learning of work skills without apparent stress, through observation, imitation, and trial and error. Children in villages and small towns do a great deal of work but, as in Zek, they are given "little independent responsibility, rather being assigned one specific task at a time" (Helling 1960:197).

> [The village judges a child directly, not with the]. . . western emphasis on the task as a problem to be solved . . . or as a testing ground of moral worth . . . [approaches] which tend to mediate between child and adult and set a performance standard. . . . Most tasks are traditional, performed unthinkingly, allocated in pragmatic and traditional ways and, for the most part, have identical minimum and maximum standards of performance. . . . Willingness and obedience rather than ability limit performance. The adult reacts to the child as another (limited) human being here and now—does not think of tasks as measuring sticks of the child's developing ability but simply as things that he wants done.
>
> . . . [Conspicuous is] the absence of verbal instruction and moralizing. There is no appeal to reason, no explanation, no purposive punishment, no effort to change the child or direct his development. *The child is what he is* [italics added]. The adult takes the responsibility for his immediate behavior but does not recognize the possibility of molding his development. [Helling 1960:200−201]

Thus the child is unlikely to fail in meeting either parental demands or the requirements of a specific task (Helling 1960:198).

Other cultural factors help to account for the low incidence of classic child abuse in Turkey. Perhaps most important are such traditional social structures as the family, kinfolk, the neighborhood, networks of friends, and the like. One way in which the relationship between social structure and child abuse is mediated is through social-psychological factors. Traditional Turkish culture is typically described as "patriarchal and gerontocratic" (Ugurel-Semin 1969:139), "coercive and constrictive" (Öztürk 1965a:127), aimed toward conformity and submission (Yürtoren 1965), authoritarian (Kağıtçıbaşı 1970:150 151), inhibiting to "autonomous ego development" (Kağıtçıbaşı 1977:64), and obsessed with "honor" and pride (Meeker 1976; Robson 1976: 248−250). Such descriptions might suggest that Turkish parents would share some of the "common characteristics" of child abusers noted by Davoren and others, particularly in terms of demands for total control and obedience. Such descriptions of Turkish culture, however, are both oversimplified and distorted, partly owing to a tendency to look at certain behaviors out of context.

In a series of publications, Turkish social psychologist Çiğdem Kağıtçıbaşı questions the alleged authoritarian character of the "traditional" Turkish personality (1970, 1973, 1977). She notes that the application of standard measures of authoritarianism at first appears to confirm the typical generalizations that Turks are characterized by a high degree of constriction and blind respect for authority, both state and parental. Owing to the Turkish sociocultural context, however, this alleged authoritarianism is something quite different from its American variant, a difference she indicates by the terms "normative" versus "core" or "personal" authoritarianism, respectively. First, respect for authority is a Turkish social norm. Obedience in Turkey reflects a rather different set of psychodynamic processes from those in the United States: "This obedience, coming from social norms, seems to carry different overtones than the blind obedience and submission, mixed with repressed hostility, that the authoritarian personality postulates on a psychodynamic basis" (Kağıtçıbaşı 1970:445). Second, the difference between American ("personal") and Turkish ("normative") authoritarianism is also corroborated by data that reveal a weaker positive relationship, or even a negative one, between authoritarianism and respect for authority in Turkish research populations (Kağıtçıbaşı 1970:448, 1977:31). Third, although Turkish students score higher than American students on respect for authority in general, an item analysis suggests that Turks show less respect than do Americans for authority that is "not justified" or worthy of respect. Thus, Kağıtçıbaşı argues, the "Turkish attitude toward authority should probably be called 'acceptance of authority,' rather than 'submission to authority,' for the latter connotes blind, unquestioning submission, acting almost as a defense mechanism, as proposed by the authoritarian personality" (1970:448).

This positive valuation of respect for authority finds expression in family relationships as well, although, as I have discussed at length elsewhere (Olson-Prather 1976:194–218), the Turkish family is neither as patriarchal nor as constrictive as is generally believed. Further, Kağıtçıbaşı argues that the average Turkish family is less authoritarian than the American family. Although the contrary is suggested by the literature, she notes that this is at least partly owing to the inappropriate combination of two separate dimensions in the measure of authoritarian family structure, a "confounding of the affection and control factors." Unlike the typical American authoritarian personality-producing family, which is strict and rejecting, the "typical Turkish family is restrictive in discipline but warm in emotional atmosphere" (Kağıtçıbaşı 1970:444). Yörükoğlu comments on this generalization: "In our traditional families parents use spanking freely and don't feel guilty about it. . . . It is so common that children accept it as the price to be paid for mischief and misbehavior. More importantly they don't see it as a sign of rejection on the part of parents. Warmth and acceptance shown toward children amply neutralize the damage done by corporal punishment" (personal communication, 1978). By keeping separate these two dimensions, which Kağıtçıbaşı also refers to as "restrictiveness-permissiveness" and "warmth-hostility," respectively, she describes the differing effects of restrictiveness in American and Turkish families. Both because of the general societal norm of restrictiveness and because of the emotional warmth of Turkish families, restrictiveness within the Turkish family does not tend to produce the typical authoritarian personality.

> . . . Strict discipline, the expected situation in Turkey but not in the States, may be perceived as rejection by the American children (and thus theoretically lead to the development of core authoritarianism), but probably [is] not perceived as rejection by the Turkish children. . . .
> In the American sample core authoritarianism correlates significantly with both family control and lack of affection. . . . In the Turkish sample . . . it correlates significantly with control . . ., but not with affection. [Kağıtçıbaşı 1970:449–450].

In summary, Kağıtçıbaşı's characterization of the Turkish family suggests that the restrictiveness of Turkish parents is not primarily a defense mechanism motivated by deep-seated fears and feelings of inadequacy as a human being, as is true of the authoritarian personality, but that it must be interpreted within the total Turkish context. Further, Turkish parents tend to be accepting rather than rejecting, warm rather than hostile, and indulgent rather than exacting toward their small children. For these reasons, stereotypes about the Turkish family as coercive and authoritarian—concepts that seem to be related to the characteristics of child abusers, despite differences in terminology—should not mislead us into expectations of a high incidence of classic child abuse.

The generalization that Turkish families tend to be warm and accepting toward infants and small children deserves further exploration. Warmth and acceptance are related to several factors. First, children are very much desired, for an impressive number and variety of values. As Kağıtçıbaşı puts it, "children are unique in the complex satisfactions that they provide" (1977:76). Her survey corroborates more ethnographic evidence that children have utilitarian value as workers and as a source of economic security in their parents' old age, especially in rural areas. They define adult status and social identity and relieve boredom by providing stimulation and fun. Children contribute to the primary group by providing love and companionship and by cementing family ties; they provide family continuity and a sort of social immortality, especially for more prosperous families (Kağıtçıbaşı 1977:65–114; Olson-

Prather 1976:299—305). Sons are particularly valued, primarily by women, who through them gain power, status, and financial security in old age. Since the mother-son relationship is also expected to be the most emotionally intense one in a woman's life, mothers indulge their sons lavishly (Kăgıtçıbaşı 1977:97—99; Kıray 1976:266—267). Daughters, though somewhat less indulged, are valued for their help in the house. As discussed below, daughters are also valued for their companionship both when young and after they marry (Kağıtçıbaşı 1977:97—99; Kıray 1964:3—17).

Second, the creation of an environment of warmth and acceptance is facilitated by the emotional and social support given to parents and children by the larger family and the local community. In "traditional" Turkey, these in-groups, in which face-to-face interaction predominates, both define and support their members to an extent rarely found in more individualistic societies like the United States.

Before proceeding with a discussion of in-groups, it is necessary to correct some common misconceptions about the Turkish family both in the past and in its current evolution. Despite the picture provided in much of the literature, there is evidence that the traditional patriarchal, patrilateral, extended family existed more as an ideal than as a reality, at least in its most comprehensive residential form (Olson-Prather 1976:198—217; Timur 1972: 31—33). For several reasons, including intrafamily stress, demographics, and economics, this is true not only of contemporary urban Turkey, but also of earlier eras and more rural communities. It does not follow, however, that the Western model of the isolated nuclear family is appropriate to Turkey. Rather, Kağıtçıbaşı describes Turkish families as "functionally," but not "structurally," extended, noting that they often are spacially proximate, include a high degree of social cooperation, and provide material support and security (1977:17—18). Even though the majority of families were and are residentially nuclear or stem (including relatives such as unmarried aunts, nephews, widowed mothers, etc.), these same residentially nuclear families are embedded in a network of kin and/or nonkin relationships that may parallel those of the ideal extended family in several ways (Benedict 1976:219—223).

Each husband and wife can draw on the daily support of a close-knit, largely same-sex social network, which may include both kin and nonkin. Turks are in almost constant verbal contact with one another, and they will in fact go to considerable lengths to be with friends and relations. For example, Helling describes a young mother in the village of Zek who, with her children, spent most of her time in other women's houses because she had no adult women sharing her own house (Helling 1960:211—215). Or, as Robson puts it, "Turkey has always been a 'conversational' culture, whose delight in sophisticated and easy conversation is reflected in the architecture of their houses with their *misafir odası, salon,* or *selamlık* appointed for entertaining guests" (Robson 1976:211–212).

For most women, the social network is primarily a neighborhood (*semt* or *mahalle*) and/or kin group, defined largely in terms of proximity (Olson-Prather 1976:243–269). The men's networks, more public and less limited geographically, often include the men who frequent their places of work (Benedict 1976:237; Kolars 1963:58–62; Magnarella 1974:96).

This pervasive, inclusive system of overlapping social groups provides support for parents and children in several ways. The sociability, warmth, and acceptance in the social environment allow a distinctive sense of security for the young child which is unusual in the urban West. For example, life in the village of Zek seems to fit this pattern and to produce a feeling of self-worth and competency in the child who lives there:

> His life, while circumscribed, is secure and involves little of the self-doubt and feelings of inadequacy so characteristic of modern western civilization. The child is wanted for his practical service to the household, for his own (or even her) prestige value, and for himself alone. He is born into a role in the extended family and the community which gives him an important and meaningful place in the life of his entire group. Everyone knows him. *He is accepted as he is and no demands are made on him which he cannot meet or cannot learn how to meet under the continuing influences of the community* [italics added]. [Helling 1960:199].

The Turkish child in such a setting, then, does not have constantly to prove his worth but is automatically assigned a secure role as a useful and valued member of his local group.[4]

Unlike the social environment of many American parents, the Turkish social structure provides many alternative sources of love and affection for parents besides their young children. As a result, it is suggested that traditional Turkish parents are unlikely to make the unrealistic and impossible demands for love and support from their immature children which Davoren described as typical of classic child abusers. Further, thanks to what might be called "orientation towards others" rather than orientation either to the objec-

---

[4]Orhan Öztürk, an American-trained Turkish psychiatrist, warns not to "interpret the data of child-rearing practices in terms of their virtues or healthy aspects." He adds that "so far there is no sound evidence to indicate that traditional societies or families have more 'secure' or 'valued' children than transitional or modern societies do" (personal communication, November 1978). Although comparisons of overall mental health are unwarranted, there seems to be considerable evidence that the traditional Turkish setting provides a certain type of security for the child and the adult which may be a factor in the apparently low incidence of child abuse. As noted above, the symptoms of stress in traditional Turkish culture do not seem to include classic child abuse, and my purpose here is to try to illuminate some of the factors that may explain its low incidence.

tive situation or to absolute standards (Helling 1960:196−200), and motivated by strong loyalties to family, in-group, and nation (Hyman et al. 1958; Kağıtçıbaşı 1970:445), the Turkish parent tends to be very skillful in social interaction. As a child he had learned "to feel out the adult, to become a skillful judge of just how far he can go, to regulate his behavior according to the signs he reads in the appearance and behavior of those about him" (Helling 1960: 200). As a parent he finds in those social skills the means for satisfying his personal needs in social interaction with a large number of adults with whom he has multifaceted and (usually) long-term relationships. This kind of parent is in contrast with the classic child-abusing parent who, having failed to develop such skills, is socially isolated.

The traditional Turkish social structure also tends to provide more tangible assistance to the parents of small children. In contrast with the relative social isolation of many American mothers, Turkish mothers are likely to share the rearing of their small children with several other people. Since the care and supervision of children is an important responsibility of girls and women of all ages (Helling 1960:194), nonparental socializers include older sisters, aunts, cousins, grandmothers, other relatives, neighbors, and teachers. Men and boys are involved, too, though not as frequently with female as with male children. Finally, grandparents of both sexes are particularly valuable in providing affection and stimulation for the children. One of the major goals of life is to have adult children who will provide one with grandchildren and the leisure to retire and play with those grandchildren (Helling 1960:121). Older children are discussed in more detail below, but it might be noted that, perhaps as early as five or six years of age, peers are also important sources of emotional support and discipline to an extent seldom seen in middle-class American communities.

The presence of other people at nearly all times can help prevent child abuse in other ways. Outsiders can fend off an explosive buildup of stress by sharing in the responsibility for discipline. The shared responsibility may be rather publicly demonstrated by men toward somewhat older boys. For example, when the men and older boys are gathered in the guest room of someone's house, everyone present takes the responsibility for controlling the smaller boys. This is especially true of the young men, one of whom might rather suddenly pull the leather belt from his waist and deliver a silent "strapping" to the transgressor. The practice of sharing responsibility both reflects and allows the diffusion of any one father's responsibility to discipline his sons directly (Helling 1960:129-130). Of course, discipline of another's child may sometimes lead to words between the discipliner and the parent (Helling 1960:154−155), but in general the effect of shared disciplining is to spread the responsibility for child rearing and thereby to reduce the stress on individual parents.

Moreover, other people constantly assist in meeting the physical and emotional needs of children. They may give advice to a worried parent, carry the toddler while its mother carries the baby, rock the cradle, play word games with the toddler while the mother chops beets in the field, take the child out to defecate while the mother chats with neighbors, or clean the soiled floor after an accident. Finally, the constant presence of other people can provide a buffer for the child, either because they can bail out the overwrought parent, which Helfer cites as an important preventive of abuse (1973:777–778), or simply because they can physically intervene between the angry parent and his intended victim. As Yörükoğlu puts it, neither relatives nor neighbors "need any invitation to come over and intervene in case of an unreasonably severe spanking" (personal communication, December 1978).

I have presented above some possible explanations for the alleged low incidence of classic abuse of small children in Turkey, abuse that would be recognized as such by most Americans and Turks alike. There is, however, some evidence of other practices and situations that might be defined as child abuse or neglect by Western standards but are seen as either nonabusive or as unavoidable facts of life by most Turks.

One of these practices is the custom of swaddling babies and strapping them in their cradles most of the time for their first six months of life (Helling 1960:195). Both Western and Western-trained Turkish observers have criticized this physically restricting practice as damaging to the emotional, social, and physical development of the child (cf. Öztürk 1965a). Such criticism, however, reflects ethnocentrism in the definition of healthy development, raising basic questions whose answers are beyond the scope of this paper. The determination of possible damage is related to such issues as the relative value of freedom versus security and of individual development versus group well-being; judgments about the importance of early stimulation and activity for later developmental stages; standards for the types and degrees of physical discomfort which are unacceptable, acceptable, and optimal; and more complex sets of values about what constitutes healthy emotional development and creates ideal personality types.

Similar issues are raised by a second traditional practice, the use of a special clay, *höllük*, dried and warmed, in the baby's diapers, which some American researchers apparently regarded as benign; (Helling 1960:70–81, 106–107; Scott 1966), but which has been strongly criticized as a "primitive custom" and a cause of infections, vermin infestation, and so forth, by at least one Turkish scholar (Kansu 1961).

A third practice involving explicit attention to the child's genitals might be viewed by some Western observers as a sexual assault on the child's body or as psychologically crippling seduction. Yet it is regarded as a desirable practice by the Turks engaging in it. It is my impression that the genitals of tiny boys and girls are much admired by adult relatives. For example, old women snatch at the bare penises of little boys as they run by, threatening to cut them (Helling 1960:87−88), but also in apparent celebration of the small boy's incipient virility. Such behavior might also be considered potentially abusive by Western standards, either because it violates the boy's sexual privacy and increases his castration anxiety or because it is a symbolic seduction of a small child by a more powerful adult who is teasing him.

Manipulation of the little girl's genitals seems to be less common, but it is more clearly positive. During our last residence in Turkey we engaged the services of an older Turkish woman as maid and nurse to our twenty-month-old daughter. She was very vocal in her admiration of our daughter's *şeker kutu* (sugar box), kissing her vulva lovingly when she changed her diaper and urging me to do the same as a part of appropriate "mothering." A teenage neighbor girl of the elite class also expressed verbal but not physical admiration (Olson-Prather 1976:278).[5] Although I viewed our maid's behavior as positive, it could be interpreted by some observers as seduction in a much more explicit form than that practiced with little boys, and thus as damaging to a girl's psychosexual development. At issue again, of course, are basic questions as to what constitutes healthy development and how to achieve it.

There remain several possible forms of abuse or neglect stemming from environmental factors and the Turkish style of child rearing. In regard to the latter, the absence of eating and sleeping schedules may lead to child abuse or neglect. For example, as noted above, Helling observed that babies in Zek were nursed whenever they cried. Despite the amount of "rooting" they might do at the breast, they were never nursed until they cried and then were nursed only briefly. As a result, a feeding usually consisted of several short nursing periods in the course of an hour. The pattern of unscheduled feeding continues in the feeding of older children, with little or no supervision as to what the child eats (Helling 1960:196). Aside from the psychological implications that might be drawn from this pattern, the unsystematic feeding of the weaned child is probably at least a minor factor in the high rates of malnutrition,

---

[5]I have seen no mention of this practice in the literature, although another American researcher, Barbara Bilge, reports that it is common among recent and earlier Turkish immigrants now resident near Detroit, Michigan. They use the terms *şeker kütü* and *fındık* (hazelnut) (personal communication, November 1978).

illness, and mortality found in Turkey (Cura 1961; Kansu 1961; Öztürk 1965a:127).

These health problems are forms of what Gil terms "collective abuse and neglect," damage to children caused by general levels of poverty and scarcity of resources (Gil 1970:15). Öztürk lays the blame for inadequate child care on the "low status of women which forces . . . [a mother] to work continuously" and thus robs her of the ability to provide adequate "time, energy, and security" for healthy child care (1965a:126). Poverty of resources also leads to other types of neglect in the area of health. Villagers and the urban poor are ordinarily unable to take advantage of professional medical services and instead rely on folk remedies and magico-religious measures, many of them ineffective. For example, a mother may leave a tiny child alone in a cemetery at night, praying that God will "bury my youngster's sickness in the earth" (Nesin 1977:19–20).

Finally, Turkish children suffer from another form of collective abuse: relatively high rates of accidental injuries and burns. Injuries reported by parents as accidents may of course be the result of unadmitted abuse, as child abuse experts are fully aware. Most accidents, however, are just that, since traditional Turkish environments, especially those of the urban poor and rural dwellers, present many opportunities for accidents. Most cooking is done over open fireplaces or pressure kerosene stoves on the floor; wood cookstoves and space heaters become red-hot but have no protective guards. Double teapots, long-handled coffee makers, and soup cauldrons full of scalding liquids are within easy reach of both infants and small children. Children are allowed access to knives, needles, axes, and other sharp implements at an age far younger than is considered safe by Western standards. Stairways to the second-floor living quarters over the stables frequently lack banisters and never boast child-proof gates. Playpens are unheard-of. It is only the watchful eyes of caretakers and the child's previous learning which protect him from these ubiquitous dangers; it is not surprising that children suffer repeated bruises, broken bones, burns, poisonings, and lacerations.

Other situations provide the potential for abuse to older children in Turkey. Although little is expected of very small children, by the age of five or six, and especially by the age of seven when they are required to start primary school, children are perceived as much less limited in their capabilities. As a result, indulgence by adults decreases while the use of physical punishment and demands for competence and conformity markedly increase (Helling 1960:119 120; Ugurcl-Scmin 1969.145). It is also at about this age that a girl begins to work more seriously alongside the women, whereas a boy leaves the world of indulgent women and small children for the world of male work and stern discipline (Helling 1960:145—147; Kăğıtçıbaşı 1977:50). Not only rural children but urban apprentices work increasingly long hours from the age of seven on, during a period regarded as an age of play by Western standards (Fallers and Fallers 1976:257—258; Öztürk 1965a:128; Ugurel-Semin 1969:141).

Although most Turks regard this transition as unremarkable, the shift from the indulgence of the early years to the hard work and harsh discipline of later childhood may be traumatic enough to be considered a source of abuse by Western standards. My own observations in a Turkish village suggest that the transition brings a radical change in adult behavior toward children of both sexes. For example, like Helling (1960:170—173), I was myself very surprised at first by the strict discipline and sudden punishment meted out by the village teachers, whom I knew to be warm, nurturant, and tolerant individuals.

The literature, both fictional and autobiographical, presents examples of harsh treatment by both religious and secular teachers which suggest that abuse of Turkish students by their teachers and masters has been recognized by more than one observer. As they near school age, boys especially are expected to be courageous, to be able to endure physical pain and frustration. Further, both teachers and apprentice masters are expected to be strict disciplinarians and are often encouraged to use corporal punishment. This pattern is reflected in a proverb sometimes said to be the standard admonition of a parent to his child's teacher: *Eti senin kemiği benim* ("His flesh is yours, his bones are mine") (Redhouse 1968:351). Given the sanction of strict discipline, the likelihood of sadistic teachers and masters—who must be assumed to exist in Turkey as elsewhere—inflicting abuse on students in the guise of discipline is possibly greater than in the ideally more permissive American school.

On the other hand, I would argue that at least three contextual factors probably reduce the potential damage of both the psychological shock caused by a sudden change in definition and treatment of children and the physical pain inflicted by teachers and other adults. First, children must be quite cognizant of the coming transition and probably approach it not only with apprehension but also with pride, since it signals a new stage of maturity. As such, punishment by teachers and other adults may prove to be more constructive than destructive to children's sense of identity and self-worth. Second, since the harsh treatment is usually viewed as necessary and appropriate, rather than unwarranted, Turkish children may not perceive it as rejection. Finally, because of the unsystematic, pragmatic style of child rearing they have experienced earlier, the children have learned to respond directly and matter-of-factly to specific demands by adults without necessarily internalizing those demands as part of an absolute set of standards. As a result, rather than seeing punishment as a condemnation of their self-worth, they may see it merely as a cue to change their behavior in order to avoid unpleasant consequences. Öztürk stresses the importance of context in noting the adaptability of children: "It can be assumed that the village child [in Turkey] learns to modulate his needs and frustration thresholds and learns to live with what can be given." Quoting Erickson, he adds: "A traditional system of child care can be said to be a factor making for trust, even when certain items of that tradition, taken singly, may seem unnecessarily cruel" (1965a:174).

In many communities the transition coincides roughly with the ceremony of circumcision for boys. As the circumcision of boys typically occurs between the ages of four and eight, within the Oedipal period, it might itself be perceived by Westerners as a form of child abuse (Kağıtçıbaşı 1977:64; Öztürk 1973:49−54). Such a view seems especially likely given the common practice of threatening in word and gesture to cut (*kesmek*) boys' penises, employing the same verb used for circumcision. This threat is made not only as playful teasing of little boys but also as a warning of punishment for misbehavior. As might be expected, Öztürk finds evidence that such practices do exacerbate the usual anxiety. Moreover, the small boy's playmates may have been terrorizing him for months (Fallers and Fallers 1976:256). An adult male friend said of his own unusually late circumcision at the age of nine that expectations of fear are far worse than the pain actually experienced in circumcision. There are also many "compensatory and counterphobic devices such as verbal preparation ahead of time, ceremonies, gifts, masculinity status, etc." (Öztürk 1965a:127). As a result, the attitudes of the family and the preparation of the boy (or lack of it) are very significant factors in the meaning circumcision comes to have for each boy. When well prepared, the experience provides both a "defensive, compensatory resource" against fears of castration and "passage from an ambiguous sexual concept of self to a more clear-cut sexual concept of self," as well as a "sense of being masculine" (Öztürk 1973:58).

Some observers have viewed male circumcision in Turkey as an initiation ceremony marking a boy's passage from childhood to adulthood. For example, Fallers and Fallers refer to it as a formal transfer into the "universal (male) Muslim community (*ümet*)" and as "*the* rite of passage for the male," somewhat like marriage for the girl and even including a similarly lavish outlay of resources by the family (1976:256−258). Öztürk, however, disagrees, arguing that circumcision is not a rite of passage, although it is essential to the development of adult male identity:

> Circumcision is needed to integrate one's self-concept and body image with one's sexuality within a societal framework. In spite of the fact that circumcision is recalled as highly associated with fears and unpleasant feelings, it is almost unthinkable not to be circumcised. [1973:57]

[In Turkey, however,] there is no specific initiation into the developmental stage except the state of being circumcised. That is, circumcision in itself develops into a powerful, autonomously felt need that must be met if one is to be able to grow with a masculine gender identity. [1973:59].

For boys not fully prepared by their parents for the experience of circumcision, the fears and conflicts not only are greater before and during circumcision but may never be fully resolved in the adult years. Öztürk reports that the failure of parents to prepare their sons adequately was usually a result of overprotectiveness and indulgence (1973:50−59). There is thus an irony in the relationship between child abuse and circumcision: parents who most wish to protect their sons from pain are the most likely to be guilty of actual though unintended abuse by subjecting them to unusual emotional trauma.

I may surprise some readers by suggesting that the analogous ceremony for a girl, her wedding, may also be considered child abuse by Western standards. In earlier years the majority of Turkish girls married while still children (twelve to sixteen years old) by Western standards and law. Many rural girls still marry at fifteen or sixteen, despite legal restrictions. Practices that might be seen as abuse of these child wives include *kiz kaçırmak* (bride kidnapping) with degrees of cooperation by the girl ranging from total resistance to total acquiescence; the sexual consummation of the marriage while kin and wedding guests wait impatiently outside the nuptial chamber for the bloodied sheet which proves the bride's virginity (and the groom's virility); the reputedly high incidence of wife beating (Nesin 1977:43−44); childbirth "early and often" by mothers who are themselves but children; the universal departure of young husbands for military service which leaves some wives without adequate means of support for themselves and their children and other wives at the mercy of overly demanding in-laws (Nesin 1977:9, 20); and even the practice of *gelinlik* (customary respect expected of a bride) when it is perverted into mental and physical abuse by her husband and in-laws.

Girls who are orphans or who have been raped or seduced by men who had no intention of marrying them are particularly vulnerable to mistreatment by husbands or in-laws because they lack family or reputation as protection (Nesin 1977:138). Seduction or rape can also lead to child abuse through prostitution, often the only other recourse for the violated young girl (Robson 1976:48−49). Further, even the ideal sexual union in Ottoman times, whether between a sultan and one of his concubines or between a peasant girl and her husband, might itself be regarded by Western observers as a sexual form of child abuse, involving as it did a girl in early adolescence and a man ten to forty years her senior.

In addition to the practices described above, which are more or less unrecognized as abusive by most Turks, other facets of Turkish culture lead to practices decried by both Westerners and Turks but seen as unavoidable facts of life by the latter. They include the occasional or even systematic child abuse or neglect which is reputed to occur in Turkish orphanages at the hands of calloused and/or overworked and untrained personnel, directors who milk or embezzle funds, and others in authority. Because of the strong orientation toward kinfolk and the in-group, an institutionalized form of child adoption has not been developed. Large numbers of children without close relatives are placed in state orphanages, where they tend to fall outside the traditional Turk's cognizance, again owing to the same in-group orientation, and thus are less likely to enjoy the protections from abuse tendered to their nonorphaned peers.

Two other categories of children are especially vulnerable to abuse, again partly because of the kin- and in-group orientation of traditional Turkish culture. The first is *evlatlık*, generally translated as "adopted child" or "foster child," but referring to the long-established practice of prosperous families taking in a female orphan or the young daughter of extremely poor parents. Theoretically, she shares equally in the resources of the household, including clothing, food, education, and so on, but she is seldom granted full status as a member of the household; instead she may be treated more like a servant and even abused. Second, a girl whose widowed mother or father marries again and who lacks the active support of her consanguineal relatives seems to be especially vulnerable to abuse by her stepparent (Nesin 1977:18, 50–52). There is little documentation of this pattern, but it is a situation worthy of further investigation.

Just as there are Turkish practices that are abusive by Western but not Turkish standards, so there are American practices that are considered abusive by Turkish standards. Space permits me to touch on only a few of these. American practices such as failing to cover the baby's head with a thick close-fitting cap in all weather, including the hottest days, giving babies brief sunbaths in the nude or clad only in diapers, and even bathing babies frequently are regarded as extremely dangerous: the baby *soğuk alacak* ("will get chilled") and become ill or even die.

These attitudes were made especially vivid to me when we took our own twenty-month-old daughter Aysha to Turkey in 1970. Our maid/nurse, a warm, independent-minded woman in her fifties, was openly critical of many of our child-rearing practices, such as subjecting Aysha to the loneliness of sleeping alone. But when we allowed Aysha to play in a washtub of water outdoors on warm summer days, the nurse was beside herself with fears and predictions of certain illness! (Fortunately for all of us, Aysha did not become ill in the ensuing months.)

Besides chilling, another common danger is *nazar*, the "evil eye," whereby one can either purposely or inadvertently cause a child to become ill, have an accident, or even die by openly admiring that child. Such admiration may release the malevolent power of envy through one's words and glance, thus the evil eye. Consequently, one should avoid open admiration or, at the very least, counteract the power of *nazar* by immediately uttering the formula, *Maşallah* (literally, "What wonders God hath wrought," but with the connotation of "May God protect"), when one admires a child. As further protection, of course, babies and children wore the ubiquitous *nazar boncuğu* (evil-eye bead) pinned to their clothing (Helling 1960:72). American neglect of these practices would be regarded by some Turks as at best ignorant and thoughtless, and at worst malevolent.

On an earlier occasion Aysha had contracted an intestinal illness serious enough to require a doctor's attention and antibiotics, which—most frightening of all—changed her from a normal two-year-old live wire to a weak, apathetic child who wanted only to lie in bed. As I sat by Aysha's bed in the typical manner of the doting mother, our nurse joined me and began muttering rapidly under her breath. Eventually I recognized that she was angrily condemning nameless acquaintances for admiring Aysha and bringing the evil eye upon her. Her next actions both moved and surprised me: clearly an exorcism in sound and gesture of the *nazar* from Aysha and out the door! (Aysha, of course, regained her health rapidly.)

An American practice that neither Western observers nor our Turkish friends found abusive illustrates the problem of definition in a slightly different way. Because of her toeing-in, Aysha's pediatrician had strongly urged that we purchase special shoes and a metal appliance to be worn while she slept. These would correct her toeing-in, which was less a physical than a psychological handicap because it would subject her to the teasing of her peers: "Someday, Aysha will thank you for correcting her walk." We took the shoes and the appliance to Turkey with us, subjecting Aysha to the discomfort of sleeping with her feet held apart at a 45° angle for a year and a half. Our maid, apparently even more cowed by technology than we were, had no objections to the device. Yet in retrospect this practice seems to me a minor form of abuse, carried out for primarily cosmetic purposes and thus resembling tattooing, foot-binding, and like practices more than we might care to admit.

Thus far I have limited my discussion primarily to traditional society and culture in Turkey. But what about the nontraditional sectors of contemporary Turkey and Turkish society in the future? First, the accelerating rate of socioeconomic change in Turkey makes it seem likely that classic child abuse will increase. Owing to such typical factors as rapidly increasing geographic and social mobility, emigré labor, industrialization, urbanization, unemployment, underemployment, mass media influence, and inflation, many changes in traditional society and culture have already occurred in Turkey and will almost certainly continue. Large-scale influence from individualistic Western culture will probably result in such changes as shifts in the locus of control from ultimate and external causes to the individual (Karpat 1960:153, 161) and the adoption of unfamiliar, more systematic, and more demanding styles of child rearing. Both changes are likely to produce more anxiety and feelings of inadequacy among parents (Kağıtçıbaşı 1977:91–92).

In addition, the competitiveness and achievement-orientation of the urban sector can be expected to put more stress on children of all ages to meet certain standards in order to make for themselves a better life than their parents enjoyed (Kağıtçıbaşı 1977:40). As a result, the child's opportunities for failure and thus the pressures pushing a parent toward abuse are sharply increased. Urbanization has increased the basic costs of raising children just as the economic value of children has decreased. Moreover, thanks to the rising expectations that accompany urbanization, parents are also attempting to raise children in new ways that require a heavier expenditure of resources. This dual process is reversing the earlier positive relationship between costs and rewards of child rearing to one in which children are major economic liabilities (Kağıtçıbaşı 1977:65).

Changes in social structure are also occurring. Although the social networks of urban migrants are frequently characterized by remarkable strength, flexibility, and continuity (Levine 1973:355), geographical mobility, a cash economy, and demands of urban life increasingly separate young married couples from parents, relatives, neighbors, and friends. This pattern is particularly prevalent among military officers and civil service officials, who are seldom stationed in their home towns and are transferred frequently, thus making the development of stable personal networks virtually impossible (Fallers and Fallers 1976:254–255). Fallers and Fallers argue that such changes tend to increase the dominance of the husband and decrease the wife's accustomed freedom. On the other hand, although the continuing development of a cash economy in Turkey permits a son to be economically independent and thus leads to residential separation from his father, other concomitant changes seem to be strengthening the ties between a young woman and her mother. Increasingly, a young married woman with two or three children not only lives in the same neighborhood as her mother, but may even have her mother living with her. Thus she can enjoy traditional forms of support, although through a somewhat different type of network from the traditional one in the patriarchal extended family (Kıray 1976:268–269). In general, however, the effect of these changes is to strengthen the pressures on the husband-wife dyad, since the various forms of assistance and protection described above, which traditionally come from family and neighborhood networks, are sharply reduced. One likely result is an increase in classic child abuse.

Kağıtçıbaşı suggests another result of the increased social and geographical mobility: children are valued more for "primary group ties, affection, and love" and less for security in old age and utilitarian values (1977:83). Ironically, as children become relatively more important as sources of love, support, and companionship to parents cut off from their family and neighborhood networks, it is possible that the parents' unmet emotional needs may lead to increasingly high expectations and unrealistic demands on their small children and thus to more classic child abuse. In addition to the children of military officers and civil officials, I believe that children of workers who accompany their parents to Europe and of apartment-house *kapıcılar* (literally "doormen," but really combination janitor—furnace stoker—general errand "boys") are among the most likely targets of such abuse. *Kapıcılar* typically occupy the basement apartment of buildings they serve and thus, like military and civil personnel, are geographically separated from their familiar social networks and are too dispersed to create new ones.

Less obvious, perhaps, are some of the new forms of collective child abuse and neglect which these and other recent changes may produce. One example is the popularity of bottle-feeding as a substitute for breast-feeding, which may lead to unintended and largely unrecognized child abuse and neglect in terms of nutrition and hygiene and perhaps in terms of the emotional needs of infants. This is particularly likely to happen under current conditions, such as the high cost and virtual unavailability of adequate infant formulas, leading to the adoption of commercial and home preparations of *mama* (substitutes for mother's milk) made of rice water or of other inadequate substances. The nutritional problem is exacerbated by the lack of commercially prepared baby food or of appliances for preparing it easily at home. The unavailability of hygienic bottles and nipples and basic ignorance of the need for sterilization create innumerable new opportunities for infection not found with breast-feeding, even as the infant loses the natural immunities normally bestowed through his mother's milk. A second simple change is also a possible source of only partly recognized child abuse of the collective type: increasing replacement of traditional foods like whole-grain breads and bulgur pilafs by such foods as white bread and milled rice as the population becomes increasingly able to satisfy its preferences for the latter prestigious but nutritionally inadequate staples.

Other expected changes illustrate vividly some of the problems inherent in an attempt to define a term as value-laden as "child abuse." The relativity of the term is illustrated by noting that the incidence of certain kinds of practices which are considered abusive by traditional Turkish standards—for example, sleeping in a room alone or exposing babies to the danger of chilling—will increase with modernization. At the same time, traditional Turkish practices deemed abusive by Western standards—swaddling, the use of clay in diapers, early marriage for girls, perhaps even the postulated crisis in later childhood—are already becoming less common. The alleged abuses of orphans, *evlatlık* daughters, and stepdaughters are receiving increased attention from influential Turkish citizens and thus may be ameliorated. Whether the improvement will occur primarily through large-scale societal changes or through specific programs is hard to predict.

Concern on the part of Turkey's political and intellectual leaders about collective abuse and neglect which result from environmental factors and poverty has a long history in Turkey. Modernization is perceived by both Turks and Americans as a way of reducing many types of collective abuse through such changes as universal education, Western medicine, malaria eradication, and land reform. Ironically, modernization also threatens to create new sources of abuse by Western standards. Thus it appears that changes now occurring promise both to ameliorate and to exacerbate child abuse in Turkey, in rather complex ways.

REFERENCES

Ateş, Suleyman
    1968 Azl veya Doğum Tahdidi (Prevention or birth limitation). Ankara University
        Ilahiyat Fakültesi Dergisi (Journal of the School of Theology) 16:123–130.
Benedict, Peter
    1976 Aspects of the domestic cycle in a Turkish provincial town. In *Mediterranean
        family structures*, ed. J. G. Peristiany. Cambridge: Cambridge University Press.
        Pp. 219–241.
Cura, Sabiha
    1961 Social aspects of child nutrition in Turkey. *Turkish Journal of Pediatrics*
        3:145–152.
Davoren, Elizabeth
    1968 The role of the social worker. In *The battered child*, ed. Ray E. Helfer and C.
        Henry Kempe. Chicago: University of Chicago Press. Pp. 153–168.
Fallers, Lloyd A., and Margaret C. Fallers
    1976 Sex roles in Edremit. In *Mediterranean family structures*, ed. J. G. Peristiany.
        Cambridge: Cambridge University Press. Pp. 243–260.

Gil, David
    1970 *Violence against children: physical child abuse in the United States*. Cambridge: Harvard University Press.
Helfer, Ray E.
    1973 The etiology of child abuse. *Pediatrics* 51:777-779.
Helfer, Ray E., and C. Henry Kempe, eds.
    1968 *The battered child*. Chicago: University of Chicago Press.
Helling, Barbara
    1960 Child rearing techniques in Turkish peasant villages. M.A. thesis, University of Minnesota.
Hyman, H. H., A. Payaslıoğlu, and F. W. Frey
    1958 The values of Turkish college youth. *Public Opinion Quarterly* 22:274–291.
Kağıtçıbaşı, Çiğdem
    1970 Social norms and authoritarianism: a comparison of Turkish and American adolescents. *Journal of Personality and Social Psychology* 16:444–451.
    1973 Psychological aspects of modernization in Turkey. *Journal of Cross Cultural Psychology* 4:157–174.
    1977 Cultural values and population action programs: Turkey. Paper prepared for the United Nations Educational, Scientific, and Cultural Organization. Istanbul: Boğaziçi Üniversitesi Matbaasi.
Kandiyoti, Deniz
    1976 Social change and family structure in a Turkish village (bachelors and maidens: a Turkish case study). In *Kinship and modernization in Mediterranean society*, ed. J. G. Peristiany. Rome: American Universities Field Staff. Pp. 61–71.
Kansu, Ceyhun Atuf
    1961 Infant mortality in Turkish villages. *Turkish Journal of Pediatrics* 3:129–144.
Karpat, Kemal H.
    1960 Social themes in contemporary Turkish literature. Pt. II. *Middle East Journal* 14:153–168.
Kıray, Mübeccel B.
    1964 *Eregli, Ağır Sanağıden Bir Sahil Kasabası* (Eregli, a coastal town before heavy industry). Ankara: T. C. Devlet Planlama Teskilatı.
    1976 The new role of mothers: changing intra-familial relationships in a small town in Turkey. In *Mediterranean family structures*, ed. J. G. Peristiany. Cambridge: Cambridge University Press. Pp. 261–271.
Kıray, Mübeccel B., and Jan Hinderink
    1970 *Social stratification as an obstacle to development: a study of four Turkish villages*. New York: Praeger Publishers.
Kolars, John F.
    1963 *Tradition, season, and change in a Turkish village*. Program Report no. 15. Chicago: University of Chicago.
Levine, Ned
    1973 Old culture—new culture: a study of migrants in Ankara, Turkey. *Social Forces* 51:355–368.
Magnarella, Paul
    1974 *Tradition and change in a Turkish town*. New York: Schenkman Publishers.

Meeker, Michael E.
1976 Meaning and society in the Near East: examples from the Black Sea Turks and the Levantine Arabs (I and II). *International Journal of Middle East Studies* 7:243–270, 383–422.

Munroe, Robert L., and Ruth H. Munroe
1976 *Cross-cultural human development*. Monterey, CA: Brooks/Cole Publishing Co.

Nesin, Aziz
1977 *Istanbul boy*. Austin, TX: University of Texas Press.

Olson-Prather, Emelie
1976 Family planning and husband-wife relationships in contemporary Turkey. Ph.D. dissertation, University of California, Los Angeles.

Öztürk, Mualla, and Orhan M. Öztürk
1977 Thumbsucking and falling asleep. *British Journal of Medical Psychology* 50:95–103.

Öztürk, Orhan M.
1965a Child-rearing practices in the Turkish village and the major area of intra-psychic conflict. *Turkish Journal of Pediatrics* 7:124–130.

1965b Folk interpretation of illness in Turkey and its psychological significance. *Turkish Journal of Pediatrics* 7:165–179.

1973 Ritual circumcision and castration anxiety. *Psychiatry: Journal for the Study of Interpersonal Processes* 36:49–60.

1978 Psychotherapy under limited options: psychotherapeutic work with a Turkish youth. *American Journal of Psychotherapy* 32:307–319.

Redhouse, James
1968 *Redhouse Yeni Türkce-Ingilizce Sözlük* (New Redhouse Turkish-English diction-ary). Istanbul: Redhouse Yayınevi.

Robson, Bruce
1976 *The drum beats nightly: the development of the Turkish drama as a vehicle for social and political comment in the post-revolutionary period 1924 to the present*. Tokyo: Centre for East Asian Cultural Studies.

Scott, Richard B.
1966 Some turkish women's attitudes towards swaddling. *Turkish Journal of Pediatrics* 9:71–75.

Steele, Brandt F., and Carl B. Pollock
1968 A psychiatric study of parents who abuse infants and small children. In *The battered child*, ed. Ray E. Helfer and C. Henry Kempe. Chicago: University of Chicago Press. Pp. 103–147.

Timur, Serim
1972 *Türkiyede Aile Yapısı (Family structure in Turkey)*. Ankara, Turkey: Hacettepe University Press.

Ugurel-Semin, R.
1969 Youth in Turkey. In *Youth: a transcultural approach*, ed. J. H. Masserman. New York: Grune and Stratton. Pp. 139–145.

Yürtoren (Timur), Scrim Gülsüm
1965 Fertility and related attitudes among two social classes in Ankara, Turkey. M.A. thesis, Cornell University.

CHILD ABANDONMENT AND INFANTICIDE: A Japanese Case[1]

7

Hiroshi Wagatsuma

In Japan, child abuse and neglect, as understood in the United States and the Western world, do not constitute a serious social problem. There is no sign of deep social concern, and very little Japanese literature on the subject.[2]

The occurrence of child abuse and neglect is quite infrequent in Japan, as indicated in a governmental survey that will be discussed later. There are good reasons to believe that the low reported incidence reflects an actual lack of instances rather than a failure to identify and recognize the problem. This is not to say that child abuse and neglect never happen in Japan. Occasionally the newspapers carry stories about battered children which sound remarkably similar to those in the United States (Kodama et al. 1977; Takaháshi and Naka 1976). When Japanese parents do aggress against their children, however, their acts tend to take a somewhat different form from abuse inflicted by American parents. Japanese parents, especially mothers, tend to abandon or kill their children more often than they keep and abuse them. Further, the so-called parent-child joint suicide (*oyako shinjū*), in which a child is killed by

[1] I am grateful to Professor Minoru Ishikawa of Seikei University in Tokyo for providing me with some of the research materials I used in this paper. I am also grateful to Erika Wagatsuma and Dr. Jill Korbin for their editorial help.

[2] The problems of child abuse and neglect in the United States are not well known in Japan. Not until 1971 did an article on "the battered-child syndrome," referring to reports by American physicians, appear in a professional journal in Japan (Satake 1971). In 1977 the American situation was reported by an official of the Japanese National Institute of Mental Health (Ikeda 1977).

the parent or parents who then commit suicide, may very well be a uniquely Japanese phenomenon.

The definition of abuse and neglect is culture-bound, and thus the form and interpretation of child abuse and neglect may differ. From the viewpoint of most Japanese mothers who spend much of their time being with their infants (Caudill and Weinstein 1966), the American use of baby-sitters may very well suggest child neglect. In prewar Japan some parents used moxa-burning ("moxabustion") or, more often, the threat thereof, to inflict a sharp, momentary pain upon an unruly child. Although no longer used as a form of punishment in postwar Japan, this practice would be considered an excessive punishment, and hence abuse, by Americans as well as contemporary Japanese. The use of moxabustion as a disciplinary measure seems to have originated from the Japanese belief in human nature as basically good. When a small child frequently threw temper tantrums, it was traditionally explained as the work of "a bug of temper tantrum" (*kan no mushi*) which somehow got into the body of the child. Such a child would be taken by the parent to a shrine, whose deity was known for its power to seal off the bug, and some sort of exorcism was performed, or an amulet was purchased. Moxabustion, which Japanese used for medical treatment of various ailments, was also believed to be effective for "sealing off the bug of temper tantrum" (Wagatsuma 1970).

Japanese parents rarely inflict physical punishment on their children (Lanham 1956, 1966). Further, the Japanese do not circumcise their infants, nor do they observe any form of initiation rites accompanied by hazing.

If in American society relatively young mothers, deprived of community support, tend to abuse their unwanted children, the existing social conditions in Japan can be said to work as an antidote for child abuse. First, Japanese marry considerably later than Americans. In the United States the peak ages for the first marriage are 21 or 22 years of age for males and 18 or 19 for females; in Japan they are 25 to 29 for males and 20 to 24 for females. Second, unlike many isolated American nuclear families, most Japanese lead their lives deeply and securely embedded in neighborhood, community, and kinship networks. Third, most Japanese women still find the greatest meaning and the deepest gratification in their lives in motherhood, that is, in being a dedicated mother of intellectually achieving and socially successful children, preferably sons (see, e.g., DeVos and Wagatsuma 1961, 1970; Wagatsuma 1977). There are very few unwanted children in Japanese homes, and those who are not wanted are usually disposed of, as discussed later.

In addition, at every Japanese school, public and private, from the first grade to the twelfth, all pupils receive physical examinations twice a year. The results are reported to the parents and records are kept at school. When a school physician suspects an illness, the parents are urged to take their child to a hospital. The so-called battered-child syndrome would not be likely to escape the eyes of an examining doctor, a helping nurse, or the several teachers who are present at the physical examinations.

In general, the outward expression of destructive human impulses against people seems less frequent in Japanese society than in the United States. For example, in 1973 the number of murders per 100,000 people in Japan was only one-fifth of that in the United States (1.9 versus 9.3). In the same year, Tokyo, with a population of 12 million, had only 196 murders, whereas the New York metropolitan area with a population of just under 12 million had 1,739 murders or nearly nine times as many. The incidence of rape in Japan is one-fifth of that in the United States. The rate of robbery with force or the threat of force in Japan is less than 1 percent of the American rate: in 1973 there were 1,876 robberies in Japan as compared with 382,680 in the United States, and 361 in Tokyo as compared with 74,381 in New York City. Overall, there are four times as many serious crimes committed per person in the United States as there are crimes of all sorts, even the most petty, in Japan (Bayley 1976). Thus, as revealed by the crime statistics, Japan is much less violence-prone than the United States. Furthermore, the crime rate has been steadily decreasing in Japan recently, while it has been increasing in America.

If, on the other hand, suicide is considered a form of destructive human impulses turned inward, such impulses among Japanese are more frequent than among Americans. In 1978 the suicide rate in Japan was 22.7 per 100,000 males and 13.5 per 100,000 females. In the United States the suicide rate in 1976 per 100,000 was 19.8 for white males, 7.2 for white females, 11.0 for nonwhite males, and 3.2 for nonwhite females.

CHILD ABUSE, ABANDONMENT, AND MURDER

In 1974 the Bureau of Children and Families in the Japanese Ministry of Health and Welfare conducted a survey on child abuse, abandonment, and murder. There are 153 Child Guidance Centers under the jurisdiction of the Welfare Ministry located throughout the country which handle all problems related to children. Each of these centers compiled a report on the cases of abuse, abandonment, and murder of children under the age of three in the period from April 1973 through March 1974.

Child Abuse

Child abuse was defined as "physical harm from violence and other behavior dangerous to the life of a child, such as starvation or confinement for many hours." During this period only twenty-six cases of child abuse were reported for the entire country. Thus, as a category, it accounted for only 6.1 percent of all the cases in the ministry report. There may be some margin of error in the compiling of reports, since child abuse can at times be justified as a disciplinary act by the parents or can be hidden from the neighbors' eyes. It is difficult, however, to believe that the government report was totally unreliable. It at least suggests that child abuse does not occur very frequently in Japan (Kōseishō Jidō Katei Kyoku 1974). As further evidence, only 59 cases of child abuse were reported by the *Asahi News* (one of the major newspapers with nationwide circulation) during the 26 years between 1946 and 1972 (Kurisu 1974). Despite a slight increase recently in reported cases of child abuse, the newspapers give no indication that abuse is a mounting social problem.

It is noteworthy that in the 26 cases of child abuse listed in the government report, the aggressor was predominantly the biological mother (16 cases); second was the biological father (6 cases) (table VII-1). The age of the abusing or neglecting parent was predominantly in the thirties (20 cases), and the age of the victim was primarily two to three years (16 cases) or one to two years (7 cases). It is of interest that children less than one year old were rarely abused (4 cases) (tables VII-2, VII-3). When the parents were asked to explain the reasons for abusing or neglecting their children, ten of them said they were unwilling to rear their children, which may suggest that these cases were more

TABLE VII-1   Results of Welfare Ministry Survey: Aggressor

Act of aggression	Number of cases	Bio- logical father	Bio- logical mother	Step- parent	Other	Unknown
Abuse or neglect	26 (6.1%)	6	16	2	2	0
Abandonment	139 (32.9%)	26	74	0	2	37
Murder- abandonment	137 (32.4%)	7	51	0	0	79
Murder	54 (12.8%)	9	40	1	4	0
Joint suicide	67 (15.8%)	12	53	0	2	0
Total	423 (100%)	60	234	3	10	116

"neglect" than "abuse." (Unfortunately, the report does not differentiate between abuse and neglect.) Other stated reasons were family conflict or financial problems (table VII-4). Of the 26 individuals who abused or neglected a child, only one was tried in court. All others received counseling by caseworkers. Of the 26 children, 16 were sent to foster homes and welfare facilities. The others were returned to their homes.

TABLE VII-2   Results of Welfare Ministry Survey: Age of Aggressor

Act of aggression	Number of cases	Teenage	Twenties	Thirties	Forties	Over fifty	Unknown
Abuse or neglect	26	0	3	20	2	0	1
Abandon-ment	139	5	52	32	7	2	41
Murder-abandon-ment	137	8	33	13	4	0	79
Murder	54	5	33	14	1	1	0
Joint suicide	67	1	45	9	3	1	8

TABLE VII-3   Results of Welfare Ministry Survey: Age of Victim

Act of aggression	Number of cases	1 day	Less than 1 month	1–6 months	7–12 months	1–2 years	2–3 years	Unknown
Abuse or neglect	26	0	0	1	3	7	15	0
Abandon-ment	139	25	37	31	13	18	13	2
Murder-abandon-ment	137	119	7	6	5	0	0	0
Murder	54	15	5	10	4	12	8	0
Joint suicide	67	0	0	9	16	21	21	0

TABLE VII-4   Results of Welfare Ministry Survey: Stated Reason for Act

Act of aggression	Number of cases	Unwillingness to rear	Family conflict	Financial problems	Other	Unknown
Abuse or neglect	26	10	9	5	2	0
Abandon-ment	139	36	25	30	3	45
Murder-abandon-ment	137	27	6	12	1	91
Murder	54	14	8	11	5	16
Joint suicide	67	6	31	8	10	12

Child Abandonment

"Abandonment" is defined in the ministry report as "leaving a child at a hospital, clinic, or other public place like a railway station or a department store." According to the ministry survey, the cases of abandonment were much more frequent than cases of child abuse and neglect (table VII-1). There were 139 such cases during the period from April 1973 through March 1974. Another report by the National Police Agency found 102 cases of child abandonment in 1973 (Nakaya 1978). These two sets of figures for child abandonment approximate each other, although the two reports cover slightly different periods. There has, however, been a decrease in child abandonment over the past ten years (table VII-5). Of the 102 identified abandoning parents, approximately three-fourths (74) were the biological mothers. Most of them were in their twenties and thirties. Nineteen of the mothers were criminally prosecuted, but the others were given counseling by welfare personnel. The ages of the deserted children varied widely, ranging from one day old to three years, the upper age limit of the ministry survey (table VII-3). In approximately two-thirds of the cases (93 of 139) the child was less than six months old. The children were abandoned at a variety of places—department stores, railway stations, public lavatories, parks and on the streets (table VII-6). In about one-third of the cases (44 of 139), the child was abandoned at a hospital or maternity clinic. In such cases the young mother, who was usually unwed, disappeared from the hospital or clinic after delivering her unwanted baby. It

TABLE VII-5   Infanticide and Child Abandonment Cases over a Ten-Year
Period*

Year	Abandonment cases	Parents arrested	Infanticide cases	Parents arrested
1967	121	107	183	152
1968	92	81	222	183
1969	116	80	185	163
1970	109	94	210	187
1971	119	101	189	149
1972	102	87	174	152
1973	102	85	196	156
1974	86	76	190	160
1975	80	69	207	177
1976	71	55	183	161

*Adapted from National Police Agency report on crime statistics, 1967–1976.

is noteworthy that the most frequently stated reason for abandonment was
unwillingness to raise the child (36 of 139 cases or 25.9 percent) (table VII-4).

The *Asahi News* reported a total of 94 cases of child abandonment during
a period of 26 years (1946-1972). The reasons given for abandonment were
unwillingness to raise the child (26.6 percent), poverty (22 percent), disappearance of the spouse (21.5 percent), marital conflict (16.6 percent), and the
spouse's criminal arrest (13.3 percent). It is significant that in both the newspaper and ministry reports, a little more than one-fourth of the parents, mostly
mothers, admitted their unwillingness to raise their babies. In contrast, a
prewar Tokyo City Office report indicated that the most frequently stated
reason for abandoning a child was poverty (59.8 percent) and that only
10 percent of the abandoning parents admitted unwillingness to raise the baby
(Kurisu 1974). In prewar Japan there was a much stronger emphasis upon the
importance of parental responsibility, the duty to raise one's children and
continue one's family lines. Under the pressure of such social norms, people
were not free to admit their wish to avoid their duties and responsibilities. We
can see the changing values of present-day Japan in the increased number of
young parents who admit that they do not want their babies.

Murder-Abandonment

In the Welfare Ministry report, the category "murder-abandonment"
(137 cases) was almost as frequent as child abandonment (table VII-1). In the

TABLE VII-6 Results of Welfare Ministry Survey: Location of Act

Abuse and neglect		Abandonment		Murder-abandonment		Murder		Joint suicide	
Own home	20	Own home	11	Own home	43	Own home	42	Own home	40
Friend's home	2	Friend's home	12	Friend's home	1	Hospital or clinic	1	River, sea, or field	20
Park or street	2	Hospital or clinic	2	Dept. store or station	5	Park or street	6	Park or street	1
Other	2	Dept. store or station	2	Public lavatory	19	Field	1	Other	6
		Public lavatory	7	Coin locker	36	Other	4		
		Park or street	20	Park or street	2				
		Other	33	Field, sea, or river	27				
				Other	4				
Total	26		139		137		54		67

127

National Police Agency report the number of infanticide cases in 1973 was 196 (table VII-5). When we combine the categories of murder-abandonment (137 cases) and murder (54 cases) in the Welfare Ministry report, the figure becomes very close to that in the National Police Agency report (196 in the latter and 191 in the former), suggesting that the reports were accurate.

The category of murder-abandonment seems to include cases in which the death of the baby was not originally intended but in which the baby died before being found. In other words, this category contains both infanticide cases and unsuccessful abandonment cases, although we have no way of differentiating between them from the reports. The children who were killed and then abandoned or those who were abandoned and then died were predominantly neonates, no more than one day old (119 of 137 cases, or 86.9 percent) (table VII-3). Of the 58 known persons who had murdered/abandoned a baby, 51 were the biological mothers and nearly three-fourths of them (41) were in their teens or twenties. Of the 46 persons who provided a reason for murdering/abandoning a baby, 27 expressed their unwillingness to raise the child (table VII-4). Of the total of 137 cases of murder-abandonment, 43 cases (31 percent) took place at the parent's own home (table VII-6). In these cases it seems clear that the babies were killed and their bodies abandoned. When dead babies were found in a department store, railway station, public lavatory, park, or on the street (26 cases), however, it is not clear if they were killed before they were abandoned or whether they were abandoned alive and died before discovery. It should also be noted that in 36 cases the dead babies were found in coin lockers for storing luggage, which first appeared in Japan's major railway stations and airports in 1965. When a baby's disintegrating body was found in a coin locker at a station a year later, the newspapers sensationalized the incident. Several women followed the example. The railway companies then initiated the practice of inspecting the coin lockers every twenty-four hours. Because of their gruesomeness, the coin locker cases drew much social attention, but the actual use of a coin locker to dispose of a baby has not been very frequent (Kurisu 1974).

Infanticide

In the Welfare Ministry report, the 54 cases of murder or infanticide were committed predominantly by the biological mothers (40 cases). These mothers were in their twenties and thirties (tables VII-1, VII-2). Fifteen babies were only one day old when murdered (table VII-3). Fourteen of the parents admitted that they did not want to raise the child (table VII-4). Thus these 14 or 15 cases of infanticide were similar to many of the murder-abandonment cases, in which an unwanted neonate was killed by its mother soon after birth. Other reasons stated by the mother included family conflict (8 cases) and financial difficulty (11 cases). We do not know the exact nature of these stated reasons, but the mother may have killed her child from despair in poverty, especially when deserted by her spouse, or out of spite against her unfaithful husband. At times a mother may also kill her physically or mentally handicapped child "out of mercy."

According to a study by the Ministry of Justice, 163 mothers were arrested in 1972 for killing or attempting to kill a child under one year of age (Sasaki 1975*a*). Of these mothers, 67 (41.1 percent) killed their neonates during delivery or within a day after birth. The methods used were dropping (often into a nonflush toilet bowl) (26 percent), abandoning (17.7 percent), suffocating (16.7 percent), and strangling (12.5 percent). The other 96 mothers killed their babies later by strangling (22.4 percent), drowning in water (20.9 percent), gassing (16.4 percent), or suffocating (11.9 percent).[3]

Joint Suicide

The last category in the Welfare Ministry report is "joint suicide" in which a parent or parents take the life of a child when committing suicide. Although the number of cases is relatively small (67), they deserve attention because they reflect certain characteristics of the Japanese parent-child relationship (table VII-1). It should be noted that these cases primarily involved the biological mother (53 of 67 cases, or 79 percent). The children tended to be older than those in the other categories (table VII-3). Unfortunately, the circumstances that drove parents to joint suicide are not always clear from the report (table VII-4). The Welfare Ministry report does not include those cases in which a child above the age of three was killed in a joint suicide. Sometimes, however, older children are killed in joint suicides in Japan.

When a husband and a wife agree to commit suicide and take their children along, it is called *ikka shinjū* (collective suicide of a whole family).

---

[3]Crime statistics in Japan are generally reliable, although the figures for infanticide may not always be accurate because it is sometimes classified as murder. Police statistics have a separate category of infanticide for killing a child less than a year old, but an unknown number of infanticide cases appear in another category as murder when the police or the court somewhat arbitrarily record the cases. When the Justice Ministry Research Institute examined the 163 mothers who had been arrested for killing their neonates or infants during 1972, 116 of them had been tried in court for murder rather than for infanticide. It is possible, therefore, that at the police level some of the cases are classified as murder rather than as infanticide (Tsuchiya and Sato 1973).

When one parent kills the child(ren) and himself or herself, it is called *fushi shinjū* or *boshi shinjū* (father-child or mother-child joint suicide, respectively).

Since suicide statistics in Japan unfortunately do not classify joint suicide as a separate category, it is not possible to follow its shifting trend in past years. A study of newspaper reports, however, may shed some light on the subject. The *Asahi News* reported a total of 1,735 cases of joint suicide in eight years in prewar Japan (July 1927—June 1935). In contrast, the same newspaper reported only 838 cases in 26 years in postwar Japan (1946—1972). In other words, while 216.9 cases of joint suicide were reported every year in prewar Japan, the number dropped to 32.2 cases per year after the war. In postwar Japan the value of human life and the fundamental rights of individuals were strongly emphasized. Parents who killed their children in joint suicides were in conflict with these new values and with individualistic norms and therefore had increased news value to the public. One may postulate that in postwar Japan joint suicide was more likely to be reported by the newspapers. Thus the decreased number of joint suicide cases reported in the newspaper most likely reflects a decrease in actual occurrences. Of the 1,735 cases reported before the war, whole family suicide constituted 13 percent, father-child suicide, 17 percent, and mother-child suicide, 70 percent. Of the 838 postwar cases, whole family suicide constituted 23.7 percent, father-child suicide, 10.1 percent, and mother-child suicide, 66.2 percent (Kurisu 1974).

CASES OF JOINT SUICIDE REPORTED BY ASAHI NEWS

	1927—1935 (1,735) (Percent)	1946—1972 (838) (Percent)
Whole family	13	23.7
Father-child	17	10.1
Mother-child	70	66.2

The proportion of father-child suicides decreased after the war, but mother-child suicides had not changed substantially and still constituted about two-thirds of all joint suicide cases. According to the Welfare Ministry report, mother-child suicide was even more frequent (53 of 67 cases, or 79 percent) (table VII-1).

CULTURAL EXPLANATIONS

Let us now return to the generalization proposed at the beginning of this chapter, that Japanese mothers tend to abandon or kill their children more often than they keep and abuse them. What factors possibly account for such a tendency?

Killing of an unwanted neonate, especially by an unwed mother, probably suggests that certain women consider infanticide an extension of artificial abortion. Artificial abortion was never objected to in Japan for religious reasons, and after World War II it was widely practiced as a measure of population control. Although by now it has been largely replaced by various birth-control devices, control of the postwar "baby boom" owed much of its success to abortion.

During the feudal period in Japan (1604—1868), infanticide was widely practiced among the impoverished peasants as a means of population control. The practice was called *mabiki* ("thinning out," as in rice seedlings). During the period of stationary population in the late Tokugawa period (1750—1868), the number of offspring was kept between one and three (Dickman 1975; Taeuber 1958). The Japanese believed that when a baby was born an ancestral spirit entered into its body. The midwife often played the supernatural role of "implanting an ancestral spirit" into a newborn baby. It was believed that when the spirit entered, the baby made the first birth cry. Only after that happened was the baby believed to have become a human being. If a killing was to be done, it had to be before the baby made the first birth cry. A piece of wet paper was placed on the face of the neonate to suffocate it, or the baby was placed underneath a stone mortar. This act was not believed to be homicide because the spirit had not yet entered into the baby; it was only a killing of a nonhuman (Inokuchi 1959). Numerous cases have been reported in which a baby, destined to be killed, was saved by its birth cry (Yanagita 1969).

Most Japanese today no longer believe that an ancestral spirit enters the neonate. Mothers who kill their infants pay no attention to the first birth cry. It may be assumed, however, that certain women have a tendency to regard the neonate as not yet quite human. It is therefore possible that a Japanese woman who can undergo an artificial abortion without guilt (thinking that abortion is not killing) can feel similarly about killing a neonate during or immediately after its birth. It is my assumption, however, that Japanese mothers tend to abandon their babies much more often than they kill them, although, as noted earlier, a number of abandoned babies die before they are found.

Traditionally, the Japanese believed that for the successful growth of a child, rearing by its biological parents alone was not enough (Miyamoto 1967). The child needed the nurturance and protection of many other people who played the role of its "ritual parents." In the past there were a series of customs of establishing ritual parent-child relationships between a child and adults of various statuses. Very often the midwife was designated as the "parent" of the newborn baby and the relationship continued for quite some time. When a mother prayed for pregnancy at a shrine or a temple, and her wish was fulfilled, a priest or a monk was asked to become the baby's "parent." The relationship lasted for a long time. In many locales, boys and girls coming of age at puberty entered a new ritual kinship relationship with an adult couple who became their ritual parents. They served as mentors, guarantors, and often employers for the youths. In certain instances the ritual parents, because of their high social status, were considered much more important for the life of the youth than were his or her biological parents. Many parents trusted and relied upon certain other people whose help they expected in raising their children. Trust and reliance also were often extended to supernatural beings. When a baby was born in the climacteric year of its parents,[4] it was believed that the baby would not live long. In such a case the baby was ritualistically abandoned at the roadside. A passerby would pick it up, give it a name, thus symbolically becoming its parent, and leave it in custody of its biological parents. It was believed that the passerby was sent by some supernatural being and, therefore, that the baby treated in such a way would receive special supernatural attention and protection. At present, most Japanese no longer believe in the supernatural protection of a baby, and the custom of ritualistic abandoning of a baby is no longer practiced. The trust in and dependence upon other people's nurturance and benevolence has, however, continued well into the present time. There have been cases of individuals who, realizing their own inadequacy as parents, abandoned a child with the hope that somebody much better qualified would find it and be better parents (Ariga 1948).[5] Expressions such as *suteru kami areba hirou kami ari* ("there are gods who forsake but there are gods who save," meaning that the world is as kind as it is cruel) and *wataru seken ni oni wa nashi* ("there is no devil in the human form in the world," meaning that people are kind, benevolent, and helpful) reflect traditional trust in human kindness and dependence upon the benevolence of unknown others.

When Japanese parents cannot trust in and depend upon others for the care of their children, they may kill the children out of despair. Basically, Japanese parents do not expect their children to be capable of being completely on their own. Interdependence among people, instead of individual autonomy, characterizes Japanese social relations. Japanese mothers and their children remain very close, both physically and psychologically, for a long time.

[4] Among the Japanese there has been a notion of *yaku-doshi* (calamity year or climacteric), a specific year during which the danger of some bad luck for an individual is thought to be greater than usual. An individual in his or her critical year observed certain practices in order to get rid of such danger and avert bad luck. The critical year varied from one locale to another but mostly it has been the thirty-third year for women and the forty-second year for men.

[5] It might be added that Japanese abandon unwanted puppies and kittens on the street, hoping that they will be picked up and cared for by other people. The Japanese were once harshly criticized for cruelty by the Britishers, who poison unwanted animals, a practice that is alien to most Japanese.

During socialization a close emotional bond develops between a child and its mother, and dependence upon such a bond is encouraged rather than discouraged (Caudill and Plath 1966; Caudill and Weinstein 1969; DeVos and Wagatsuma 1961, 1970; Doi 1973; Lanham 1956; Norbeck and Norbeck 1956; Vogel and Vogel 1961; Wagatsuma and Hara 1974). Very often Japanese children are not psychologically weaned until after adolescence. From the mother's standpoint, her children, especially her sons, remain extensions of herself. In contrast with American society, in Japan psychological differentiation between a mother and her children occurs late and often remains incomplete. It is for this reason that many Japanese parents, especially mothers, kill their children when they commit suicide. They do not feel guilty about killing their children and, further, they hesitate to leave their children behind in a world they cannot trust to care for them. If it is true, as some scholars have suggested (Minamikawa 1973; Nakaya 1977), that parent-child joint suicide increased in the 1910s and 1920s, the increase may reflect the weakening of community solidarity and the decline of trust in and reliance upon unknown others as a result of the processes of industrialization and urbanization. Westerners may find it incomprehensible that Japanese parents can kill their children in joint suicide. For the Japanese, however, it is not killing of "others" but only a part of their own suicidal act because their children are, after all, extensions of themselves. The following are a few cases of joint suicide (Imamura 1978).

In a gas-filled apartment, a husband (age 39), his wife (age 38), and two children (aged 8 and 3) were found dead in bed. They were lying with their heads pointing to the north (it is a Japanese custom to lay a dead person with the head pointing to the north). The husband and wife each held a Buddhist rosary. A note written by the husband said that he had failed in his business and become bankrupt and that he could not abandon his children, therefore he had decided to take them along with him.

A real estate agency employee (age 37) suddenly disappeared, deserting his 34-year-old wife and three children (aged 1, 3, and 6). The wife tried to eke out a living but became exhausted in poverty. Six months later she jumped onto a railway track in front of an approaching locomotive. She carried her three-year-old daughter on her back and her one-year-old baby on her right arm and held the hand of her oldest son. They were all killed. They had been wearing their best clothes. A brief note written by the mother simply said, "I am mentally and physically tired but I cannot abandon my children."

In present-day Japan, parent-child joint suicide is disapproved by a majority of the people, and parents are criticized for killing their child(ren). There is evidence, however, that some people are not sure about making such a judgment. In a survey, 623 mothers of preschool children and 330 female university students were asked to express their opinions regarding infanticide by the mother. The majority of the mothers (81.4 percent) and students (71.2 percent) answered that no mother should be "allowed to kill her child under any circumstances." Since questionnaire respondents may express what they think they should answer, rather than revealing their deep feelings, it is noteworthy that 12.4 percent of the mothers and 21.2 percent of the students responded that "there are cases in which a mother cannot always be blamed for killing her child."

ATTITUDES TOWARD INFANTICIDE

	Mothers		Students	
	No.	%	No.	%
No mother is allowed to kill her child(ren) under any circumstances	507	81.4	235	71.2
In certain cases a mother can not be blamed for killing her child(ren)	77	12.4	70	21.2
Don't know	22	3.5	25	7.6
No answer	17	3.7	0	0
Total	623	100	330	100

The same mothers and students were presented with newspaper reports of five actual cases of infanticide by a mother, together with the reasons given for the act, including marital conflict, poverty, an unwanted illegitimate baby, and exhaustion from caring for an incurably ill child. In one of the five cases the mother committed suicide after killing her child. In expressing their opinions about these cases, the majority of the respondents disapproved the mother's act in every case. However, 11.4 percent of the mothers (71 of 623) and 13.9 percent of the students (46 of 330) said, with regard to at least one of the five stories, that they might act in the same way if they were in the same situation. Thus there still seems to be a slight tendency among Japanese women to accept or sympathize with, if not openly approve, a mother's killing of her child, especially when she too commits suicide (Sasaki 1977b; Sasaki et al. 1974, 1975a, 1975b).

One more observation, which has been reported elsewhere (DeVos and Wagatsuma 1961), is pertinent here. In 1954 we examined responses to the Thematic Apperception Test in a Japanese village. We found a number of stories involving the chastisement of an errant son (and, much less frequently, of a delinquent daughter) by the mother. It was clear that both men and women of the village saw mothers as capable of violence in disciplining their children. The chastisement, however, was not depicted as the expression of uncontrollable anger or of fury, but as arising from the mother's deep sense of responsibility to society for the behavior of her child. The bad behavior of a child, especially when directed against societal norms, threatens the reputation of the parents or violates their sense of responsibility to society. As noted earlier, parents and their children in Japan are emotionally tied and are not altogether differentiated from the psychological unity of the whole family. The children's conduct therefore tends to have a direct emotional effect upon their parents. Parents often experience their children's behavior almost as if they themselves were responsible for it. Accordingly, when their children's behavior is negative and threatens their own ego ideal, they may react by chastisement, which primarily expresses their resentment against the uncontrollable part of themselves. Parents may even want to kill their children, which actually means punishing themselves, in order to be faithful to their own ego ideal and to maintain their psychological security. Parents expect their children's behavior to support parental aspirations for the children's success and to brighten the reputation or uphold the honor of their parents. Thus, all that is required of children can be phrased in terms of fulfillment of the parents' sense of duty and responsibility to both family and society. Parents may not know how to cope with a child who flouts the expectations of the parents. The response of a parent in an extreme situation, in fantasy at least, as in response to the TAT, may be to kill the child who is the product of the failure in parental responsibility and duty, and then to commit suicide. In the traditional pattern, parental pressure, expectation, or control was exerted more strongly on a son than on a daughter. Important social status and roles were usually limited to men and thus much more social responsibility was required of them. When children act in opposition to parental expectations, it is more often the mother who is exposed to a strong sense of failure, because to raise socially laudable children is considered the most important female responsibility. Thus, in many TAT responses the mother was seen as chastising her son. The responses also included stories of a mother killing her delinquent son and then killing herself to atone for his and her crime. It is not clear how often cases of chastisement and mother-child joint suicide actually happen in present-day Japan. Whether the psychodynamics of the mother-child relationship described above is weakening or disappearing with changing social norms is a question that can be answered only in the light of further empirical research.

REFERENCES

Ariga, Kizaemon
   1948 *Nihon konin shi ron* (A study of the history of marriage in Japan). Tokyo: Nikko Shoin.

Bayley, David H.
  1976 *Forces of order: police behavior in Japan and the United States.* Berkeley, Los Angeles, London: University of California Press.

Caudill, William, and David Plath
  1966 Who sleeps by whom: parent-child involvement in urban Japanese families. *Psychiatry* 29:344–366.

Caudill, William, and Helen Weinstein
  1969 Maternal care and infant behavior in Japan and America. *Psychiatry* 32:12–43.

DeVos, George, and Hiroshi Wagatsuma
  1961 Value attitudes toward role behavior of women in two Japanese villages. *American Anthropologist* 63(6):1204–1230.

  1970 Status and role behavior in changing Japan. In *Sex roles in changing society*, ed. G. Seward and R. Williamson. Pp. 334–370.

Dickman, Mildred
  1975 Demographic consequences of infanticide in man. *Annual Review of Ecology and Systematics* 6:100–139.

Doi, Takeo
  1973 *The anatomy of dependence.* Tokyo: Kodansha International.

Ikeda, Yoshiko
  1977 Jido gyakutai no mondai ni tsuite, seishin eisei to fukushi no tachiba kara (On the problems of child abuse, from the standpoint of mental health and welfare). *Seishin Igaku* 19(9):4–20.

Imamura, Hiroshi
  1978 *Kogoroshi: sono seishin byōri* (Child killing: its psychopathology). Tokyo: Seishin Shobo.

Inokuchi, S.
  1959 Tanjó to ikuji (Birth and child rearing). *Nihon Minzoku Taikei* (Japanese Folklore Series), vol. 4. Tokyo: Heibonsha. Pp. 181–213.

Kodama, Hiroko, et al.
  1977 Deprivation syndrome and battered child syndrome: kyōtsū suru hassei yōin oyobi shakaiteki haikei ni tsuiteno kōsatsu. (Observations on the common causative factors and social backgrounds). *Shōnika Gakkai Zasshi* 81(7):546–554.

Kōseisho Jidō Katei Kyoku (Ministry of Health and Welfare, Bureau of Children and Families).
  1974 Jidō no gyakutai, iki, satsugai jiken ni kansuru chōsa kekka (The research results of cases of child abuse, abandonment, and infanticide). Mimeograph.

Kurisu, Eiko
  1974 Kodomo no yōiku ni kansuru shakai-byōriteki kōsatsu: eijisatsu oyobi jidō no iki, gyakutai nado o megutte (A social pathological observation on child rearing: infanticide, desertion, and abuse of the children). *Jurisuto* 557:121–127.

Lanham, Betty
  1956 Aspects of child care in Japan: a preliminary report. In *Personal character and cultural milieu*, ed. D. G. Haring. Syracuse: Syracuse University Press. Pp. 564–584.

  1966 The psychological orientation of the mother-child relationship in Japan. *Monumenta Nipnica* 26(3–4):321–333.

Minamikawa, Taizo
1973 *Chiisana hitsugi* (A small coffin). Tokyo: Buronzu Sha.

Miyamoto, Tsuneichi
1967 *Chosaku shú (Collected works). Vol. 6.* Tokyo: Miraisha.

Nakaya, Kinko
1977 Kaku kazoku-ka to eiji goroshi (Nucleation of the Japanese family and cases of infanticide). *Kēsu Kenkyu* 135:2−10.

1978 Josei hanzai zōka no jittai to sono haikei (The reality and its background of the increase of female crimes). *Hōritsu no Hiroba* 31(1):35−49.

Norbeck, Edward, and Margaret Norbeck
1956 Child training in a Japanese fishing village. In *Personal character and cultural milieu*, ed. D. G. Haring. Syracuse: Syracuse University Press. Pp. 651−673.

Sasaki, Yasuyuki
1977*a* Kosute kogoroshi (Killing and abandonment of children). *Jurisuto*, Special Issue no. 6:235−240.

1977*b* Oyako shinjū ni miru oyako no aijō no shinri to ronri (The psychology and logic of parental love observed in the parent-child double suicide). *Jidō Shiori* 31(9): 145−151.

Sasaki, Yasuyuki, et al.
1974 Kogoroshi no shinrigakuteki kenkyū: haha oya no ishiki chōsa (A psychological study of infanticide: the mothers' attitudes). *Utsunomiya Daigaku Yóji Kenkyú Kyógikai Kenkyú Hokoku (Utsunomiya University Child Research Council Research Report).* No. 1.

1975*a* Kogoroshi no shinrigakuteki kenkyū: chichioya no ishiki chōsa (A psychological study of infanticide: the fathers' attitudes). *Utsunomiya Daigaku Yóji Kenkyú Kyógikai Kenkyú Hokoku* (Utsunomiya University Child Research Council Research Report). No. 2.

1975*b* Kogoroshi no shinrigakuteki kenkyū: joshigakusei no ishiki chósa (A psychological study of infanticide: the female university students' attitudes). *Utsunomiya University Department of Education Bulletin* 25(1):63−79.

Satake, Yoshio
1971 Shōni no gyakutai (Child abuse: battered child syndrome). *Shōnika Shinryō* 34(2):89−94.

Taeuber, Irene
1958 *The population of Japan.* Princeton: Princeton University Press.

Takahashi, Taneaki, and Ichiro Naka
1976 Hahaoya no yōikutaido no yugami ni kansuru kenkyū (A study of anomalies in maternal attitudes toward children). *Nihon Sōgō Aiiku Kenkyujo Kiyō* 9:173−174.

Tsuchiya, Shinichi, and Noriko Sato
1973 Eiji goroshi ni kansuru kenkyū (A study of infanticide). *Homushō Sōgō Kenkyūjo Kiyō (Justice Ministry Research Institute Bulletin)* 23:45−62.

Vogel, Ezra, and Suzanne Vogel
1961 Family security, personal immaturity and emotional health in a Japanese sample. *Marriage and Family Living* 23:161−166.

Wagatsuma, Hiroshi
   1970 Study of personality and behavior in Japanese society and culture. In *The study of Japan in the behavioral sciences*, ed. Edward Norbeck and Susan Parman. Rice University Studies. Vol. 56 (4):53–63.

   1977 Some aspects of changing family in contemporary Japan: once Confucian, now fatherless? *Deadalus* 106(2):181–210.

Wagatsuma, Hiroshi, and Hiroko Hara
   1974 *Shitsuke* (Child rearing and discipline). Tokyo: Kobundo.

Yanagita, Kunio
   1969 *Teibon Yanagita Kunio shū (Collected works)*. Tokyo: Chikuma Shobo. Vol. 5.

CHILD ABUSE IN TAIWAN   8

David Y. H. Wu

I. INTRODUCTION

Child abuse has become increasingly recognized in Western nations, particularly the United States where the literature on child abuse has been growing rapidly since pediatrician C. Henry Kempe and his associates, coining the term "the battered child syndrome," aroused public and professional concern (Kempe et al. 1962). Since the concept of child abuse is relatively new, it is not well understood in many non-Western countries, and little attention has been paid to research concerned with the pathological aspects of child rearing and the parent-child relationship. In Taiwan, maltreatment of children is a negatively sanctioned behavior, and offenders are subject to public criticism and legal prosecution. Nevertheless, scholars in Taiwan have thus far made no attempt to collect empirical data on child abuse, nor have they researched the etiology of maltreatment of children in the Chinese sociocultural context.

It is therefore not surprising that our initial visits in 1977 to various health agencies and major hospitals in Taipei for statistics on battered children and on nonaccidental injuries to children yielded no results. We realized that neither the government health department at various administrative levels nor public hospitals had records of this nature. A social worker at the Taipei Municipal Children's Hospital recalled no cases of abused children. Initial discussions with parents and health practitioners about ill-treatment of infants in Taiwan led to their denial that such incredible incidents were possible. Cases of battered babies in the United States, which we cited for the purpose of eliciting information about similar cases in Taiwan, were taken to be a unique occurrence in American or Western society. It was pointed out, as illustrated in a Chinese proverb, that if even a cruel, ferocious animal like a tiger would never harm her cub, a human mother could hardly hurt her own child.

Yet, contrary to the general belief in benign, benevolent Chinese parents, newspapers in Taiwan print stories of parents who beat or torture their children to death. A sporadic check of 1977 news items yielded such incidents: a "mentally abnormal" mother (age 27) poisoned her two children (2 and 4 years old) before she hanged herself; a mother (age 28) threw her one-year-old baby to the ground three times and killed it when the baby "cried endlessly" during feeding; and a divorced young mother (age 18) left her baby with a wet nurse, paid one month's fee, and was never heard of again (*Lian He Bao*, Aug. 14, 1977, p. 6; Aug. 19, 1977, p. 6; *Da Hua Wan Bao*, Aug. 8, 1977, p. 8). In most of these cases of serious child abuse the parent was regarded by the reporters as temporarily insane. Furthermore, such instances are believed by police, press, and health agencies to be isolated cases rather than part of a widespread phenomenon. We were aware that understanding the parameters of child abuse in Taiwan according to the definition accepted in the West requires epidemiological research on a large scale. Our preliminary study in 1977–78, however, though small in scale, yielded significant information. Based on anthropological fieldwork and library research, we gathered sufficient data to warrant a discussion of Chinese cultural values in regard to children, the ideal parent-child relationship, and general child-rearing and disciplinary practices.[1] We believe that these findings may provide clues to understanding culture-specific modes of child abuse and suggest preventive measures for child abuse in Chinese society in Taiwan.

Before discussing child-rearing practices in contemporary Taiwan, I shall analyze a fundamental Chinese cultural value on the ideal parent-child relationship which is centered on the concept of *xiao (hsiao)*, or filial piety. This concept (discussed in Sec. II), is central to understanding the possible social

---

[1]Data are based on my previous fieldwork on socialization processes in Taiwan and overseas Chinese societies; library work on classic Chinese writings; review of a major Chinese newspaper in Taiwan for the years 1951–52 and 1970–71; distribution of a questionnaire on child rearing and discipline; and a field survey, interviews, and observations in Taiwan in the summers of 1977 and 1978. My wife, Wei-lan, was mainly responsible for data collection during the summer field trips to Taipei. I am most grateful to her for the data and for her assistance in many other ways during my preparation of this paper. I wish also to express my appreciation to the following people for their help in many ways, from literature search, comments, and interviews to computer analysis: Mutsu Hsu, Brenda Foster, Yeo-hsien Han, Victor Askman, and Jonathan Okamura. To Jill Korbin, I owe a great deal for introducing me to this new and exciting field of child abuse. I am also indebted to her for providing me with references and constant encouragement.

and psychological mechanisms that either contribute to or prevent child abuse. Next I discuss (in Sec. III) our field material on child-rearing practices and disciplinary measures in Taiwan which could be regarded as abusive by outsiders. Then institutionalized abuse against adopted daughters in Taiwanese society is examined (in Sec. IV). The chapter concludes (Sec. V) with hypotheses relating a trend toward increased child abuse and neglect to rapid socioeconomic change in Taiwan.

II. FILIAL PIETY AS FUNDAMENTAL VALUE IN PARENT-CHILD RELATIONS

Filial piety is one of the oldest moral codes of the Chinese, who have emphasized it since the first millennium B.C. Scholars, philosophers, and political elites considered it the essential moral principle as well as the pivot of social order in Chinese society. To this day, the teaching of filial piety is pursued in Taiwan in schools, public speeches, theatrical performances, children's story books, and promotional articles in newspapers and magazines. As Wilson (1970:62) points out, "Overt training in filiality begins in kindergarten and is most marked in the early years of school." During the heyday of the so-called Cultural Renaissance Movement in Taiwan between 1966 and 1971 (to counter the Cultural Revolution in China), the government sponsored some 400 articles and speeches, either written or delivered by high officials and well-known scholars, to echo President Chiang's emphasis on Confucian moral teachings (Hsiao 1973:19). About 100 of them explicitly stressed filial piety as one of the most important moral tenets for the restoration of Chinese culture—the beginning of the ultimate task of retaking mainland China. Although these articles and speeches can be seen as relevant to this specific political context, they can also be viewed in the literary tradition of classic Chinese writing, which for centuries glorified filial piety. We cannot fully understand Chinese child rearing without first understanding the historical, cultural, political, and psychological background of filial piety.

Filial examplars are still cited today in newspaper articles and school texts. Twenty-four were selected by Guo Jujing (Kuo Chu-ching) of the Yuen dynasty (13th century A.D.) for a children's story book, the modern version of which is read by almost every Chinese child in Taiwan (cf. Hsu 1970; Koehn 1944, one of the best English translations; Solomon 1971; Tseng and Hsu 1972). In 1970 and 1971 the Taiwan government issued special postage stamps, illustrating these stories of filial piety, "in order to honor the virtue of filial piety as well as to promote the Chinese Cultural Renaissance campaign" (as the government put it).

Because filial piety toward parents and elders was so strongly emphasized in China throughout time, records of model filial persons regularly appeared in personal biographies, local gazettes, and official historical books in every part of China. From time to time court historians would be asked to compile an encyclopedic document in which a section or a chapter would usually be reserved for the illustration of filial deeds of extraordinary nature. Two chapters of one such book, *Tai-Ping Yu-Lan* (Imperial Review of the Grand Peace), compiled during the Sung dynasty (960–1279 A.D.), illustrate model filial behavior as esteemed in traditional Chinese society. The chapter entitled "Xiao Gan" ("Hsiao-Kan") (Filial Move) comprises sixty[2] short accounts of remarkable filial deeds performed by commoners, officials, and even emperors, which moved heaven, animals, and people. All except one of these deeds of "filial move," the highest filial deed, were performed by males. A later chapter, "Xiao Nu" ("Hsiao Nu") (Filial Daughters), recounts twenty-nine stories of filial deeds performed by a girl or an adult woman.

A review of these cases reveals that filial piety was expressed not only toward parents but also toward patrilineal elders of the third, or even the fourth, ascending generation. Table VIII-I shows more instances in which filial deeds are directed by the son to his mother and by the daughter to her father than to same-sex parents. We should not speculate about an Oedipal relationship, however, without first analyzing the cultural context. Another point worthy of mention concerns filial behavior toward a stepmother. In these stories stepmothers were invariably described as mistreating their stepchildren. Ironically, the stepchild's submissive and tolerant behavior won him or her a place in the documentation of model filial behavior. We shall return to this point about stepmothers.

The ages of the filial children ranged from three years to adolescence, and some of the subjects were elderly. According to the manner in which filial behavior was displayed, the stories may be classified into nine categories, described as follows.

CATEGORY 1.   Sacrifice of one's own life or one's child's life for the parents' sake

Several stories portray a father who committed a crime and was sentenced to death. When a son or a daughter offered to die in the father's place, the emperor was so moved that he pardoned the father. In one case a poor man decided to bury his infant son alive in order to provide properly for his elderly

[2] *Xiao gan (hsiao-kan)*, "filial move," refers to the phenomenon of moving heaven or the gods by one's virtue or, as here, by an exceptional behavioral expression of filial piety. The resulting miracles are considered rewards from heaven, as shown by later explanations in this chapter.

TABLE VIII-1   Persons to Whom Filial Deeds Are Directed

BY BOYS OR MALE ADULTS*	
Filial object	*Number of cases*
Biological mother	27
Foster mother	2
Stepmother	2
Father	17
Parents (unspecified)	8
Parents plus older brother's wife	1
Grandmother	1
Grandfather	1
Great-grandmother	1
Total	60
BY GIRLS OR FEMALE ADULTS	
Father	16
Biological mother	2
Stepmother	1
Parents (unspecified)	2
Grandmother	2
Grandfather	0
Grandparents	2
Parents-in-law	4
Total	29

*In one case a daughter is involved.

mother. While digging the grave intended for his son, the man struck gold, a reward from heaven.

CATEGORY 2.   Mourning in excess of the normal rites
     When a parent died, these filial sons and daughters cried day and night until their eyes bled, or until they fainted repeatedly. Some of them prolonged the mourning period; one son mourned his father continuously for thirty years without taking off his mourning costume and remained a vegetarian bachelor all his life. Filial sons and daughters sometimes committed suicide in their mourning.

CATEGORY 3.   To accomplish an impossible task or to suffer self-inflicted bodily pain in fulfillment of a parent's (especially a mother's) wishes or demands

In these stories we see obvious manifestations of child abuse. In two of them a stepmother mistreated a stepson, who accepted her unreasonable demands obediently. In the first story a nine-year-old boy, Wang Yen, was asked by his stepmother to find live fish in a severe winter when the river was frozen. When Wang Yen was unable to provide the fish, he was beaten until he bled. He went to his own mother's tomb and cried. A live fish, which was said to be five feet long, suddenly appeared on his mother's tomb. He therefore was able to please his stepmother and thereafter was spared her harsh treatment. It is noteworthy that in a different version of the story of Wang Yen's filial behavior his biological mother rather than his stepmother mistreated him. As an apparent indication of his mother's deliberate maltreatment, it was pointed out that he did not have decent clothing to cover himself in the severe winter.

The second story worthy of special mention tells about a boy named Wang Xiang (Hsiang) who, in order to catch live fish for his stepmother in winter, lay on the ice to melt the frozen river. On another occasion his stepmother ordered him to watch a fruit tree at night. When the wind blew, the boy clung to the tree trunk in order to stop the fruit from falling off the tree. His stepmother was still not satisfied with him, however, and intended to kill him with a dagger. The boy miraculously escaped his stepmother's attack during his sleep. When he realized his stepmother's intention, he kneeled before her and offered his head. It was said that his stepmother's heart was suddenly moved and that she thereafter treated him as if he were her own son.

Mention should be made here of another model filial child whose deeds are acclaimed (*Tai-Ping Yu-Lan*, chap. 413):

> Wu Meng, who lived during the fourth and fifth century, showed already at the age of eight years, great love for his parents. . . . Every summer night when the mosquitoes annoyed his parents, Meng took off most of his clothes and lay down near their bed to attract the mosquitoes away from them to himself. Stoically he suffered, and gladly endured the bites for those whom he loved and reverenced.[3] [Koehn 1944:20]

CATEGORY 4.   To attend sick parents or to seek medicine or a cure through extraordinary behavior or miracles

To take special care of a sick parent is another popular expression of filial piety. In the stories under review, even a wealthy official who possessed

---

[3]The deeds of both Wang Xiang (Hsiang) and Wu Meng are included in the book of twenty-four ideal filial stories, as are many others cited in this section.

hundreds of servants or slaves would personally attend to a parent's sickbed, sacrificing his own proper diet and sleep to show his concern. To cook the herb medicine oneself and to test the medicine before it is served to the sick parent is considered an essential part of filial behavior under such circumstances (cf. Hsu 1970:78). It seems that filial piety through concern and sharing of the suffering (by not eating or sleeping) adds to the efficacy of the medicine. Another example of extraordinary behavior in attending to a sick parent concerned a son who sucked his parent's boil or tumor to relieve the swelling. The story explicitly pointed out that "the son's face displayed not the slightest expression of hesitation or unwillingness [while sucking his parent's boil]."

The belief that a child's suffering and pain could assist a parent's recovery from illness has developed through time to such an extent that as a last resort—believed to be a sure cure—a filial son or daughter would cut a piece of flesh from his or her arm or thigh to be used as one of the ingredients for the parent's medicine. News of such filial behavior was reported until not too long ago in Taiwan (see Hsu 1970:79 for occurrences in China).

CATEGORY 5.   To provide parents with a proper, decent burial

One of the prevalent themes in filial piety concerns an impoverished child trying to find a way to provide the deceased parent (especially the father) with a decent tomb. Some children worked hard to accumulate the needed burial fee; others sold themselves into slavery in order to raise funds for construction of a tomb. In two cases, a son who grieved over the impossibility of finding his father's bones among thousands of remains on the battlefield was advised to use his own blood as a detector. It was believed that if a son's blood touched his father's bones it would penetrate into the bones. The son cut his arms and legs to bleed upon hundreds of skeletons and finally, before killing himself through loss of blood, he was able to locate his father's bones for a proper burial.

CATEGORY 6.   Extreme bravery in protecting a parent or a parent's corpse from harm or damage

The stories ranged from a young boy or girl who shielded a father or a mother from an attacking tiger or a threatening bandit to an adult son who refused to leave his parent's coffin when a fire in a neighbor's house threatened to spread. The tiger was so touched that he retreated; the bandit was moved to spare the parent, the parent's corpse was saved when the fire stopped short of the coffin and the weeping son. In one case, however, the filial son threw himself onto the flames and died when the house in which his father's coffin lay caught fire and was beyond saving.

CATEGORY 7. Attachment to parents (especially a son to his mother) through extrasensory or supernatural communication

One story portrays a mother-son attachment so strong that, when visitors unexpectedly arrived while the son was collecting firewood on the mountains, the mother needed only to bite her fingers. The son suddenly felt a heartthrob and rushed home to see if anything had happened to his mother.

CATEGORY 8. To avenge a father's death

CATEGORY 9. To support parents despite difficult circumstances or through self-sacrifice

These cases describe filial sons or daughters who faithfully provide for parents despite their own hardships. In most of the cases concerning women, a daughter or a daughter-in-law would remain single or refuse to remarry in order to stay with parents or parents-in-law and support them.

Although for the sake of clarity I have classified the filial behaviors reviewed into the above nine categories, many of the stories could easily fit into more than one category. The typology of the stories is summarized in table VIII-2. Although these stories may be regarded today as cultural myths, as only a few of them would be acted out in real life, they still have implications

TABLE VIII-2 Summary of Filial Deeds in Two Chapters of Tai-Ping Yu-Lan

	NUMBER OF CASES	
Behavioral category	Filial move*	Filial daughters
1. Sacrifice own life for parent's sake	2	6
2. Excessive mourning	14	7
3. Suffering in meeting parent's demands	7	1
4. Attending sick parent	7	1
5. Providing parent with proper burial	11	2
6. Extreme bravery in protecting parent	4	5
7. Profound attachment to parent	7	0
8. Avenging father's death	1	3
9. Supporting parents through hardship	4	4
10. Other	3	1
Total	60	30

*All except one were performed by males.

for parent-child relationships and influence child training in modern Taiwanese society.

The following moral and cultural tenets can be inferred from the above analysis of historical cases of model filial children:

1. From a very young age children are expected to show great devotion to their parents, especially the mother.
2. The parent's welfare comes before the child's welfare or that of a son's wife and children. One should not be happy when one's parents are not happy.
3. At the loss of a parent one is expected to express one's grief openly and dramatically. Those whose mourning behavior exceeds that prescribed by the rites are considered filial. The most filial would rather die than continue to live without the parent's company. This last point is again an extension of the emphasis of attachment even after a parent's death.
4. No matter how unreasonable a parent's demands, or how harsh the treatment inflicted by a parent, a son or a daughter should obey and endure and make sure that the parent's wishes are fulfilled. Children should be considerate and pleasing in order to make their parents as comfortable as possible, even though they may thereby suffer bodily pain or damage. Children's submissiveness to a stepmother's maltreatment is praised.

In short, the parents' pleasure is the children's suffering.[4] Psychiatrists T'seng and Hsu (1972) make two useful remarks in their study, "The Chinese Attitude towards Parental Authority as Expressed in Chinese Children's Stories," which is based in part on modern versions of the historical accounts of filial piety. They say, first, that the "extremely close and prolonged relationships between son and mother may appear pathological to a Western psychiatrist. In most cases, this close relationship is considered virtuous in Chinese culture and is not highly sexualized." Their second noteworthy comment is: "From a Western point of view, these sons serve their fathers in a masochistic way" (referring to the son who warmed his father's bed in winter and to the son who allowed the mosquitoes to bite him) (T'seng and Hsu 1972:29). Indeed,

---

[4] Many of the stories of filial behavior in the present analysis are focused on food. Filial behavior thus reflects the central importance of food in Chinese culture. Fried (1976:52–53) calls this emphasis on food, as evidenced by its central place in ritual activities, the Chinese "orality." Thus a mother craving fish in winter could be regarded as a symbolic representation of Chinese orality, a desire for reverse nurturance. Taiwanese Buddhists believe that those who let their parents starve will themselves be tortured after death in a special hell (Eberhard 1967).

many daring Chinese scholars have questioned the "unnatural" behavior required of children, but they were overruled by public and political pressure.

Recent articles in Taiwan newspapers also have begun to subtly argue the relevance of these traditional models in the modern world (*Min Zu Wan Bao*, Oct. 1, 1978, p. 10; *Min Sheng Bao*, Sept. 24, 1978, p. 5). A recent newspaper item (*Min Sheng Bao*, Oct. 1, 1978, p. 4), reported that the Ministry of Education, in preparation for the 1979 nationwide "teaching filial piety month" in April, decided to edit a new textbook of the twenty-four stories on filial piety so that the "traditional ethics of filial piety can be expanded and developed, exerting a long-lasting influence." Even though this project means little more than rewriting the stories to fit the contemporary reality as well as adding new stories, it stimulated protests from conservative extremists who argued that historical-model personalities need not fit the modern reality.

One could argue that the emphasis on and the teaching of traditional values of filial models enhance parental control but ignore children's rights. Furthermore, I believe that the stories concerned with stepmothers help to legitimize, at least in the minds of the stepmothers, institutionalized abusive treatment of stepchildren and, further, of adopted daughters in Taiwan (to be discussed later).

There is another piece of evidence that traditional Chinese cultural values uphold the absolute rights of parents to inflict harsh physical punishment upon children while the children are obliged to endure or even to show enjoyment of parental punishment. The classical writing *Shuo Yuan* (cited in *Tai-Ping Yu-Lan*) contains a story about one of Confucius's disciples, Tseng Tzu, believed to be one of the authors of *Xiao Jing (Hsiao Ching)* (The Classics of Filial Piety):

> When Zeng Zi [Tseng Tzu] was working [weeding] in the field he accidentally broke the roots of a young plant. His father Tseng Hsu was so angry that he picked up a big pole and hit him. Zeng Zi [Tseng Tzu] was knocked to the ground and was unconscious for quite a while before he came around. He jumped up, approached his father, and said, "I have offended your lordship. You beat me with such strength I am worried whether you might have hurt yourself." Zeng Zi [Tseng Tzu] then retreated to his own room, played *chin* and sang. [This was intended to show his father that he was happy and had no hard feelings at all.]
>
> When Confucius heard about this incident, he ordered his doorman not to let Zeng Sen in should he come. [His name is Sen. Zi (Tzu) is an honorary address by the writer.] Zeng Zi [Tseng Tzu] thought he had not done anything wrong, so he sent someone to Confucius for an explanation. Confucius said, "Have you not heard about the 'blind man' who had a son named Shun [a legendary emperor of a prehistoric dynasty] who served the old man [his father] with such devotion that whenever he was sent for he would present himself at his father's side. However, whenever his father wanted to kill him he would not present himself. He would wait on his father when his father demanded his

beating with a small stick. He would run away when his father wanted to beat him with a thick rod. Now you have submitted yourself to your angry father's beating with a huge pole. Are you trying to get your father to kill you? If you do not submit yourself to your father's beating you would not be right. But if you do let your father beat you to death then you are not filial [because he would be leaving his father heirless]. Which is more wrong? You tell me."

It is clear that according to Confucian logic a son should use his judgment in voluntarily submitting himself to his father's beating. He should run for his life when the stick is large enough to kill him. The question, then, is: What if the son makes the wrong decison? He would be either an unfilial son or dead.

That the Chinese culture encourages a son's masochistic submission to parental physical punishment is also clear from another story in *Shuo Yuan*:

Han Boyu [Puo Yu] was at fault. After his mother beat him he cried. His mother asked, "You never cried when I beat you before, why should you cry this time?" He replied, "Your son Yu suffered from pain when you beat him in the past. Today I did not feel the pain which indicates mother's strength has weakened [hence becoming old and unhealthy]. Therefore I cried."

Han Boyu (Puo Yu) was an adult, but there are stories about a young child who learned to endure pain rather foolishly, that is, according to the perspective of the Western world. The following story indicates how the Chinese appreciate a young child's exhibition of extreme consideration toward elders.

A five-year-old "filial girl" endured the pain caused by injury, not uttering a word of protest, when her grandmother, who was giving her a haircut, mistakenly cut the girl's skin because of poor eyesight. The girl accepted the pain rather than let the grandmother know of her bad eyesight which would indicate her age and failing health. [*Tai-Ping Yu-Lan*, chap. 415]

Children's consideration of their parents is supposed to last all their lives. Another well-known story is about an old man, Lao Laizi (Lai-tzu), whose deed was selected for the modern twenty-four stories of filial piety. This seventy-year-old man, in order not to hurt his aging parents' feelings and aware that they were very old, would wear multicolored clothes of children's fashion. One day when he was serving drinks to his parents Lao Laizi lost his footing and fell to the ground. While lying on the floor he imitated a baby's cry so as to create an illusion that the parents were still young enough to have a baby son (*Tai-Ping Yu-Lan*, chap. 413). This Confucian exemplar symbolizes the Chinese value that a son remains a son all his life (Solomon 1971:34–35).

Whatever the reality of actual treatment of children in Taiwanese society today (to be discussed later), I am concerned with the possible effects of sociocultural values that overemphasize parents' rights at the expense of children's rights. The traditional moral principle of filial piety could legitimate parents' abusive and unreasonable behavior toward their children. Infanticide, for instance, is known to have been a tolerated Chinese custom, and during famines children could even be sold for food (Ho 1959). Although these phenomena can be explained in economic terms as owing to the scarcity of resources and to population pressure, they nevertheless manifest how cultural values permit the Chinese to sacrifice the young generations for the older. Cohen (1976), for instance, maintains that in rural Taiwan children are regarded as property to be disposed of at will by their parents, and in many parts of traditional China children could be sold into slavery or to entertainment institutions without their consent. Traditional legal codes provide for extremely harsh punishment of children who harm or kill their parents, yet parents who commit the same acts on their children are lightly dealt with or excused. The precedent for this anomaly can be seen in the following example from the legal records of the Qing (Ch'ing) dynasty (1644–1911 A.D.):

> Chen Wenxun [Wen-hsun] scolded his son when the latter brought him a cup of cold tea. The father poured the tea on the ground and picked up a stick with which to beat his son. The son ran away and the father chased after him. The ground was slippery because of the spilled tea and Wen-hsun lost his footing, struck his head, and died as a result of his injury. The son was charged with a crime and the verdict was "detention in prison for strangling." [Scharfstein 1974:8]

In his discussion of legal enforcement of filial piety in traditional China, Scharfstein (1974:7–8) says that a father is within his rights to beat his adult son until blood is evident. Furthermore, a "child, of whatever age, who scolded, cursed, beat or seriously disobeyed his parents, could be put to death by them without fear of intervention by the law." Although the present law in Taiwan would hold parents responsible should they harm their children, public opinion is often on the side of the parents.

We must understand that continuing efforts to promote filial piety in Taiwan are based on sociopolitical motives. These motives in turn are historically based on the merit system, which operated in old China as it does in modern Taiwan. It is interesting to note that in many of the stories of filial deeds the heroes or heroines were at the end rewarded by the emperor or local officials with material goods (silk, rice, exemption from taxes and labor), public citation or honor in the form of stone tablets or arches, and even official positions or promotions. One should not take the bestowal of these rewards as grounds for the accusation that sons and daughters behaved in extraordinary ways in order to receive them. We can reasonably say that most of them acted in response to their feelings and impulses which were culturally inculcated. Yet we cannot rule out the possibility that some people have exploited cultural circumstances by a deliberate demonstration of filial behavior for the sake of personal sociopolitical advancement. Sociopolitical activities in Taiwan and in the early People's Republic of China are replete with examples of this kind of exploitation. According to Fried (1959, quoted in Abbott 1976:84), during the first ten years of Communist rule in China "the practice of *xiao* (filial piety) by children (even after they become adults) is still a 'virtue of socialist youth.' " Solomon (1971) attributes the successful establishment of a Communist state in China to the Chinese socialization process and its fundamental emphasis on filial piety. Wilson's (1970) study leads to the conclusion that the "socialization of filiality" in Taiwan accounts for the people's willing submission to authoritarian rule despite the government rhetoric of liberty and individual freedom and a democratic political system.

III. CHINESE CHILD REARING AND DISCIPLINE

Filial piety thus embraces the entire Chinese cultural system and functions as the foundation of Chinese personality as well as of political organizations. Solomon (1971:75) aptly characterizes Chinese socialization for filiality as a security pact or social contract between parent and child. Parents raise children, and children are expected to provide for parents in their old age. We shall see that to maintain the "agreement" or "contract," as Solomon puts it, certain child-rearing techniques and punitive actions are necessary for the assertion of parental authority in order to gain children's submission, dependence, and unconditional support.

Two mechanisms to train for filiality are emphasized in child rearing: (1) the inducement of both physical and emotional closeness so that a lifelong bond is assured; and (2) the maintenance of parental authority and children's obedience through harsh discipline.

Child-rearing practices that induce parent-child attachment may be summarized as follows. Infants sleep in the same bed with their parents. Whenever a baby cries the mother quickly responds by picking it up and rocking or feeding it. Feeding is frequent, either by breast or by bottle, in response to the infant's cry. Changing of diapers is also frequent; a good mother usually gets up at night to change and to nurse her baby. The mother and other adults in the family are very responsive to a young child's dependent behavior, as when it seeks help. Young children's physical mobility is kept rather limited, yet there are few restrictions on children's boisterous behavior as long as they seem to be happy. Few parents have a strict rule as to children's bedtime. School-age children are encouraged to go to bed early, but if the family is engaged in a social party or other celebration children are allowed to stay up late. Since the culture encourages parent-child attachment, Chinese children's physical contact with their mothers through clinging and following lasts longer than it does for American children. Chinese infants and young children are more frequently held in an adult's arms. In rural Taiwan a mother normally carries her young child on her back while doing household chores, shopping, visiting, or working in the field. Older siblings often help the mother in looking after younger children while under their mother's surveillance. Many mothers almost never part with a child during its first and second years. A good mother does not seek pleasure alone, such as going to a movie and leaving her baby with somebody else; therefore, children almost always take part in adults' social gatherings.

Our data on child rearing in Taiwan were collected during brief field trips in the summers of 1977 and 1978. Field interviews were conducted with eight families in Taipei and five in southern Taiwan. Additionally, a questionnaire concerning punishment, attitudes toward children, and observed techniques of child rearing was administered to 10 working parents and to 30 college students taking psychology courses. The working parents were between 25 and 56 years of age; among the students there were 9 males and 21 females between the ages of 21 and 28. Many of the students were employed but were also attending evening classes; all except one man were single.

Most of the informants who were interviewed agreed that nonresponsiveness to an infant when it cries—letting it cry without either holding, rocking, or feeding it—and not checking frequently to change a baby's diapers qualify as maltreatment of infants. Confirmation of this opinion came from our questionnaire respondents. Paying a lot of attention to infants, frequently checking on their comfort, meeting their demands, and, most of all, the biological mother serving as the major caretaker were valued by respondents of both sexes and across the age range of the sample. In response to the questionnaire item concerning the most abusive behavior against infants of one year and younger, 17 cited ignoring or nonresponsiveness, 10 cited beating, 9 cited deprivation of food and drink, 2 said not changing diapers frequently enough, and 2 referred to other practices. With regard to children between the ages of 5 and 10, more than half of the respondents (23) referred to heavy beating or inappropriate punishment as abusive treatment, 7 cited nonresponsiveness, and 5 cited deprivation of food.

In a related question, the respondents were asked whether they themselves had actually seen child abuse according to the definitions given above. Twenty-five percent of our respondents reported having seen abused children 1 year of age; 32.5 percent had seen abused children between 1 and 3 years of age; and 40 percent claimed to have seen abused children between the ages of 5 and 10. In other words, the older the children, the more likely they are to be subjected to child abuse.

It is noteworthy that several Chinese mothers in Papua New Guinea commented that European mothers (predominantly Australians) did not change their infants' diapers frequently enough to keep the babies comfortable. European mothers were also criticized for not giving enough attention to their children and depriving them of the pleasure of being with adults when the adults were enjoying themselves. On the other hand, European mothers resent the Chinese practice of letting children participate in social gatherings.

The second mechanism to establish filiality is discipline. Anthropologists and psychologists usually portray the period of Chinese childhood under the age of five or six as one of indulgence or, in Solomon's (1971:39–60) words, as the "golden age" of life. This stage is said to be characterized by gratification of food and comfort needs as well as by absence of punishment. Based on my own observations and interviews, I tend to disagree with the belief in a golden age for young Chinese children. Aside from my own observation of mothers spanking young children for disagreeable behavior, informants from both sexes and all ages almost unanimously agree that discipline is necessary as soon as a child begins to "understand things" (*dung shi*) (*tung shih*); that is, when he is able to talk, to walk, and to comprehend adults' instructions.[5] Common methods of discipline include punitive measures such as kneeling on the floor and being beaten on the buttocks, legs, or palms with a bamboo rod. One Taiwanese mother (age 30) vividly described her disciplining of her three-year-old son.

> Disobedience always ends with my beating. For example, when he was drinking milk he did not hold the glass properly and the milk appeared to spill. I warned him, "Watch your glass! Hold your glass upright or the milk will spill!" He did not pay any attention to what I said and eventually spilt his milk. Then I hit him. You see, I beat him because I told [warned] him beforehand, yet he did not listen to me. If I did not tell him ahead of time and he did not know he had done wrong, I would not beat him. For example, the other day I told him not to get near to the

---

[5] A child normally learns to talk and walk before reaching the age of two, when it is expected to take adults's commands. Young children are not subject to parental discipline and correction because of their inability to "tell right from wrong" (*ben-be shi-fei*) (*pien-peh shih-fei*). With regard to how old a child must be to be able to tell right from wrong himself or herself, our respondents provided us with varied answers: 8 (20 percent) said 1 to 3 years; 17 (42.5 percent) said 4 to 6 years; 8 (20 percent) said 7 to 9 years; 4 (10 percent) answered 10 years and above; 3 respondents (7.5 percent) did not give precise answers. One replied that some children can never tell right from wrong until they themselves become parents.

ditch [small and shallow] in the kitchen. He did not obey me, fell into the ditch, and dirtied his clothes. I beat him. He understands perfectly why I hit him.

Chinese parents are faced with a dilemma regarding disciplinary beating of their children; the choice is between unwillingly inflicting pain on the child or allowing the child to become a delinquent by not punishing him. As a father said, "We know that beating too heavily or too frequently is not right, but a most 'abusive' parent is one who does not discipline his or her child, hence 'drowning the child with love.' " *Ni-ai* (literally, "drowning with love") was condemned by 38 of our 40 questionnaire respondents. Although Solomon (1971:65) describes *ni-ai* as Chinese parents' anxiety over their indulgence or show of affection to their children, 28 (70 percent) of our respondents defined it as "answering to whatever children demand" and 9 (22.5 percent) responded with the definition, "no disciplinary punishment or no physical punishment." To show how Chinese parents punish their children against their own wishes, we cite a popular proverb: "[A parent] beats on [the child's] body, but pain is in the [parent's] heart." Chinese children are trained to accept their parents' beating and other forms of punishment as necessary and beneficial to them. Wilson (1970:102) conducted a survey among 695 schoolchildren in Taiwan and received predominately positive answers about the need to be punished.

Among my questionnaire respondents many subscribed to this popular Chinese view that early disciplinary measures toward young children are necessary (even though the college students were taking educational psychology courses). The respondents were first asked to indicate their own approval or disapproval of various types of punishment for children of a specific age. They were then asked to think about a family (their own, a neighbor's, a friend's, or a relative's) and decide whether or not they had observed such punishments being administered. The children concerned were divided into two age groups: those below three and those between five and ten (the one-year gap was intentional so as to make a clearer distinction between the two groups). Table VIII-3 shows the results of this study.

People who study child abuse may be alarmed to note that our respondents appear from their attitudes to be highly punitive toward young children. Also, a high frequency of severe punitive behavior (categories 7, 8, and 9) was observed, although it was disapproved by our respondents. For instance, many of our respondents approve of punishing children below the age of three by means of ignoring (temporary rejection or withdrawal of love; category 1), scolding (category 2), and spanking or beating (category 6). Spanking or beating of children under three, as respondents observed, occurred quite frequently. This fact supports my own observation that it is culturally approved (note that in table VIII-3 the approved attitude is higher in frequency than is observed occurrence). Twisting ears or pinching cheeks (category 7), kicking

TABLE VIII-3   Attitudes toward and Observed Practices of Punishment*
(N = 40)

Age of child	Method of punishment	Attitude				Observed occurrence			
		Approve		Disapprove		Yes		No	
		Freq.	(%)	Freq.	(%)	Freq.	(%)	Freq.	(%)
Under 3 years									
	1. Ignore	22	(55)	15	(37.5)	18	(45)	22	(55)
	2. Scold	25	(62.5)	9	(22.5)	24	(60)	16	(40.5)
	3. Kneel	10	(25)	24	(60)	15	(37.5)	25	(62.5)
	4. No meal	2	(5)	33	(82.5)	11	(27.5)	29	(72.5)
	5. Lock up	5	(12.5)	30	(75)	12	(31.5)	28	(70)
	6. Spank†	29	(72.5)	8	(20)	26	(62.5)	15	(37.5)
	7. Twist ear, pinch face	1	(2.5)	34	(85)	13	(32.5)	27	(67.5)
	8. Kick and beat	0	–	35	(87.5)	8	(20)	32	(80)
	9. Hit head	1	(2.5)	34	(85)	11	(27.5)	29	(72.5)
5 to 10 years									
	1. Ignore	25	(60)	13	(32.5)	17	(42.5)	23	(57.5)
	2. Scold	33	(82.5)	2	(5)	25	(62.5)	15	(37.5)
	3. Kneel	25	(62.5)	9	(22.5)	22	(55)	17	(42.5)
	4. No meal	6	(15)	30	(75)	15	(37.5)	25	(62.5)
	5. Lock up	8	(20)	26	(62.5)	14	(35)	25	(62.5)
	6. Spank†	34	(85)	2	(5)	25	(62.5)	14	(35)
	7. Twist ear, pinch face.	6	(15)	28	(70)	21	(52.5)	18	(45)
	8. Kick and beat	4	(10)	30	(75)	17	(42.5)	23	(57.5)
	9. Hit head	3	(7.5)	31	(77.5)	17	(42.5)	23	(57.5)

*Missing values in the table due to no answers from some respondents.
†Includes beating on buttocks and palms with a stick.

and beating or beating while hanging (category 8), and hitting a child's head
(category 9) are considered harsh punishments, causing severe pain or injury.
While most of the respondents disapprove (again, we must note that some do
approve), the observed occurrences, particularly for older children, are high.
Since the respondents came from both city and countryside, this reported
harsh punishment of children may have significant implications in Taiwan.

A further indication of parental abusive behavior was found in the answers to a questionnaire item asking if the respondents had seen children beaten so severely that they bore marks, bruises, or other injuries. Three respondents (7.5 percent) saw many cases, fourteen (35 percent) saw some cases, and eleven (27.5 percent) saw one or two cases, but only twelve (30 percent) respondents maintained that they had never seen or heard of such incidents.

Among the common reasons for punishment listed by the respondents were disobedience, arguing with parents, refusal to yield or stubbornness, playfulness to the extent of neglecting homework, and endangering oneself. Cheng (1944:51) points out that in traditional Chinese society "Chinese children were not allowed to talk back to their parents, to ignore their commands or thwart their wishes. They were discouraged from criticizing the acts of their father and mother even if these acts were heinous and wicked."

Aside from beating and scolding, the most favored punitive method is to order the child to kneel down for a period of time. As seen in table VIII-3, ten respondents approve of this punishment even for children under three years of age. As a respondent reported, a nine-year-old boy who went to swim in the river without prior parental permission was first beaten on the buttocks with a stick then was told to kneel on the ground "to self-examine himself." The most severe punishment a college girl could remember was to kneel by the door, facing the street, so that all the passersby could see her in that situation. (See Wilson 1970 for a description of public shaming as a technique of child discipline and group control in schools.) The girl was then nine years old, and in her answer she said she forgot why she was punished in that manner. Punishment by kneeling apparently causes psychological humiliation along with pain, though physically it is less painful than being beaten. Boys above the age of seven or eight may receive beatings quite frequently. In rural Taiwan it is not uncommon to see a boy running and crying aloud, pursued by his mother with a stick in hand, while bystanders watch with amusement.

Most of our informants and respondents condemn the beating of children for no apparent reason and severe beating to the extent of harming the children. Several informants believe that beating too harshly or too frequently will not correct the child's behavior; it may, in fact, have the reverse effect. A good, virtuous parent, especially a father, should win a child's respect without resort to force. Also, a father is expected to be kind in order to gain his children's filial devotion. We observed, both in Taiwan and in some overseas Chinese communities, that Chinese parents use the technique of intimidation much more frequently than actual beating. With a duster in hand, a mother may threaten to use it, but she almost never needs actually to beat the child. Furthermore, punishment by kneeling (within reasonable duration), though shameful for the child and effective, appears to be less harmful in physical terms. For example, a boy of twelve, after he had failed an examination and received a zero mark, was ordered to kneel down and eat a boiled egg. This treatment is perhaps the best example of symbolic humiliation, for the egg symbolizes zero; eating an egg is a symbolic reenactment of the failure.

There are other safeguards against excessive punishment by parents. A Chinese child, a son in particular, does not belong to the parents alone. He is also a grandson, a nephew, and a young relative. A child is usually cared for by a wide range of kin, friends, and neighbors. Chinese adults, whether or not related to the family, are obliged to punish a child for his wrongdoing. Schoolteachers in the old days, for instance, were encouraged to cane pupils on behalf of the parents. Adult relatives and neighbors, in addition to being responsible for punishing a child, may also act as rescuers when the time for punishment arrives. They may beg or mediate on the child's behalf with the parent for a shorter (in the case of kneeling) or a lighter (in the case of beating) punishment. Mothers usually take a more active part in disciplining younger children (Muensterberger 1951:48), whereas fathers are responsible for punitive actions against older boys. Fei's (1939:37) vivid description of child punishment in rural China could also be true of Taiwan: "Very often in the evening a big storm will burst out in a house and show that a child is being beaten by a bad-tempered father. As a rule this is ended by the mediation of the mother. Sometimes, the result is a dispute between husband and wife."

Especially in dealing with young children, parents often play a game: one acts as the "good guy" and the other as the "bad guy," so that either one can always interfere with the other's "sentence" or "execution." Our respondents confirmed the existence of this practice in families they had observed. In answering the question whether a mother will mediate when the father beats the child, 9 respondents indicated that it was frequently done, 15 that it sometimes occurred, and only 7 said that it never happened (9 provided no answers). The respondents reported more frequent interference in punishing children by elders in the family (16 frequent, 9 sometimes, and 6 never). Even neighbors sometimes act as mediators. Large numbers of child caretakers and mediators in Chinese society seem to support the cross-cultural evidence in pointing to the benefit of alternate caretakers in alleviating a mother's stress of daily child care (Rohner 1975:114). Our findings also support the ethnographic indication that when the society respects elders, child abuse is less likely to happen, since the elders may act as a brake against extreme child punishment.

In summary, two socialization mechanisms—emphasis on attachment and discipline for obedience—support the cultural tradition of filial devotion of the young to the old. As I have proposed (Wu 1974), on the basis of Bowlby's (1971, 1973) ethological theory, Chinese child-rearing practices focus particularly on mother-child attachment, which contributes to the strong emphasis on achievement motivation in Chinese individuals and social life. An obedient son would be a good, obedient student in school and an obedient subordinate in the government, and thus he would be guaranteed a good position as a prosperous individual in the social hierarchy. According to the classical ethic of filial piety, the highest filiality a son can achieve is to become "somebody" (in terms of social attainment) in order to bring glory to his parents. Disciplinary punishment is necessary for children because "rods produce filial sons" (Wu 1966: 741). This cultural value is still valid in Taiwanese society, according to our data of people's attitudes toward harsh punishment.

On parent-child attachment, Western scholars may introduce a paradoxical point regarding the observed emotional reserve among Chinese parents toward children older than six or seven. This reserve means the lack of verbal and physical expressions of affection in the form of kissing, hugging, and touching. Although we may argue that the Chinese express affection in culturally meaningful ways and through subtle and symbolic gestures, we may still fail to explain how the parent-child bond is maintained and intensified in later years. For years I have observed Chinese parents freely express or display their negative emotions toward children (anger, rage, disgust, frustration), but they hesitate to show affection or pleasure. Mothers in particular are prone to demonstrate (or mock) pain, frustration, sufferance, or sadness as a means to elicit children's sympathy and, consequently, submission to parental control in order to alleviate the parent's suffering. In a sense, Chinese children may suffer (though unconsciously) a kind of emotional abuse which is not found in Western cultures. Yet this very negative emotional demonstration on the part of the parent may intensify the desirable parent-child bond, both for young children and for adult offspring. Thus the mother-child bond and a weaker father-child bond are psychologically long-lasting relationships and are very profound in social reality.

Contemporary Chinese families express the desire to have children without explicitly noting their utilitarian value. Most of our female respondents (21 of 24) thought children are treasured because they "provide pleasure for life." But, interestingly enough, male respondents still stress the cultural value of having children to carry on the lineage or descent line. This interesting contrast is statistically meaningful:

REASONS FOR VALUE OF AND DESIRE FOR CHILDREN
(N = 40)

	Carrying on descent line	Other reasons
Males	8	5
Females	3	24

$$x = 10.36 \quad \alpha < 0.01$$

It can be hypothesized that if a Chinese parent is aware of the social-contract nature of reciprocal protection under the concept of filial piety, and if he or she has established a bond with the child, then child abuse is not likely to occur. Of course, this hypothesis does not rule out nonabusive disciplinary punishment, and its validity must be tested both in Taiwan and cross-culturally. If, however, we accept the idea as plausible on the basis of the data presented here, we may have a clue to institutionalized child abuse against adopted daughters in Taiwan. To follow through on the hypothesis, we may propose that a mother figure (stepmother or foster mother) who has not gone through a period of socialization for attachment with the child would be more likely to apply harsh, cruel treatment to the child. A foster mother who adopts a child to ensure future security will be especially harsh toward the child if the child shows any sign of disobedience.

IV. INSTITUTIONALIZED CHILD ABUSE AGAINST ADOPTED DAUGHTERS

To accept a little girl into a family as an adopted daughter, a maid, a slave, or a future daughter-in-law was a common practice in many parts of China. It has a long history and probably originated in ancient law which condemned a criminal's wife and daughters to slavery even though they had no part in the crime. In times of hardship or famine, Chinese parents could resort to selling their daughters to more prosperous families. In his study of peasant life in central China, Fei (1939:53–55) mentions both the "foster maid" system and the "foster daughter-in-law" or *siaosiv* system. Both practices stemmed from economic depression, according to Fei. The term "foster maid" was known in Taiwan as *za-bo-gan* (*tsa-bo-kan*), but the custom was legally abolished during Japanese rule. According to early accounts (Wolf 1974:147), *za-bo-gan* are girls who were taken from poor peasant families at the age of five or six to work for wealthy families as unpaid servants. To a Taiwanese, the term connotes either maids or slave girls. We found little documentation on this system, but like foster daughters-in-law, *xim-bua* (*sim-pua*), foster maids are perceived as a miserable lot whose lives are full of suffering. Both Freedman (1957) and Wolf (1974) comment on the jural status of the foster maid's kinship position in her new family, but little is said about her welfare. In his discussion of the *za-bo-gan* system among the Hokkien, or of the *muizai* (*mui-tsai*) among the Cantonese in Singapore, Freedman (1957:65) calls it a form of female adoption rather than slavery: "Their social sphere was the kitchen and they were treated with some severity." The misfortunes and the harsh life of the *muizai* in prewar Hong Kong are well documented (Mai 1933). Contrary to the ideal practice of adoption, some of the less fortunate *za-bo-gan* and *muizai* ended up as concubines or were sold to brothels (Wee 1963:386).

Similar fates awaited adopted daughters-in-law in Taiwan until a decade ago. Wolf (1975) marshals excellent demographic evidence of child abuse directed against adopted daughters or daughters-in-law. Statistics on childhood mortality in northern Taiwan between 1906 and 1935 (Wolf 1975:95, table 2) reveal a higher mortality rate among adopted daughters than among biological daughters. The death counts for girls from birth to about three years of age (adopted daughters from the age of about six months are included in the statistics) were 1,458 adopted daughters and 834 biological daughters. In comparing female and male child mortality rates, Wolf (ibid.) concludes: "Mortality among female children exceeded that of male children solely because of the very high mortality rates among adopted daughters." But he fails to explain why adopted daughters had a higher mortality rate than biological daughters. I think it is caused by maltreatment and neglect.

Although I have seen no scientific research report on differential treatment of children by sex in Taiwan, it is known that girls are often sacrificed for the sake of boys. For instance, Rin's (1969) study of sibling rank and mental disorders among Chinese in Taiwan reveals an overrepresentation of youngest females. Rin explains that the youngest daughter often suffers from tension and aggression within a family and that she is likely to be given for adoption when the family is in financial straits.

Child abuse against adopted daughters was common in Taiwan in the early 1950s. A survey of a leading Taiwan newspaper, *Lian He Bao*, during 1951–52 reveals numerous articles on maltreatment of adopted daughters. By 1970–71, however, the press carried almost no stories about adopted daughters, perhaps because the government launched a movement in 1951 to protect them. An association for the protection of adopted daughters was organized, and the public was encouraged to report maltreatment of adopted daughters to the association or to the police. But in 1976, when the legislative Yuan of the Republic of China for the first time passed a child welfare law, the main concern was adoption and the rights of adopted daughters. Either the law was out of date or maltreatment of adopted daughters was still a problem.

According to the government census of 1951, there were 125,343 adopted daughters in Taiwan, with the majority concentrated in Taipei county (21,481) and Taoyuan (11,538) (*Lian He Bao*, Jan. 23, 1952, p. 7). Six months later a newspaper report (ibid., July 24, 1952, p. 5) estimated an even larger number (180,000) of adopted daughters. A third of them reportedly faced the threat of being resold or sent to the "fire dune" (prostitution). Twenty cases of prosecution for maltreatment of adopted daughters, ranging in age from 3 to 24, were found. Among the younger girls, five were beaten to death, several were severely beaten or tortured (with knife cuts or burns), and others were deprived of food. One girl of ten was raped by her adopted father.

Another mature adopted daughter conceived a child by her foster father, who killed the baby when it was born. Two girls reportedly were forced into prostitution at the age of twelve. Among the cases concerning adult adopted daughters were three attempted suicides and one successful suicide. More details about the reason for adoption and the manner of mistreatment were available for one girl:

> A twelve-year-old girl peddling fruits on the street was found weeping. A customer discovered fresh burn marks on her face and arms and took her to the police. She was an adopted daughter, sold to her foster mother at the age of five [for the equivalent of U.S. $3.50]. The money was needed to cover her biological mother's burial expenses. The girl was ordered to peddle fruits and cakes for her foster mother, and whenever business was slow she would receive a beating and no meal as punishment. On the day of the incident, the girl had not sold much because of bad weather. When she came home the adopted mother blamed her for her laziness and, after beating her, tortured her with hot iron rods. After her face, arms, and belly had been burned, she was sent back to the street again. [*Lian He Bao*, Nov. 6, 1951, p. 7]

It is worth noting that none of these girls were adopted as infants. According to newspaper reports, they were adopted between the ages of three and nine. Several were adopted around the age of five. This finding leads me to relate the maltreatment to the lack of socialization for attachment during early childhood as well as to the foster mother's uncertainty about having a guaranteed future provider. Of course, other cultural factors contribute to institutionalized child abuse, such as the cultural tradition of harsh treatment of servants and discrimination against daughters during childhood. The psychological basis of violence against children who are not one's own may have cross-cultural relevance. The Chinese have a saying that in ancient times people exchanged their sons to render disciplinary punishment, since parents are always lenient toward their own sons.

V. RECENT SOCIOCULTURAL CHANGE AND CHILD ABUSE

Further study of the sociocultural factors in child abuse in Taiwan should explore recent social changes and their effect on child rearing. Two court cases that recently made newspaper headlines in Taipei can be summarized as follows:

> A retired dance-hall hostess (age 27, residing in Taoyuan) was sentenced to three and half years in prison for abusing her illegitimate daughter, aged eleven. The

daughter was raised by a private nurse until she was four years old. When her mother took her back, the mother and a boyfriend were living together. The woman began to mistreat her daughter (when she was 7), frequently beating her and sometimes kicking her and knocking her head against the wall. When the neighbors finally sent for the police, the woman was found cutting her daughter's hands and feet with a fruit knife. [*Zi Li Wan Bao*, Sept. 25, 1978, p. 2]

A couple and a neighboring man were prosecuted for murdering a three-year-old girl who had been in the couple's care. The girl's parents were separated. The girl lived with her father, and he paid a neighbor woman in the same apartment NT$3,000 a month to look after her while he was at work. It was reported that the girl often urinated and defecated on her nurse's bed and sometimes on her father's roommate's bed. One day, after the girl again defecated on the nurse's bed, the nurse, her husband, and the girl's father's roommate all beat the girl so hard that they eventually killed her. [*Zhung Guo Shi Bao*, Oct. 8, 1978, p. 3]

Several aspects of these two cases are related to recent social changes that have affected child-rearing practices in Taiwan. Both maltreated girls were nursed by others at a young age, and both came from a broken family. Since both parents had to pay nurses to care for their children, they apparently had no relatives to rely upon. This circumstance is a typical urban phenomenon. In the process of urbanization and rapid industrialization, broken families and nuclear families with young, working couples and their infant children are increasing in Taiwanese cities. Many people have migrated from rural to urban areas for employment and have to maintain a partial or a small family; working parents have to leave their infants or young children with someone who is willing to care for them for a fee, unless relatives are available. Some parents require only day-care service, but others prefer to leave their children with a nurse for a longer period, even months or years. These private nurses are ordinarily housewives who want to earn extra income by taking in one or more children.

Our respondents made some interesting observations on this development. When asked whether they had seen parents who did not take care of their own infants or young children, 16 respondents (40 percent) said they had seen parents who did not take care of their children during the day, and 22 (55 percent) said they knew parents who did not have their children both day and night. Concerning the reasons for parents not taking care of their children, the majority referred to occupational necessity. Some pointed out other reasons, such as irresponsibility, not being able to stand the baby's crying, and pleasure seeking. As to where to find help for child care, 12 respondents answered grandparents, but 17 listed nursery, wet nurse, or "temporary fosterage" (hiring a long-term private nurse). Ironically, during a field visit, a kindergarten teacher was found to have left her nine-month-old baby with a private nurse while she looked after other people's young children. Whereas most of our informants and respondents approved of having grandparents nurse grandchildren, they were not certain whether a nurse would take equally good care of the child as would a close relative. With the decreasing interaction between a young couple and their older relatives, the decreasing and interrupted socialization for attachment, and changing values and lifestyles, more problems in child rearing for the young generation, especially in urban situations, will arise.

VI. CONCLUDING REMARKS

In this paper I have proposed a functional relationship between cultural values bearing on the parent-child relationship and child-rearing practices in Taiwan. The concept of filial piety is crucial for understanding how Chinese parents and children establish and maintain a relationship of attachment which obligates parents to assert authority and inflict punishment and children to obey and support parents. At the conceptual level it may appear that filial piety implies unrealistically high parental expectations of children. As a Chinese proverb says, "Every parent hopes his son will become a dragon [symbolizing social and moral attainment]." Such an expectation certainly may contribute to, and justify, rigid parental control and severe punishment of older children. But, paradoxically, the highly ritualized disciplinary measures and indoctrinations, both at home and in school, help to deter the battered-child syndrome. Furthermore, the pragmatic side of the cultural logic of filial piety makes Chinese parents not only bear with, but enjoy, the arduous task of bringing up children. Although Chinese usually argue that parental love is natural, they are quite aware of and explicitly describe the painful experience of child rearing. It is because of the suffering, the burden, and the sacrifice the parents have endured that children are expected to reciprocate with love, respect, sacrifice, and support. It would therefore be to the parents' ultimate disadvantage to abuse their children.

REFERENCES

Abbott, Kenneth
    1976 Culture change and the persistence of the Chinese personality. In *Responses to change*, ed. George DeVos. New York: D. Van Nostrand. Pp. 74–104.
Bowlby, John
    1971 *Attachment and loss*. Vol. I: *Attachment*. Harmondsworth, England: Penguin.
    1973 *Attachment and loss*. Vol. II: *Separation*. London: Hogarth Press.

Cheng, Ch'eng-k'un
    1944. Familism the foundation of Chinese social organization. *Social Forces* 23(1): 50–59.
Cohen, Myron L.
    1976 *House united, house divided: the Chinese family in Taiwan.* New York: Columbia University Press.
Da Hua Wan Bao (Ta Hwa Wan Pao) (Da Hua Evening News). Taipei.
Eberhard, Wolfram
    1967 *Guilt and sin in traditional China.* Berkeley and Los Angeles: University of California Press.
Fei, Hsiao-tung
    1939 *Peasant life in China.* London: George Routledge and Sons.
Freedman, Maurice
    1957 *Chinese family and marriage in Singapore.* London: H.M.S.O.
Fried, Morton H.
    1959 The family in China: the Peoples Republic. In *The family: it's function and destiny*, ed. Ruth Anshen. New York: Harper & Row. Pp. 146–166.
Ho, Ping-ti
    1959 *Studies on the population of China, 1368–1953.* Cambridge: Harvard University Press.
Hsiao, Hsin-I
    1973 A study of Hsiao-Ching with an emphasis on its intellectual background and problems. Ph.D. dissertation, Harvard University.
Hsu, F. L. K.
    1970 *Americans and Chinese.* New York: Doubleday.
Kempe, C. Henry, Frederic N. Silverman, Brandt F. Steele, William Droegmueller, and Henry K. Silver
    1962 The battered child syndrome. *Journal of the American Medical Association* 181: 17–24.
Koehn, Alfred
    1944 *Filial devotion in China.* Peking: Lotus Court.
Lian He Bao (Lian Ho Pao) (United Daily News). Taipei.
Mai, Mei-shen, comp.
    1933 *Fan-Tui Hsu-Pi Shih Lueh* (A short history of the anti-foster maid practice). Hong Kong.
Min Sheng Bao (Min Sheng Pao) (People's Life Newspaper). Taipei.
Min Zu Wan Bao (Min Tsu Wan Pao) (Nationality Evening Newspaper). Taipei.
Muensterberger, Warner
    1951 Orality and dependence: characteristics of southern Chinese. In *Psychoanalysis and the social sciences*, ed. G. Roheim. New York: International University Press. Pp. 37–69.
Rin, H.
    1969 Sibling rank, culture, and mental disorders. In *Mental health research in Asia and the Pacific*, ed. W. Caudill and T. Y. Lin. Honolulu: East-West Center Press. Pp. 105–113.

Rohner, Ronald P.
   1975   *They love me, they love me not: a worldwide study of the effects of parental acceptance and rejection*. New Haven: HRAF Press.
Scharfstein, Ben-Ami
   1974   *The mind of China*. New York: Dell Publishing Co.
Solomon, Richard H.
   1971   *Mao's revolution and the Chinese political culture*. Berkeley, Los Angeles, London: University of California Press.
Tai-Ping Yu-Lan (Imperial Review of the Grand Peace). First compiled by Li Fang in Sung dynasty.
   1574   Revised edition in Ming dynasty, year of Wan-Li.
T'seng, W. S., and J. Hsu
   1972   The Chinese attitude toward parental authority as expressed in Chinese children's stories. *Archives of General Psychiatry* 26:28–34.
Wee, Ann
   1963   Chinese women of Singapore: their present status in the family and in marriage. In *Woman in the new Asia*, ed. Barbara E. Ward. New York: UNESCO. Pp. 376–409.
Wilson, Richard W.
   1970   *Learning to be Chinese*. Cambridge: M.I.T. Press.
Wolf, Arthur
   1974   Marriage and adoption in northern Taiwan. In *Social organization and the applications of anthropology*, ed. Robert Smith. Ithaca: Cornell University Press. Pp. 128–160.
   1975   The women of Hai-shan: a demographic portrait. In *Women in Chinese society*, ed. M. Wolf and R. Witke. Stanford: Stanford University Press. Pp. 89–110.
Wu, David Y. H.
   1966   An anthropologist looks at Chinese child-training methods. *Thought and Word* 3(6):741–745. Text in Chinese.
   1974   An immigrant minority: the adaptation of Chinese in Papua New Guinea. Ph.D. dissertation, Australian National University, Canberra.
Zhung Guo Shi Bao (Chung Kuo Shih Pao) (Chinese Times). Taipei.
Zi Li Wan Bao (Tsu Li Wan Pao) (Independent Evening News) Taipei.

"VERY FEW CASES": Child Abuse and Neglect in the People's Republic of China[1]

9

Jill E. Korbin

As you know, cases of child mistreatment are very few in China, and still fewer are brought to the courts. The main reason is that everybody is aware that children are not private property to be dealt with at will. As the future of our nation, they are taken care of by the whole society. Physical punishment is strictly forbidden in all schools. If a child is ill-treated by his parents, the neighbors usually interfere. Sometimes the neighborhood committee (the grass-roots level) comes and criticizes the parents; sometimes they are educated by the leadership of their working places. But if the case is a serious one or the child is badly hurt, then it is brought to the community committee or even the local public security bureau (the local police headquarters, as called here) where the parents are questioned or detained. Whether or not legal procedures are taken depends on the gravity of the offense and the attitude of the offenders. Once the case is brought to court, there will probably be a public trial and they will be convicted of child mistreatment. There is a feeling among the people that child mistreatment is something intolerable. So anyone who does harm to children is condemned by public opinion and is punished by law. [Wu 1978]

Representatives of the People's Republic of China acknowledge that child abuse and neglect occur but report that there are "very few cases." Such an

[1]This chapter is based on a review of the literature and on information gathered in 1977 as a member of the International Union for Child Welfare Delegation to the People's Republic of China. I am indebted to the International Union for Child Welfare, to the China Travel Service, and to our interpreters, Wu Chao-yi, Chao Shu-li, and Chen Gen-fa, for their helpfulness and concern during our stay in China. I would also like to thank Ruth Sidel and Wu Chao-yi for commenting on an earlier draft of this paper, and L. L. Langness for his helpful suggestions.

assertion is often met with incredulity by Westerners familiar with conditions in China as recently as thirty years ago. Children, according to the ethic of "filial piety," were considered the sole property of their parents. As such, they could be dealt with in whatever manner the parents chose, with little or no interference from outsiders. Severe beatings, infanticide, child slavery, the selling of young girls as prostitutes, child betrothal, and foot-binding were not uncommon.

In the past thirty years the structure of Chinese society has undergone dramatic change. Similarly, the experience of childhood in China has undergone a transformation. "When I am asked if the Chinese of today are happier than those of yesterday, there is at least one answer that I can give with certainty. That is that the Chinese children have never been as happy as they are today; or as clean, as well dressed, and as well behaved; or as cheering a sight" (Robert Guilian, cited in Sidel 1972:109).

No research has been carried out specifically on child abuse and neglect in the People's Republic. Nevertheless, support for the Chinese assertion that child abuse is indeed rare may be inferred from what is known about the dynamics of child abuse and neglect in Western nations and what is known about the nature and structure of contemporary Chinese society. It is important to note that information on the mainland Chinese family as it exists today is largely limited to studies of child care facilities and schools and to brief visits in homes and neighborhoods (Kessen 1975; Sidel 1972, 1974). Another limitation is imposed on the present discussion by the difference between rural and urban areas of China. While some facilities are well developed in the cities, preschool child care for example, progress has lagged behind in rural areas. Because the bulk of China's population lives in the countryside, and also because of the diversity of China's population, generalizations are necessarily limited. This chapter, unless otherwise specifically stated, deals with the urban situation.

One need not search far to find reports of severe child abuse and neglect, both on a societal and on an individual level, in pre-Liberation China. Joshua Horn (1969:19) cites the reactions of a Canadian who lived in Shanghai for twenty years before Liberation and who returned in 1965:

> I searched for scurvy-headed children. Lice-ridden children. Children with inflamed red eyes. Children with bleeding gums. Children with distended stomachs and spindly arms and legs. I searched the sidewalks day and night for children who had been purposely deformed by beggars. Beggars who would leech on to any well-dressed passer-by to blackmail sympathy and offerings, by pretending the hideous-looking child was their own. I looked for children covered with horrible sores upon which flies feasted. I looked for children having a bowel movement, which, after much strain, would only eject tapeworms. I looked for child slaves in alleyway factories. Children who worked twelve hours a

day, literally chained to small press punches. Children who, if they lost a finger, or worse, often were cast into the streets to beg and forage in the garbage bins for future subsistence.

In 1965 he searched in vain for these sights, which were all too familiar during his previous experience in China.

One must temper one's judgment of, but certainly not justify, such conditions in China with the knowledge that similar abuses of children occurred in Western society (Bakan 1971; Radbill 1968; Solomon 1973; Spargo 1913). The description of child labor in Europe, for example, differs only slightly in its overall bleakness:

> Children from five years of age upward were worked sixteen hours at a time, sometimes with irons riveted around their ankles to keep them from running away. They were starved, beaten, and in many other ways maltreated. Many succumbed to occupational diseases and some committed suicide; few survived for any length of time. . . . Sometimes they were dipped head first into cisterns of cold water to keep them awake. [Radbill 1968:11–12]

Female infanticide, based largely on a cultural bias toward sons, was also practiced in China.[2] Of her childhood in the early 1900s, a woman reported that "even a club-footed son is of more value than a daughter with the virtues of eighteen Lohans, while to educate a daughter is said to be like watering another man's garden" (Smedley 1976:7). Daughters went to live with, and work for, the families of their husbands while sons remained in the households of their parents and continued the family line.

> If one was unfortunate enough to be born female, before 1949, one might very well not survive. Female babies were an economic liability; they would never become part of the family's work force and would only bring a marriage price. Often, parents did not know how they could feed a daughter, and, in fact, the practice of drowning girl babies was common. [Sidel 1972:11–12]

In times of economic hardship or famine, female children were particularly vulnerable to being sold as slaves, child brides, concubines, or prostitutes

---

[2]The strength of this preference for sons presented a substantial obstacle to Chinese population planning, or planned-birth program (Chen 1976). Particularly in rural areas families may have seven or eight children rather than the officially sanctioned two children, in the hopes of having a male child. The success of the population-control program depended not only upon convincing the people of economic and health reasons for limited family size, but also upon altering values so that girl children would be equally valued with boys. Although it can be argued that sexual equality has not been achieved, nevertheless the official doctrine that women are equal to men, that they "hold up half the sky," and the status of women as workers who can support their parents in their old age have contributed to the success of population planning in China.

(Belden 1949; Chow 1978; Hinton 1966; Sidel 1972; Smedley 1976). Sons were sometimes sold, but more frequently the selling of daughters was a means for parents to assure their own survival and that of their culturally required male descendants. Some of these girls were reportedly treated well, particularly those adopted by childless wealthy families (Pruitt 1967), but many were subjected to considerable abuse.

> One of my earliest memories was of the slave trade in which my grandmother took a part. . . . The slaves in whom she dealt were always girls . . . . and their owners have the power of life and death over them; they can be resold whenever or wherever it pleases the fancy of their owners; they may be sent as workers into the factories to earn money for their owners; they may be used as prostitutes; they may be sold to . . . men as concubines. [Smedley 1976:8]

The trauma of being sold as a young child as well as the trauma to the parents cannot be minimized.

> There were three famine years in a row. The whole family went out to beg things to eat. In Chinchang City conditions were very bad. Many mothers threw new-born children into the river. Many children wandered about on the streets and couldn't find their parents. We had to sell our eldest daughter. She was already 14. Better to move than to die, we thought. We sold what few things we had. We took our patched quilt on a carrying pole and set out for Changchin with the little boy in the basket on the other end. Because the boy wept so bitterly a woman came out. We stayed there three days. On the fourth morning the woman said she wanted to buy the boy. We put him on the k'ang. He fell asleep. In the next room we were paid five silver dollars. Then they drove us out. They were afraid when the boy woke up he would cry for his mother. My heart was so bitter. To sell one's own child was such a painful thing. We wept all day on the road. [Hinton 1966:42−43, also cited in Sidel 1972:7]

Similar stories are recounted about the selling of daughters. One woman, whose opiate-addicted husband sold their eldest daughter, reported: "I said that I would hang myself. . . . I rolled on the ground in my agony, my anger, and my pain" (Pruitt 1967:71).

Just as children could be killed or sold at their parents' discretion, so too could they be beaten or neglected, forced to work long hours, or given in marriage. Children, and also women, had little hope of rescue from an abusive father or husband. The Marriage Law of 1950, among the first legislation enacted in the People's Republic of China, was specifically aimed at changing this situation. It sought to break the life-and-death hold of the patriarchal head of the family and prohibited various forms of family violence, including that between parents and children: "Neither the parents nor the children shall maltreat or desert one another. . . . Infanticide by drowning and similar criminal acts are strictly prohibited" (Marriage Law 1950, Art. 13).

Comparing the situation of children in the "old" and "new" Chinas, one cannot fail to be struck by the contrast. And, while optimal conditions have not been produced, the changes "made hitherto unbearable conditions bearable" (Belden 1949:131). In her study, *Women and Child Care in China*, Ruth Sidel noted:

> Much of this book may sound unduly optimistic; people may seem unbelievably happy; there may seem to be a striking lack of conflict. . . . First and of prime importance, the Chinese compare their present life not to life in other societies but to life in the "bitter past," prior to the revolution of 1949—and, in comparison, life does seem fine indeed. Second, the matters on which we concentrated—the role of women, the care of children, and medicine—are those in which the Chinese have made astonishing progress, and they are justifiably proud of their accomplishments. [Sidel 1972:xiii]

Child mistreatment in the People's Republic of China is broadly defined. Parents or caretakers may be called into account for any actions that harm the physical, moral (political), or intellectual development of the child. The functioning of each individual as a member of the group is seen as a valid concern of the entire society. This is particularly true for children since they are considered the future of the country (Sidel 1974).

Although the use of physical punishment is strongly disapproved, the Chinese do not claim that parents never resort to spanking their children. Spankings are not severe, however, and apparently do not turn into beatings. Visitors to China repeatedly report that it is rare to see children crying or to see parents scolding or hitting their children (Horn 1969; Kessen 1975; Sidel 1972, 1974). Spankings are seen by the Chinese as arising from parental frustration that overtakes reason. The strict prohibition of physical punishment in the schools reflects the belief that spanking or physical sanctions are not effective methods for changing children's behavior. In Western nations, paradoxically, the educational system often maintains the right to discipline a child physically in order to control his or her behavior while parents are cautioned against using physical discipline on the same child at home.

In addition to physical harm that can come to children, neglect of children's needs as developing members of Chinese society is also of concern. The state has the ultimate responsibility for assuring adequate food, clothing, housing, and education for children. The parents have the responsibility, however, for ensuring that these resources actually reach their children. In addition to the basic necessities, children tend to get the best of everything, as indicated by the fact that children are the most nicely dressed members of the family (Horn 1969; Sidel 1972). The priority given to the needs of growing children is also seen in the differential allocations of food items that are rationed. For example, adolescents are usually allocated more rice that adult office workers who are sedentary and whose energy needs are presumed to be less. Giving a child so many tasks and errands that the child has insufficient time for schoolwork is also considered a parental behavior that needs correcting so that the child can develop into a productive member of society.

Neighborhood vigilance concerning child welfare is well developed. Such watchfulness not only prevents child mistreatment, but it is built into the structure of a society whose members are all concerned with and responsible for the welfare of others. Neighborhood vigilance enforces conformance to social rules, and as such it is a crucial element in contemporary Chinese society (Li 1973; Sidel 1974). If a child is heard screaming or crying excessively, all the neighbors are expected to investigate or take some action. Indeed, should a child be injured, either through an accident or by mistreatment, and should no one come to help and/or find out what the trouble is, the neighbors would be criticized and held accountable for the harm to the child.

> If truly no man is an island and the actions of each person directly affect the lives of all others, then the "group," however defined, has a real and direct stake in controlling the actions of its members. This is entirely contrary to the Western approach of legally, though possibly not morally, discouraging the intrusion by one person into the lives of others, except when something very serious is involved. [Li 1973:151]

That neighborhood involvement is built into everyday activities may be illustrated by the provisions for child supervision after school. Once a child begins attending primary school, at approximately seven years of age, the child is considered sufficiently competent and mature to "manage himself/herself." Often a grandparent lives with the family and watches out for the child after school. If there is no grandparent living in the household, the child is given a key to the house. Such keys are worn around the children's necks. The term for these children is translated as "latchkey children," which connotes lack of supervision and even neglect in the United States. In China, however, it carries no such meaning. While children of this age are considered responsible enough to be unsupervised, they are by no means entirely on their own. If the child is being "naughty" (a term that seems to be broadly used for most child misbehavior) or is involved in an accident the neighbors will intervene. Because the structure of the community is based upon mutual cooperation, if a child is injured one does not need to be concerned about authorization to provide needed medical care, as often happens in the United States. Parents can thus be free from worry at work because someone will be able and willing to care for their child in the event of an emergency. Parents can also be free from concern about their child's possible misbehavior, since one of the neighbors can be counted upon to intervene. Although parents can be summoned home if there is a behavior problem with their child, reportedly this rarely occurs.

Because of the nature of the community, intervention occurs before potential abuse or neglect reaches the level at which the child is damaged or the parent labeled a child abuser. Virtually all Chinese adults belong to small study groups which meet to discuss laws, appropriate behavior, and political thought. As members of these groups most Chinese either internalize norms for behavior or adhere to approved standards in order to avoid peer criticism (Li 1973; Sidel 1974). If inappropriate behavior begins, intervention can be prompt:

> Most people do not commit serious crimes without warning. Such actions are a part and perhaps the culmination of an entire pattern of dissatisfaction, unhappiness or confusion. This pattern is manifested in many ways and grows gradually, with minor problems becoming increasingly serious. The Chinese, through the small groups, treat these symptoms of unhappiness and possible deviation as soon as they appear. The effort is to solve problems before they get entirely out of control, somewhat like treating a physical disease. [Li 1973:152]

The individual who deviates from approved behavior, be it in terms of child mistreatment, thievery, or other prohibited actions, is helped within the context of the entire society. If a person exhibits problems with his or her child, the underlying cause of trouble or dissatisfaction is sought within the entire fabric of the individual's life. Is there a problem at work that is causing the individual to take out his or her frustrations on the family? Is an unhappy marriage causing the parent to resent the child? Is an in-law interfering with parental instructions? Once the cause of the problem is ascertained, members of the community—fellow workers, family members, neighbors—seek to remedy the problem by pointing out the proper behavior both to the individual and to others concerned in the troublesome situation (Li 1973; Sidel 1974). Because problems tend to be identified early, "before the offender has strayed too far or caused too much damage" (Li 1973:153), the possibilities are greater that the offender will alter his or her behavior and be redeemed in the eyes of society. Additionally, deviations or "wrong thinking" may be attributed to subjective factors such as capitalist tendencies or external factors such as poverty and unequal distribution: "One ramification of this approach is that no offender should be blamed for all of his actions, since some portion of the offense might be traceable to external factors. If care is taken in one's phrasing, it is possible to condemn an act without condemning the inner man" (Li 1973:153).

The Chinese approach to deviant behavior, including child mistreatment, thus differs rather significantly in its basic orientation from that of the United States. In China, "This gradual process differs considerably from falling off the edge of the cliff" (Li 1973:153). Contrast this approach with Gelles' characterization of the response to child abuse and neglect in the United States as "an ambulance service at the bottom of the cliff" and his suggestion that we need to "fix the road on the cliff that causes the accidents" (1973:620).

Foot-binding may serve as an example of how the integration of individual well-being with societal well-being effected changes in the welfare of women and children. In the process of foot-binding the toes of young girls were bent back against the sole of the foot and wrapped in bandages to hold them in place. Over several years the girl was provided with smaller and smaller shoes as the bandages were tightened. The resulting badly deformed foot, between 3.5 and 4 inches long, made even walking exceedingly difficult. Small bound feet were considered a mark of beauty as well as a sign of the subservience of women (Chan 1970; Sidel 1972). "A girl's beauty and desirability were counted more by the size of her feet than by the beauty of her face. Matchmakers were not asked 'Is she beautiful?' but 'How small are her feet?' A plain face is given by heaven but poorly bound feet are a sign of laziness" (Pruitt 1967:22).

The life history of one Chinese woman reflects the extreme pain caused by this practice. Because of her illness, the foot-binding was delayed until a somewhat late age.

> When I was nine they started to bind my feet again and they had to draw the bindings tighter than usual. My feet hurt so much that for two years I had to crawl on my hands and knees. Sometimes at night they hurt so much I could not sleep. I stuck my feet under my mother and she lay on them so they hurt less and I could sleep. But by the time I was eleven my feet did not hurt and by the time I was thirteen they were finished. . . . My feet were very small indeed. [Pruitt 1967:22]

Although foot-binding was banned in 1911, it continued into the 1940s. Early in that decade the Communists attempted to abolish the practice in areas under their control. An order making foot-binding illegal was issued and a fine was imposed on families of women with bound feet. Nevertheless, the practice continued. ". . . in 1942 we abolished foot binding. We issued an order and adopted a slogan: 'Emancipate feet.' The family of any woman with bound feet was fined. Such bureaucratic methods were not effective. So we canceled the order and adopted propaganda methods and the people emancipated their feet by themselves" (Belden 1949:82). "Propaganda" efforts were directed toward educating the people about the benefits to themselves as workers and to the building of the new society. For example:

> Old Lady Wang and Young Lady Li have little feet like red peppers. They cannot farm land; they cannot carry water, and they walk one step, sway three times,

and topple over when the wind blows. Third Sister Chang and Liu Yu-lin have natural feet that are big. They go down to the river to carry water, go up to the mountain to cut kindling, and plow the land to plant crops. They are just like males. [Belden 1949:122]

In this fashion foot-binding was relegated to the "old" society and changed from a mark of beauty to a mark of oppression and an obstacle to women's contributing to the progress of the "new" society. Similar strategies were employed to gain the people's support for and compliance with other desired goals, such as compulsory education, population planning, and the eradication of venereal disease (Belden 1949; Sidel 1972; Sidel and Sidel 1973).

The possibility that the Chinese do not have the means to detect child abuse, or that they are hesitant to acknowledge that parents harm their own offspring, is minimized by the structure of the health care delivery system. Virtually all children receive regular physical examinations from the time they are born throughout their school years. It would be unlikely that bruises or other physical injuries would go undetected. Further, parental excuses that a child is accident-prone, or explanations of circumstances which did not fit with the injuries, would be unacceptable. As child abuse was becoming recognized in the United States, similar excuses and explanations often obscured or masked cases of child abuse (Kempe et al. 1962), and are currently utilized as diagnostic factors in identifying abuse (Schmitt 1978). In China, the issue that causes concern and triggers intervention is not solely whether the physical trauma was inflicted purposely. Even if the physical trauma was not recognized as inflicted, the parent or caretaker would be held accountable. If a child is injured, the overriding concern is that someone failed to provide safe conditions for the child. The parents, grandparents, or caretaker would, at best, be criticized and educated regarding their carelessness and, at worst, castigated for the abuse or neglect that allowed harm to come to the child. These strictures help to prevent an environment conducive to child abuse or to the concealment of its occurrence.

Further, children are not held entirely responsible for accidents resulting in injury to themselves. This is particularly true for young children and is reflected in the safety precautions taken in nurseries, kindergartens, and elementary schools. At the Beijing (Peking) Number Four Kindergarten, for example, the children were considered old enough to learn not to touch the heating grills on the walls. Nevertheless, the radiators were covered by wire screens so that the children could not possibly reach the hot metal. A child who burned himself or herself would not be held accountable with the chastisement that he or she was old enough to know better. The experience might be used as a concrete lesson to point out the danger to the injured child and the other children. The teachers and the school, however, would be open to accusations of failing to provide proper care and supervision of the children—of neglecting not only the children but also their social responsibility. Such criticism is a serious matter, for the biological parents and the society as a whole entrust the care of children to the school.

Rarely does a child escape the notice of the health care delivery system. Although education from primary school onward is compulsory, provisions for preschoolers (children under seven years of age) are more flexible. Parents may elect to have their children cared for at home by a grandparent or may send the child to a nursery or a kindergarten. Mistreatment of children cared for at home is not more amenable to concealment than mistreatment of children in nurseries or kindergartens. Regular physical examinations and health care are an integral function of child care facilities, but children who remain at home receive the same kind of care from neighborhood health stations or centers. Health stations are within close walking distance, and health care workers live in the neighborhood and are well known to the families. If a parent, grandparent, or caretaker fails to bring the child to the neighborhood health center, the health care provider visits the household to determine why the child is not being brought to the facility. If there seems to be an acceptable reason—for example, if the grandmother has bound feet and thus has difficulty in walking—the health care worker conducts the physical examination and provides immunizations in the home. If there is no sufficient reason, the caretaker is encouraged to bring the child to the health station. If necessary, pressure from neighbors and co-workers is brought to bear. Regardless of the behavior of the caretaker, adequate medical care of the child is the first concern. The efficiency and comprehensiveness of the health care delivery system are reflected in the high immunization rates for Chinese children (Sidel 1972; Sidel and Sidel 1973). This system is in marked contrast with the system in the United States, where a child may be "lost" and thereby denied society's interest and notice between the time the child and mother are released from the hospital after birth and the time the child starts school at approximately age five (Helfer 1976).

In assessing child mistreatment in China, it is worthwhile to explore those factors that have been linked with child abuse and neglect in Western nations. While there is some difference of opinion as to the primacy of causal factors, the literature indicates that child abuse results from a complex inter-action of parental characteristics, characteristics of the child, and environ-mental and social conditions and stress (Green et al. 1974; Helfer 1973; Kempe and Helfer 1972; Martin 1976).

Social isolation and a lack of support networks have been linked with child abuse and neglect in Western nations (Bronfenbrenner 1976; Elmer 1967; Evans et al. 1974; Garbarino 1976; Gelles 1973; Gil 1970; Helfer 1973; Johnson and Morse 1968; Spinetta and Rigler 1972; Young 1964). Abusive parents tend to have limited social networks within which to glean the adult interaction necessary for their own healthy functioning or for the assistance that is needed in child rearing. Cross-culturally, women who are isolated in their child-care tasks, with little or no periodic relief, are the most likely to be punitive and harsh with their children (Minturn and Lambert 1964; Rohner 1975).

In China parents are not isolated in the responsibility of child rearing, since extensive support networks exist. When a child is born the mother is given a 56-day maternity leave.[3] While the mother is at home with her new baby, she receives assistance in child care and housework. The help is usually provided by a grandmother who comes to stay with the new parents if she is not already living with the couple in an extended household. When a grandmother or other relative is not available, the parents may hire a retired woman to help during maternity leave. Even though the father continues working, he also provides extra help to the new mother. It is of interest that under these conditions postpartum depression is rare (Sidel and Sidel 1973).

Once the maternity leave is over, the new parents have a choice of support systems available to assist with their child-rearing responsibilities. Not only do parents have options for assistance in child care, but their options are valued by society at large. As both parents usually work, the contributions of grandparents in running the household are particularly valued. Although considered to be perhaps overly indulgent of their grandchildren, grandparents are nevertheless valued child caretakers. In the Chinese family, "the old take care of the young and the middle-aged take care of the old":

> . . . in order to maintain a continuity, a connectedness within society, the ties between the generations must be preserved. . . . even in the massive effort of the Chinese to "root out feudal ideology," they have not severed the bonds between grandparent, parent, and grandchild, but rather they have strengthened them. . . . Thus, the three-generational family is seen as a mini-collective, a small mutual-aid group. [Sidel 1972:160]

It seems to be a regularity in the cross-cultural record that extended households act in a variety of ways as a deterrent to harsh and punitive child-rearing practices (Minturn and Lambert 1964; Rohner 1975). It could easily be postulated that this mechanism is in operation in China.

Whether or not a grandparent is living in the household, the parents may elect to send their child to the nursery and then to the kindergarten before the

---

[3] Mothers living in cities receive their full salaries while on maternity leave. In the countryside, women are not entitled to pay while on maternity leave but do not lose seniority. Also, in rural areas women may return to light work somewhat earlier, perhaps in 30 days, and to regular work assignments after four months (Sidel 1972).

child starts school. These child care facilities not only free both parents to work, but also function for the convenience and well-being of the individual parent, child, and family unit. Facilities are usually available at the parents' place of work (or within close proximity) for the care of infants. Regular breaks for mothers to nurse their infants are incorporated into work schedules. Because some parents work the night shift, child care facilities are available at night as well as during the day. If a parent has a meeting or a study group after work hours, the child may be left at the nursery or kindergarten. Similarly, if a parent has additional or unexpected time off, the parent may take the child at these irregular times.

The teachers and caregivers in the nurseries and kindergartens are considered excellent caretakers and socializers. In the United States and other Western countries, one is accustomed to thinking that the socialization of children in institutions, away from their parents for the majority of the day, is somehow harmful to the child and to the family. Nevertheless, children in China "belong" to a wider network of individuals than the nuclear or extended family. Thus individuals outside the family, including institutional care-takers, share in the responsibility and the task of rearing the next generation. Because of the high level of consensus in Chinese society, there is not a pushing and pulling between the socialization that takes place in the schools and child care facilities and the socialization that occurs at home. Rather, there is a congruence of socialization goals such that the institution and the family are in close contact and actively cooperate with each other (Sidel 1972).

In addition to this integration of socialization goals, there seems to be a genuine affectional bond between the children and their teachers and care-takers. Our interpreters repeatedly commented that the "aunties" take very good care of the children in the nurseries and kindergartens, a finding that has been echoed by other visitors to China concerned with child care (Kessen 1975; Sidel 1972). When a new child comes to the Beijing (Peking) Number Four Kindergarten, for example, the teacher goes to the home to visit with the parents and grandparents and also to the nursery or kindergarten that the child previously attended. Thus the teacher can better understand the child and his or her "habits" and make the child comfortable in adjusting to the routine of the kindergarten. In explaining the role of the three teachers in each of the classes at this kindergarten, an interpreter, a mother whose children had attended a similar boarding kindergarten, noted that one of the teachers was for "lessons" and the other two were for "love." "Love" was meant to encom-pass making the child feel comfortable and at home as well as teaching the child to take care of his or her hygiene (brushing teeth, bathing, and so on). While it was readily acknowledged that the children miss their parents at first, it was also reported that most of them adjust rapidly with the help of their teachers and peers. Since 1954 not a single child at the Beijing Number Four Kindergarten has had to be sent home because of disciplinary problems or a failure to adjust.

An extensive support network for the individual and the family is built into the structure of contemporary Chinese society. Medical care, education, employment, housing, clothing, and food are ensured for all individuals by the state. The economic crises and unemployment often connected with child abuse in the United States (Gelles 1973; Gil 1970; Light 1973) are unlikely to occur and therefore cannot contribute to child mistreatment.

Young, immature parents and unwanted, numerous children have also been connected with child abuse and neglect in Western nations (Gil 1970; Helfer 1973; Johnson and Morse 1968; Rohner 1975). Such conditions have been minimized in China. With the rationale that young people can better contribute to the building of the society if marriage is delayed, the officially encouraged minimum age for marriage is 25 for women and 28 for men. If a young couple wishes to marry earlier, members of their work or study group try to persuade them to wait. If the couple insists, they are permitted to marry. Since the force of peer pressure is so effective (Chen 1976; Li 1973; Oksenberg 1973; Sidel 1974), the majority of urban Chinese approximate these prescribed ages for marriage. In addition to late marriages, couples are encouraged to have a maximum of two children and to space them by a period of several years.[4] Contraceptive devices and abortions are readily available to all married couples. Again, group pressure acts against couples having more than two children. It is unlikely that very young parents in the cities of China will have unwanted children in rapid succession.

Because information on psychological problems in China is sparse, and because no single consistently reported psychological profile of the abusing parent exists even in the West (Gelles 1973; Spinetta and Rigler 1972; Steele and Pollock 1968), a discussion of the relationship between individual psychopathology and child mistreatment in China is not presently feasible. Still, it is worthwhile to speculate on the role that the parent's own childhood plays in the etiology of child mistreatment. That abusive parents were themselves abused in their own childhoods is the most consistently reported factor in the literature on child abuse.[5] While this assertion requires further research and

---

[4] Recent information from the People's Republic of China (*Los Angeles Times*, Sept. 8, 1980) indicates that official policy now limits families to one child.

[5] Those who have noted the cyclical nature of child abuse include Bakan 1971; Blumberg 1974; Curtis 1963; Evans et al. 1974; Feinstein et al. 1964; Fontana 1964, 1973; Galdston 1971; Gelles 1973; Gil 1970; Green et al. 1974; Helfer 1973; Helfer and Kempe 1968; Kempe 1973; Kempe and Helfer 1972; Kempe et al. 1962; Melnick and Hurley 1969; Morris et al. 1964; Nurse 1964; Oliver and Taylor 1971; Paulson and Blake 1969; Smith et al. 1973; Spinetta and Rigler 1972; Steele 1970; Steele and Pollock 1968; Wasserman 1967; Young 1964.

verification, the situation in China is of interest. Considering the abuses of children that occurred thirty years ago, what of these abused children who are now parents in China? Little evidence is available, but one can postulate that the vast restructuring of society has somewhat mitigated the individual consequences of childhood abuse. Group discussions of the "bitter past," which attribute the cause of mistreatment of women and children to the "old society" rather than to one's own parents, may minimize the psychological consequences for individuals. As Mead (1970) has noted, a regularity of American child rearing may be that one generation is committed to a child-rearing strategy different from that of their own parents. A similar mechanism may be operating in China, but strengthened by support from the entire society.

Although legal sanctions and cultural rules may act to prevent mistreatment of children in general, certain children may be more vulnerable to abuse and neglect than others. Studies in the United States and England suggest that characteristics of the child may contribute to abuse. These characteristics may be tangible, as in prematurity, illness, separation from parents in early infancy, and developmental delays, or they may be perceptions on the part of the parent that the child is somehow "different" or resembles a disliked person (Lynch 1976; Martin 1976; Milowe 1962; Milowe and Lourie 1964; Steele and Pollock 1968). In many societies there are categories of children who may fall outside the range of protective standards, such as illegitimate children, orphans, deformed children, adopted children, and stepchildren (Korbin 1979).

The People's Republic of China has taken special steps concerning children who might not be protected by general standards. Protection of stepchildren in the Marriage Law is an example: "Neither husband nor wife may maltreat or discriminate against children born of a previous marriage by either party and in that party's custody" (Marriage Law 1950, Art. 16). Illegitimate children, adopted children, and orphans are similarly protected.

Although illegitimacy has been vastly reduced in the cities, provisions have been made for the protection of children born out of wedlock: "Children born out of wedlock enjoy the same rights as children born in lawful wedlock. No person is allowed to harm them or discriminate against them" (Marriage Law 1950, Art. 15).

Adopted or foster children are also specifically protected by a clause in the Marriage Law (Art. 13) which assures them of all the rights of biological children. Because of the success of the planned-birth program (Chen 1976), there is a scarcity of children available for adoption. Couples unable to have children of their own may wait years to adopt a child. Consequently, it was reported that adopted children are more indulged than other children.

The state also takes responsibility for orphans. Many orphans are adopted by relatives of the deceased parents. If there is a family member who is willing to adopt the child, the state subsidizes the adoption. The rationale behind this practice is that the orphan might otherwise cause financial pressures resulting in resentment toward the child. Nonrelatives may also adopt orphans. Orphans that are not adopted are cared for in state institutions similar to the boarding kindergartens, which are highly valued for their excellent care of children.

Despite all these efforts toward universal child protection, certain children may be ill-treated:

> . . . we observed at least one instance of rather unfeeling treatment of a child. . . . He stood out from the other children immediately; for example, he was always bare-bottomed rather than clad in trousers of any kind. . . . Whenever there was any trouble in the courtyard, it was taken for granted that the imp was at the bottom of it. Even his mother and father treated him as though they didn't really expect him ever to behave like other children.
>
> This puzzled us, for we found him unusually bright and appealing. An older cousin let slip a possible explanation. The imp had been born with two thumbs on his right hand; one had been rather skillfully amputated, leaving what appeared, at first glance, to be a normal hand. Closer examination revealed, however, that the remaining thumb projected at an awkward angle, which made it inefficient in grasping. Certainly this abnormality would be with him for the rest of his life, but why did such a small disability lead his family to adopt such a contrary attitude toward him? Was it that he would be unable to do his share of work in the fields as a member of the comune? Certainly the thumb was not that serious. Another likely explanation is that peasant wisdom associated the polydactyly with incorrigible behavior. [Galston 1973:181]

Who, then, if there are "very few cases," are the abusive parents in China? The Chinese report that fathers (including stepfathers) and stepmothers are more likely to mistreat children than are biological mothers. Fathers are reported to be more likely than mothers to strike out at their children in frustration and anger. This difference is in part a carry-over from the "old" society in which men had the right to beat their wives and children. It also reflects the belief that, in general, women are better with young children than are men. The preference for women in the care of young children is indicated by the fact that teachers and staff in nurseries and kindergartens are nearly universally women (Sidel 1972). The reason explicitly stated for the prevalence of women in such positions is that they are more patient and thus are better with small children. In the "new" society, women and men are expected to participate equally in the rearing of their children and in other household tasks. The failure of a father to share in household activities, including child rearing, exposes him to criticism and to peer pressure to mend his ways. Nevertheless, women are preferred for child care.

Stepmothers are also specified as the individuals who mistreat children in the "very few cases" of child abuse. Most of the hypothetical situations presented to us in which children were mistreated involved stepmothers as the perpetrators. In fact, we were told that stepmothers have to be especially cautious in order to avoid accusations of child mistreatment.

In conclusion, it seems a tenable proposition that changes that have occurred in the People's Republic of China over the past thirty years have diminished the likelihood of child abuse and neglect. With the current emphasis on modernization by the end of this century, and the concomitant changes taking place in China, it will be of interest and importance to see if and how child welfare will be affected. In the absence of statistical information on the incidence and prevalence of child mistreatment in the People's Republic, and in light of our knowledge about child abuse in Western nations, a consideration of the nature and structure of contemporary Chinese society would seem to substantiate the Chinese position that, whereas child abuse and neglect are known and are a fact of human behavior, there are "very few cases."

REFERENCES

Bakan, David
  1971 *Slaughter of the innocents: a study of the battered child phenomenon.* San Francisco: Jossey-Bass.
Belden, Jack
  1949 *China shakes the world.* New York: Monthly Review Press.
Blumberg, Marvin L.
  1974 Psychopathology of the abusing parent. *American Journal of Psychotherapy* 28: 21–29.
Bronfenbrenner, Urie
  1976 Who cares for America's children? In *The family—can it be saved?* ed. V. Vaughan III and T. B. Brazelton. Chicago: Year Book Medical Publishers. Pp. 3–32.
Chan, Lily
  1970 Foot-binding in Chinese women and its psycho-social implications. *Canadian Psychiatric Journal* 15:229–231.
Chen, Pi-chan
  1976 *Population and health policy in the People's Republic of China.* Interdisciplinary Communications Program Occasional Monograph Number Nine. Washington: Smithsonian Institution.
Chow, Chin-li
  1978 *Journey in tears: memory of a girlhood in China.* New York: McGraw-Hill.
Curtis, George C.
  1963 Violence breeds violence—Perhaps? *American Journal of Psychiatry* 120: 386–387.

Elmer, Elizabeth
  1967 *Children in jeopardy: a study of abused minors and their families.* Pittsburgh: University of Pittsburgh Press.

Evans, Ian, Richard A. Dubanowski, and Annette A. Higuchi
  1974 Behavior therapy with child-abusing parents: initial concepts underlying predictive, preventive, and analogue studies. Paper presented at eighth annual convention of the Association for the Advancement of Behavior Therapy, Chicago.

Feinstein, Howard M., Norman Paul, and Pattison Esmiol
  1964 Group therapy for mothers with infanticidal impulses. *American Journal of Psychiatry* 120:882—886.

Fontana, Vincent J.
  1964 *The maltreated child: the maltreatment syndrome in children.* Springfield, IL: Charles C. Thomas.

  1973 *Somewhere a child is crying: maltreatment—causes and prevention.* New York: Macmillan.

Galdston, Richard
  1971 Violence begins at home: the parents' center project for the study and prevention of child abuse. *Journal of the American Academy of Child Psychiatry* 10:336—350.

Galston, Arthur W., with Jean S. Savage
  1973 *Daily life in People's China.* New York: Thomas Y. Crowell.

Garbarino, James
  1976 A preliminary study of some ecological correlates of child abuse: the impact of socioeconomic stress on mothers. *Child Development* 47:178—185.

Gelles, Richard J.
  1973 Child abuse as psychopathology: a sociological critique and reformulation. *American Journal of Orthopsychiatry* 43(4):611—621.

Gil, David
  1970 *Violence against children: physical child abuse in the United States.* Cambridge: Harvard University Press.

Green, Arthur, Richard Gaines, and Alice Sandgrund
  1974 Child abuse: pathological syndrome of family interaction. *American Journal of Psychiatry* 131:882—886.

Helfer, Ray E.
  1973 The etiology of child abuse. *Pediatrics* 51(4):777—779.

  1976 Comments. First International Congress on Child Abuse and Neglect. Geneva.

Helfer, Ray E., and C. Henry Kempe, eds.
  1968 *The battered child.* Chicago: University of Chicago Press.

Hinton, William
  1966 *Fanshen: a documentary of revolution in a Chinese village.* New York: Vintage Books.

Horn, Joshua
  1969 *Away with all pests: an English surgeon in the People's China, 1954—1969.* New York: Monthly Review Press.

Johnson, Betty, and Harold A. Morse
    1968 Injured children and their parents. *Children* 15:147—152.
Kempe, C. Henry
    1973 A practical approach to the protection of the abused child and rehabilitation of
        the abusing parent. *Pediatrics* 51(4):804—809.
Kempe, C. Henry, and Ray E. Helfer, eds.
    1972 *Helping the battered child and his family*. Philadelphia: Lippincott.
Kempe, C. Henry, Frederic N. Silverman, Brandt F. Steele, William Droegmueller,
        and Henry K. Silver
    1962 The battered child syndrome. *Journal of the American Medical Association* 181:
        17—24.
Kessen, William, ed.
    1975 *Childhood in China*. New Haven: Yale University Press.
Korbin, Jill E.
    1979 A cross-cultural perspective on the role of the community in child abuse and
        neglect. *Child Abuse and Neglect: The International Journal* 3(1):9—18.
Li, Victor
    1973 Law and penology: systems of reform and correction. In *China's developmental
        experience*, ed. Michael Oksenberg. Proceedings of the Academy of Political
        Science 31(1). New York: Columbia University. Pp. 144—156.
Light, Richard J.
    1973 Abused and neglected children in America: a study of alternative policies.
        Harvard Educational Review 43:556—598.
Lynch, Margaret
    1976 Risk factors in the abused child: a study of abused children and their siblings.
        In *The abused child: a multidisciplinary approach to developmental issues and treatment*,
        ed. Harold P. Martin. Cambridge: Ballinger, Pp. 43—56.
Marriage Law of the People's Republic of China
    1950 Peking: Foreign Language Press.
Martin, Harold P.
    1976 *The abused child: a multidisciplinary approach to developmental issues and treatment*.
        Cambridge: Ballinger.
Mead, Margaret
    1970 *Culture and commitment: a study of the generation gap*. Garden City: Natural
        History Press.
Melnick, Barry, and John R. Hurley
    1969 Distinctive personality attributes of child-abusing mothers. *Journal of Consult-
        ing and Clinical Psychology* 33(6):746—749.
Milowe, I. D.
    1962 Patterns of parental behavior leading to physical abuse of children. In *Protecting
        the battered child*. Denver: Children's Division, American Humane.
Milowe, I. D., and R. S. Lourie
    1964 The child's role in the battered child syndrome. *Journal of Pediatrics* 65:
        1079—1081.
Minturn, Leigh, and William W. Lambert
    1964 *Mothers of six cultures: antecedents of child rearing*. New York: John Wiley and
        Sons.

Morris, M. G., R. W. Gould, and P. J. Matthews
  1964 Toward prevention of child abuse. *Children* 2:55—60.

Nurse, S. M.
  1964 Familial patterns of parents who abuse their children. *Smith College Studies in Social Work* 35:11—25.

Oksenberg, Michael, ed.
  1973 *China's developmental experience.* Proceedings of the Academy of Political Science 31(1). New York: Columbia University.

Oliver, J. E., and A. Taylor
  1971 Five generations of ill-treated children in one family pedigree. *British Journal of Psychiatry* 119:473—480.

Paulson, Morris, and P. Blake
  1969 The physically abused child: a focus on prevention. *Child Welfare* 48(2):86—95.

Pruitt, Ida
  1967 *A daughter of Han: the autobiography of a Chinese working woman.* Stanford: Stanford University Press.

Radbill, Samuel X.
  1968 A history of child abuse and infanticide. In *The battered child*, ed. Ray E. Helfer and C. Henry Kempe. Chicago: University of Chicago Press. Pp. 3—17.

Rohner, Ronald P.
  1975 *They love me, they love me not: a worldwide study of the effects of parental acceptance and rejection.* New Haven: HRAF Press.

Schmitt, Barton D.
  1978 *The child protection team handbook: a multidisciplinary approach to managing child abuse and neglect.* New York: Garland STPM Press.

Sidel, Ruth
  1972 *Women and child care in China: a firsthand report.* Baltimore: Penguin.
  1974 *Families of Fengsheng: urban life in China.* Baltimore: Penguin.

Sidel, Victor, and Ruth Sidel
  1973 *Serve the people: observations on medicine in the People's Republic of China.* Boston: Beacon.

Smedley, Agnes
  1976 *Portraits of Chinese women in revolution.* New York: Feminist Press.

Smith, Selwyn, Leo Honigsberger, and Carol A. Smith
  1973 E.E.G. and personality factors in baby batterers. *British Medical Journal* 2:20—22.

Solomon, Theo
  1973 History and demography of child abuse. *Pediatrics* 51(4):773—776.

Spinetta, John J., and David Rigler
  1972 The child-abusing parent: a psychological review. *Psychological Bulleton* 77(4): 296—304.

Spargo, John
  1913 *The bitter cry of the children.* New York: Macmillan.

Steele, Brandt F.
  1970 Violence in our society. *Pharos of Alpha Omega Alpha* 33(2):42—48.

Steele, Brandt F., and Carl B. Pollock
    1968 A psychiatric study of parents who abuse infants and small children. In *The battered child*, ed. Ray E. Helfer and C. Henry Kempe. Chicago: University of Chicago Press. Pp. 103–147.

Wasserman, Sidney
    1967 The abused parent of the abused child. *Children* 14:175–179.

Wu, Chao-yi
    1978 Personal communication.

Young, Leontine
    1964 *Wednesday's children: a study of child neglect and abuse.* New York: McGraw-Hill.

CHILD REARING AND CHILD ABUSE: 10
The Polynesian Context

Jane Ritchie and James Ritchie

After fifty years of modern ethnographic research a body of literature has accumulated which makes possible a definitive description of the Polynesian child-rearing style. We have recently undertaken an extended review of this literature (Ritchie and Ritchie 1979), and we summarize it here. This traditional style had certain features and mechanisms which prevented child abuse and neglect, but culture change and migration have eroded these practices. Currently there is a virtual explosion of incidence in urban New Zealand (Fergusson et al. 1972), urban Hawaii (State of Hawaii Statistical Reports 1974, 1975), and probably in other areas to which Polynesians have migrated. At the time of writing there has been no corresponding upsurge in incidence in island homelands, presumably because a traditional child-rearing style persists in most places.

We are immediately confronted with an apparent contradiction between two reputed facts. From a first reading of ethnographic accounts, there is so little evidence of child abuse that one might be tempted to say it is totally absent from the Polynesian context. The second so-called fact, the reputed high incidence of child abuse and neglect among Polynesians in New Zealand, compared with Europeans, seems irreconcilable with the first. This problem is our main focus in this paper. With all the reservations that must be kept in mind as one compares incidence rates, especially if they are based on conjecture rather than on counting, it is still highly probable that, under the stress of migration, the Polynesian child-rearing style is vulnerable to disturbance, inadequate support, misinterpretation, socioeconomic stress, and other evidence of acculturative strain. These factors might well lead to a higher incidence of child abuse, and while the statisticians are sorting out their side of the matter, the anthropological perspectives can be clarified.

From earlier work (Ritchie and Ritchie 1970) we know that in the process of migration Maori parents do not simply switch from a Polynesian child-rearing style to that of the surrounding European culture, even though that would seem to be their intention. Maori mothers in the small-town sample of our earlier study actually presented a more extreme form, almost a parody, of the European child-rearing style. They attempted to toilet train earlier, used more rigid feeding schedules, were less warm, more punitive, and harsher in their judgments of their children's behavior. We attributed this phenomenon to social forces: on the one hand the surrounding pressures to conform to an alien environment, including Polynesians' desire as a minority to protect themselves from criticism, and on the other their imitation of what they perceived to be the major features of the European pattern. They considered it desirable to switch to severe scheduling of feeding and the use of tough rather than tender methods of correcting children's behavior.

There was also evidence that Polynesians moving into a large city could escape the circumspection of the small-town community, and that long-standing or second-generation migrant families were far more relaxed in their child rearing, yet basic supports for the traditional Polynesian pattern were still not really in evidence. The accommodation that Polynesian parents seem forced to make in large urban settings is essentially that of abandoning Polynesian practices.

We will return to the question of migration and its effects, for it is central, indeed crucial, to all aspects of contemporary Polynesian life. Now let us discuss the nature of Polynesian child rearing in its classical ethnographic form in island settings.

Polynesia is the name given to a culture area traditionally defined by a triangle with New Zealand, Hawaii, and Easter Island at the points and including the many islands dotted over approximately a third of the surface of the Pacific Ocean. Although the origins of Polynesian culture are still in dispute, the traditional view is that the islands were colonized by migration from an original mythical homeland. In effect, we can reasonably assume that over the past two thousand years these related cultures settled more or less permanently in one or another island group and there proceeded through their local processes of evolution and adaptation. In some instances considerable interisland contact was maintained, but in others, especially for scattered Polynesian islands lying outside the triangle—the outliers—there was virtually complete cultural isolation. In what follows we have drawn upon the most recent anthropological literature we have been able to find for the following cultures: Hawaii, the Marquesas, the Tuamotus, the Society Islands (the Tahiti group), Cook Islands, the atolls of the Northern Cook group, Tonga, the Samoas, and New Zealand. We also have information for some isolated islands—Niue, Rotuma, Tikopia, and Anuta.

For some of these islands—for example, Pukapuka (Beaglehole and Beaglehole 1938), Tikopia (Firth 1936), and Tonga (Beaglehole and Beaglehole 1941)—we have descriptions at one point of time of cultures that might be called intact; an intact culture, although subject to contact and Western influences, is one whose authority has not been impaired. In other areas, notably Hawaii (Gallimore, Boggs, and Jordan 1974; Howard 1974), New Zealand (Beaglehole and Beaglehole 1946; Ritchie 1963; Ritchie 1957; Ritchie and Ritchie 1970), and Samoa (Holmes 1974; Mead 1928), we have a number of different ethnographers for each culture writing at different periods of time.

There are other ways of contrasting these Polynesian islands. For example, some are atolls and others are so-called high islands of volcanic origin; the two types are ecologically and economically different. The colonial influence of six major metropolitan cultures—France, Britain, United States, Germany, Australia, and New Zealand—has had an impact on the different islands. Nevertheless, throughout this area, a common family and child-rearing style continues. Any one of the features we discuss below may be found in many other cultures around the world, but we believe that the intensity and the patterning of these cultural features are unique to Polynesia.

Polynesians have many, many parents. The kinship terminology gives the key to the practice. In New Zealand all persons older than one's own generation are termed *matua* regardless of age. The term means parents, and there are equivalent words in all Polynesian languages. Again, all female relatives of the age of one's biological mother are termed *whaea*, or its dialectic equivalent meaning mother. Similarly, males on both sides of the lineage, mother's and father's, are functionally equivalent in terminology and parenting role. In New Zealand they are called *matua tane*. Practically speaking, only during the earliest part of life, say the first two years, might one expect to find a child sleeping every night in the home of its biological parents, and on all ritual occasions the collective parenting function of many people is acknowledged.

Illegitimacy is virtually of no importance, for one is the child of the lineage, not of any particular set of parents. Adoption is widespread and is an open and public act of generosity in sharing children (Carroll 1970). In adoption, as in any other aspect of parenting, collective action applies because kinship is involved.

Thus the child has many parenting resources, many more than are implied by the term "extended family," which connotes extension from the nuclear basis of the household to include a few grandparents and the odd aunt and uncle and possibly their offspring. In writing about child rearing we need to recognize the existence of the collective family—which was not invented by modern Israel, the Haight-Ashbury generation, or the Soviet industrial collective—as well as that of solo, nuclear, and extended families.

Just as there are many cultures where multiple parenting is found, so too there are many cultures that place a high value on early infancy and lavish upon children of that age almost unstinted warmth and nurturance. This may seem self-evident. Have not all people everywhere at all times valued young children?

Historically speaking, the answer is clearly no (deMause 1975). In Europe and America, measures to protect children from abandonment, neglect, and ill-treatment hardly existed before the latter part of the nineteenth century, and the process of remedying the situation required extended and cumbersome cooperation between voluntary societies and legal agencies. Even now the agencies of public welfare dealing with children are unable to give practical effect to the lip service paid to our desire to protect young children. At no time in the history of Polynesia has there existed anything like the aggression and neglect that have been documented for the West for centuries past.

Traditionally, young children in Polynesia were not considered trainable, so nobody bothered to train them until early infancy was over (at about 2 years). From long before the birth of the child its advent was heralded. Although both abortion and infanticide were practiced (though not everywhere within the culture area), the ethnographic accounts give little prominence to either. These practices were apparently rather rare except in Tahiti where, according to Oliver (1974), in precontact times between three-fourths and two-thirds of live infants were killed within half an hour of birth. We do not know why Tahiti should be so different in this respect, if in fact it was. We discussed the matter with Bengt Danielsson who thought the Oliver estimate for Tahiti much too high and who gave various reasons for infanticide and abortion. These included a woman's wish not to have a child at the time, mismatches across social class boundaries, and involvement of women in sacred and priestly duties. Whatever the reasons, they constitute a quite different social phenomenon from child abuse. The whole question of infanticide and other methods of population control in Polynesia needs more research.

Infanticide and abortion are ways of controlling the population when fertility exceeds the need for more people. They reflect a social desire to give the survivors the best possible chance rather than disregard for the value of life. In modern Tahiti, contraception and abortion have replaced infanticide. A painless death is different from the induction of pain; contraception and abortion, which are rational and premeditated, are culturally accepted, and the mother is to be comforted and supported.

The Beagleholes (1946) describe the early period of Polynesian life as the "golden age of childhood." The child is so constantly attended to and frankly and openly enjoyed by so many people that the phrase is indeed apt. Ethnographers agree, however, that the golden age abruptly ends with the arrival of the next child or, in any event, after the second year of life.

A number of notable features characterize the shift in parental orientation. First, Polynesians hold the cultural belief that a child aged two is trainable. Second, talking and walking are clear indications of competence which should be recognized and developed. The child progresses from being a lap child, a mat child, or a child on the back to being a yard child. He or she moves from being inside the house most of the time to being outside most of the time. There is a clear transition from being a constant and accepted part of the adult world, the object of its activity and concern, to being part of the world of children, which is tolerated in adult company only if adult rules are recognized. These two worlds, the world of adults and the world of children, are really two separate cultures inhabiting the same space. An individual remains in the world of childhood until puberty and its traditional markers (circumcision for boys, menstruation for girls) herald the transition to the adult world.

From the adult point of view, the discontinuity when infancy ends reflects the value placed both on the child's independence and on the parents' freedom from the dependency of children. How do parents promote the change, and how do children react? When the time comes Polynesian parents gently but firmly stop attending to the toddler's demands. In behavioral terms, it is a straight extinction run. Western observers may be somewhat shocked to observe that whining and clinging and crying get no apparent adult response at all and that the adults show so much firmness. But this stage soon passes, especially since other cultural resources come into play. In general, punishment is not used at this time of transition, though it certainly is later. Parents do not act coldly toward very young children, nor do they display hostile attitudes. They may, however, be quite harsh with older children. They are not rejective in the sense in which Rohner (1975) uses that term. As adults, Polynesians do not as a rule display the psychological characteristics of early rejection which Rohner has identified: a hostile and aggressive personality, excessive dependency, emotional unresponsiveness, a negative self-image, and negativism about people and the natural and supernatural world.

Furthermore, the preconditions of a rejective pattern which Rohner (1975) has identified cross-culturally are not present. Rejection is likely to occur, he says, when mothers are the sole caretakers, when caretaking is their primary responsibility and they have no other outlets, when those around them place heavy moral pressures upon them to fulfill their role, and when they have few emotional resources available to them: that is, when they are insufficiently nurtured themselves, when their working role drains them of energy, and when they never really did have the time to indulge themselves in enjoying their babies. Rohner reports that adults around the world who were accepted as children (instead of being rejected) are more generous, responsible, responsive, and nurturant in all their social relationships, particularly with young children and babies, their own and those of other people. They tend to be optimistic, cheerful, and expressive. The latter list of qualities, rather than the former, seems to apply to Polynesian character structure.

Rohner's cross-cultural work on rejection is directly relevant to child abuse. The literature on child abuse, largely derived as it is from studies of pathological conditions in Western families, comes back again and again to the theme of rejection. Indeed, other aspects of Western culture, especially creative expressions in novels, drama, and poetry, show rejection along with fear of rejection to be a deeply ramified cultural theme. Rejection is a Western phenomenon. It would be bold indeed to claim that it is absent from Polynesian cultural expression in song and poetry, but, relatively speaking, it has low frequency. Early independence in Polynesia does not constitute rejection either in intent or effect. Early training in independence is a clearly identified, positively sanctioned, cultural practice regarded by Polynesians as evidence of good parenting.

Europeans expect parents to maintain control over their children until the end of the second decade. This concept is enshrined in the law giving parents rights over children, including the right to use reasonable physical punishment, and is endorsed by the judicial system. It is also reinforced by subjural personnel such as schoolteachers, social welfare officers, and so on. In 1967, of complaints in New Zealand about children who were judged not to be under proper control and were reported to and registered by child welfare, 54 percent concerned Polynesian children even though Polynesians and Maoris constituted only 10 percent of the total child population. Especially in respect to independence, cultural standards as to what constitutes proper control are very different and may be subject to sharply contrasting cultural interpretations.

The consequences of pressures toward early independence, especially given the high levels of initial indulgence, could be hard on the child were it not for compensating features of Polynesian family life. Two cultural resources reduce the negative effects. One is multiple parenting, already mentioned; the other is peer and sibling socialization. In traditional settings, a younger child was often placed in the care of an older sibling. Considerable folklore developed from such relationships, especially in the deference that younger children give to older ones: the *tuakana* (elder)/*teina* (younger) relationship in its various cultural forms. Throughout Polynesia, respect of one age for another is prevalent. Younger siblings must always give respect to elder siblings; elder siblings should always care for younger ones. Younger children remain silent in the ceremonious presence of older children, and in some islands they must even avoid the latter, in maturity as well as in youth.

Beyond the sibling group, but usually incorporating it, is the village peer group. As a social structure it is relatively independent of family in the narrow sense. In a wider sense it is the sibling group of sibling groups within the village as one big family. Western literature on child development generally presents peer group influence as in opposition to parental authority, as potentially antisocial, since the group comprises age-mates only, and as emphasizing adolescence and the Western mythology of *Sturm und Drang* (Bronfenbrenner 1970). None of these features apply to the Polynesian peer group, which is entrusted by parents with a socializing role as part of the parenting process. In the village setting the peer group, far from being antisocial, is like a small tribe in which one learns social responsibility. Because it comprises an age range all the way from two to fifteen, it has a wide range of age-graded models, all of them immediately and continuously available to the growing child. By comparison, Western children's almost exclusive use of their parents as models seems psychologically implausible. Polynesian children do not need to imitate only their parents; they can imitate their older siblings.

Peer socialization is a widespread human phenomenon (Weisner and Gallimore 1977). Its real significance in Western child development has not yet been fully assessed or appreciated (Bronfenbrenner 1970). It is by no means unique to Polynesia, but as an essential part of the collective ethic of Polynesian culture it mediates some of its most important cultural messages (Ritchie and Ritchie 1979).

Linking the complexities of cultural ethos to child-training variables becomes extremely complicated, especially since the Polynesian value system seems to endorse simultaneously what Western logic regards as polar opposites: hierarchical and collateral authority, competitive and cooperative strategies, democratic and autocratic decision making. All these can be related to the kind of learning strategies that are developed in Polynesian peer group experience.

Some aspects of Polynesian culture have developed from the way in which children were cared for and therefore relate to the relative absence of child abuse. First, status is traditionally the most salient feature of Polynesian life. It was after working in the Marquesas that Ralph Linton made the now classic distinction between ascribed and achieved status (1936) and Irving

Goldman (1955) recognized status rivalry as a vital Polynesian cultural dynam-
ic. Polynesians have it both ways. Not only is status ascribed in genealogical
terms but in all Polynesian societies it must be validated and maintained by
achievement; the Samoan *matai* system is the most obvious example.

Second, the nature of the status system is learned as one learns respect.
The foundation of respect for status rests in the consequences of early indulgence and its discontinuity. It is then that the child learns about the gap
between the statuses of adult and child and about other statuses he or she will
later adopt and respect. These messages are reinforced by multiple parenting
and peer socialization. Child abuse is unlikely in any social system that
requires one to give respect to people of high status who are continuously
present in the immediate day-to-day environment. Potential abusers cannot
get away with it, for high-status people are always there and have a right to
intervene—and do. In Polynesia, elders intervene directly to require that
parents impose punishment or exercise proper control, when needed, and step
in when parental conduct gets out of hand. In Tikopia, in times of famine and
disaster, the chiefs by their collective authority could enforce infanticide.

Third, Polynesian political systems are marked by open and democratic
methods of social control. As Firth (1936) points out for Tikopia and Ritchie
(1963) for Rakau, mutual surveillance and gossip are important social sanctions. In addition, many parts of Polynesia permit open communal debate,
during the course of which one is almost obliged to report any grievance
against another person. It is an older form of the encounter group.

Anthropologists who have tried to describe the Polynesian family system have been baffled. Even defining households in a village may prove
difficult: one house is primarily for elders (but may be inhabited by anyone);
another serves as a clubhouse for young men or young women or both and is a
place where they sleep, sometimes together; and considerable movement
occurs from one primary family dwelling to another. Essentially a household is
a matter of convenience, since all members of the village are of one lineage and,
in that sense, of one family. This collective sense of family and multiple
parenting guarantees adequate nurturance for any one child and also provides
a high degree of vigilance by all adults over the parenting activities of any one
of them.

Finally, gender roles in Polynesia did not traditionally preclude males
from child care activities. With men sharing nurturant activities as well as and
as much as women, Polynesian children had double the chance of good-quality
child care.

It is obvious from the foregoing description of Polynesian culture that
child abuse was virtually absent from the Polynesian scene. The whole ethos
and ecology of child rearing precluded it. Only in two respects did Polynesian

cultures authorize physical mutilation: tattooing and circumcision. Both were minor, applied to males only (for the most part) and undertaken voluntarily. While undoubtedly the pressure to submit to these practices was strong, they are acts that initiate adulthood and are not performed by adults on unwilling child victims. Nor is it likely that these acts could lead to justifications for child abuse in a disorganized or deculturated setting. Why is it, then, that in a modern culture-contact setting there appears to be a high frequency of child abuse?

The New Zealand Department of Social Welfare report, *Child Abuse in New Zealand* (Fergusson et al. 1972), concludes that "the reported incidence of abuse amongst Maori children was six times greater than amongst European children, that the incidence amongst Pacific Island children was nine times greater" (p. 149). Maori females were the most abused group, and abuse tended to increase rather than to decrease with age. The authors consider that "the present day Maori family is in a state of transition and consequent disruption" (p. 151), marshaling in evidence statistics from unpublished data which show that the incidence of family problems coming to the attention of the children's court was then considerably higher for Maoris than for non-Maoris. Of complaints of indigency, 38 percent were Maori; of neglect, 51 percent; of detrimental environment, 41 percent; of not being under proper control, 54 percent; of children committed to the care of the state, 46 percent. In that year Maori children constituted only 12 percent of those under 16 years of age. These data are ten years old and regrettably the research division of the Department of Social Welfare has not updated them. There is no reason to believe, however, that the general picture would have changed much, except that in the past decade the Polynesian population increased dramatically through migration until 1977, when immigration restrictions began to limit it.

The picture of Polynesian family life presented by Fergusson, Fleming, and O'Neill (1972) contrasts sharply with all that we have said so far in this paper. Before we discuss the social dynamics that lie behind this picture, some caveats must be applied, as is always true in discussions of the incidence of child abuse.

It is quite likely that the authorities picked up a high proportion of the child abuse that occurred among Maoris and Pacific Islanders because, like ethnic minorities elsewhere, they have become identified as groups prone to social problems. They are simply subject to a higher degree of community and official scrutiny; they are in the public eye; they attract media attention; they have high visibility. Second, whereas European, especially middle-class, child abusers go to great lengths to conceal the effects of their practices as well as the practices themselves, such covert concealment is less likely to occur to most Polynesian parents in the context of their own child-rearing practices. In a village context it cannot be concealed, but in any event it is less likely to occur because of the communal child-rearing style. Hence, these incidence figures may be comparing our estimate of about 90 percent of the actual Polynesian child abuse cases with perhaps 30 percent of those detected in the European population. Furthermore, differences in population distribution in terms of socioeconomic status must be taken into account, since in New Zealand proportionately more detected child abuse comes from lower-level families and proportionately more Polynesian families are in this category (Fergusson et al. 1972). Again, because of more relaxed cultural attitudes, Polynesian children are proportionately more likely to be technically illegitimate. The illegitimate child is more likely to be abused when the mother is under stress and culture loss has destroyed traditional supports and attitudes.

For all these caveats, however, there is no denying that, according to the only existing authoritative study for New Zealand, of a total of 252 cases of abuse detected in a single year a staggering 172, or 63 percent, were Maori, Pacific Island, or mixed-race children. Thus, of every three cases detected, two came from an ethnic background that was to some extent Polynesian. In some way, and often within one generation, Polynesians have shifted from a profile of no child abuse to one of high child abuse. What has happened?

When Maori women become mothers in an isolated suburban setting the situation is generally more stressful for them than for their non-Polynesian neighbors. A number of years ago one of us (Ritchie 1964) reported very high stress scores for Maori mothers in a large New Zealand city. In 1958, when the data were collected, the rates of psychiatric disorder for this category of people were not conspicuously high. Ten years later we obtained identical data for a further sample and again we found evidence of high stress levels and commented that the need to attend to this matter was urgent (Ritchie and Ritchie 1970). The stress, which was undifferentiated and very general, represented no recognizable patterning of scores into the usual categories, such as anxiety states, depression, mental breakdown, conversion hysteria, or other neurotic problems. So far as we know, neither in 1958 nor in 1968 was this information utilized in community or mental health services for the population concerned.

Since this stress does not fall into a recognized pattern, it is possible that the usual ways in which stress is reduced are not available to Polynesian migrant women, or perhaps to men (though we have no evidence concerning their stress levels). We postulate that there are patterns of handling stress within Western families which have not yet developed in Polynesian families. The Western woman converts the stress arising from the situation into which she has been forced into neurotic or psychosomatic symptoms, into strategies and tactics in her marriage, into visits to her doctor to procure more Librium or

Valium, and increasingly into alcohol dependence (Bernard 1972). The Maori or Polynesian mother simply acts out. None of these strategies are satisfactory, but since we see little being done to provide women with other and better ways of removing stress or coping with it we think Maori and Polynesian women may slowly adopt the same tactics as European women. They may then display less child abuse (or learn to conceal it), but will they really be any better off? The matter, we repeat, urgently needs to be researched.

Obviously, the features of Polynesian child rearing we have described are local and tribal and are best supported in a rural or small-village setting. The dwellings in a typical Polynesian village are of low-technology construction. When new houses are needed they can be rather easily provided, so overcrowding is no problem. Furthermore, since houses are used chiefly as sleeping quarters, at least in tropical Polynesia, a large number of people can be accommodated without creating unsanitary conditions or contravening housing regulations. Polynesians in Honolulu, San Jose, Los Angeles, Auckland, or any other metropolitan city simply cannot live in their accustomed way; therefore they find that housing, working, and other conditions make multiple parenting unlikely, if not impossible. Furthermore, Europeans do not engage in multiple parenting, do not like it, and do not understand it. In their endeavors to adapt to a new environment and culture, Polynesians stop doing it too. The lack of multiple parenting puts a heavier strain on nuclear parent caretakers who have little cultural preparation for stress of this kind.

A combination of high fertility rates and higher infant survival still leads to very large families, even though the rate of Polynesian population increase has started to fall. There is still a reluctance, particularly among men, to accept birth control measures even though they are available. While the Polynesian system can well handle large numbers of children in the natural setting, nothing is more likely to disturb and disrupt the Polynesian child-rearing system than nucleated suburban living. Once the surrounding community is no longer palpably and visibly present, the major check on abusive parental practice is gone. In the village setting multiple parenting operated as a quality control on the parenting of all adults and, far from reducing the individual responsibility of any one adult, probably increased it, but in conjunction with collective responsibility. In the urban situation there has not yet been sufficient time to develop the concept of individual responsibility which will prevent aggressive actions toward children. Most tribal people operate on a public rather than a private system of ethics. The Protestant ethos may encourage some parents to beat their children in the interests of virtue (spare the rod and spoil the child), but it cautions against beating to excess (Ritchie and Ritchie 1981).

The latter part of the Protestant ethos is rather weak, and with a reduction of the power and effectiveness of a collective ethic, when the nuisance value of children has exceeded their capacity to give pleasure the way is wide open for ordinary punishment to spill over into child abuse. The urban ecology is so different from that of the islands; the weather is often cold, so that a lonely mother is shut up with too many preschool children in an over-crowded house. She is not able to take advantage of preschool services since they are limited in number and are less accessible to the underprivileged (Ritchie 1978). Where is the taro patch to which she can retire to share her troubles with other women and do useful work while a solution is being worked out? Where is the lagoon, the beach, or the reef where children can have fun, find food, and escape from parental surveillance? Where are the elders who will direct that someone give assistance? Where are the dwellings of kinsfolk to whom a frightened child may run for comfort?

Undoubtedly there are ways in which multiple parenting can be restored to Polynesian child rearing in urban settings. With suitable arrangements of dwellings and by fostering the urban equivalent of the caring community, multiple parenting is a possibility. We know that Polynesian communities in New Zealand towns are developing their own social structures, but many families slip through the holes in these networks. There has not yet been enough time for a fully functioning and viable pattern to have developed.

Just as the urban environment fails to support multiple parenting, the practice of early indulgence also seems vulnerable. We have noted in all our research on child rearing the increasing harshness of early parenting once Polynesian families become nucleated (Ritchie and Ritchie 1970). One indicator of the disappearance of infant indulgence we have noted is that Maori mothers, like European mothers, breast-feed for a short time only. The whole pattern of city living, time-bound and scheduled, is not conducive to relaxed enjoyment of little babies. In the traditional setting children received indulgent treatment because a lot of people were on hand to give a little. It is a different matter when one person has to give a lot and give it all the time.

Perhaps no other feature of Polynesian child rearing is as dependent upon the whole of the pattern as is early indulgence. Its vulnerability is probably greater because early independence as a cultural value can be pushed earlier and earlier into infancy. Unquestionably early independence survives strongly as a training practice, and indeed independence itself is a valued Polynesian child-training goal. It may lead to child abuse in two ways. First, to lighten their own responsibilities parents may force autonomy upon children to a degree that leaves their dependency needs unmet. Second, acting inde-pendently may lead children into conflict with neighbors, the school, and the law and may lead girls into pregnancy or the risk of it. Children may be abused for the very acceptance of the independence that their parents seem to have forced upon them.

The degree of independence appropriate in the low-technology village situation may place impossible, even lethal, demands on a young Polynesian city child, especially in regard to sibling caretaking. Older homes, in which the poor, including Polynesians, are more likely to live, catch fire more easily. A child of five or six who is looking after his or her younger siblings simply may not know what to do in such an emergency. The modern urban environment is undoubtedly the most dangerous in which human beings have ever tried to live.

The Fergusson (1972) report notes that the rate of abuse against Polynesian female children is higher than against males and that the incidence of abuse increases rather than decreases with age. It is possible that, while both sexes are expected to be independent at an early age, parental commitment to the independence of children is less firm and more ambiguous for daughters. Unfortunately, it is not clear from the Fergusson report which parent is abusing which child and at what age, but we suspect that strongly expressed independence at adolescence may be more disturbing to fathers than to mothers because it is the father's authority which is being challenged. Mothers may be the primary agents of socialization, but fathers have the ultimate authority. Fear of pregnancy and a sexual double standard no doubt contribute to this situation; parents do all they can to prevent pregnancy, but they accept it once it happens.

In an island situation, once parents have given independence to their children it is possible for them to live with it and never really want to take it back, however often they may rant and rail. In the urban environment, however, it is assumed that parents are individually responsible for keeping their children dependent until the law says they may cease to do so. Under New Zealand law, parents must keep their children at school until they are fifteen and must continue to provide for them and keep them under proper control until they are sixteen. Parents are responsible for their children's debts until age eighteen. In insurance, hire purchase, and other money transactions parents have the ultimate responsibility and liability until their dependent offspring are eighteen (Ritchie and Ritchie 1978).

Urban European social structure and life-style are poorly adapted to accommodate the degree of independence which Polynesians customarily grant to their children. European parents are supposed to know where their teenage children are at any time and certainly during the hours of darkness. Recently, for example, the media have given considerable publicity to children as young as seven or eight coming from the suburbs of Auckland on weekends to attend all-night disco dances in the inner city, returning home only when the buses begin to run the next morning. It should be pointed out, however, that these children do not go out alone but are accompanied by an older sibling to whom responsibility has been given. What may seem to Europeans to be gross parental neglect is simply the persistence of a cultural pattern functioning in an alien and rather hostile environment and over distances far longer than those of the original habitat.

The disco phenomenon must be understood as the direct equivalent of ordinary peer socialization transferred into an urban setting. Many other examples show how misunderstandings and distrust of peer processes lead to the identification of young Polynesians as problem groups and of Polynesian parents as problem parents, even though they are just following the proper Polynesian customs. Motorcycle gangs, school dropouts who seem to form groups that sometimes resemble truancy clubs, runaways from home who squat in deserted houses, monocultural playground gangs often forming a hostile presence within the school environment—all these are negative exemplifications of the peer socialization phenomenon. Maori cultural, church, and other youth organizations are more positive expressions. Whatever evaluation the surrounding society places upon these groups, they are not only a powerful source of psychological satisfaction but also a learning environment. For Europeans, learning is thought to take place at home or at school, and when it occurs elsewhere, as in gangs or through the media, it is suspect (Ritchie and Ritchie 1978). In Polynesia there were no schools and the family did not act as the major socializing agent once infancy had passed. Rather, there was a direct interaction between peer groups and the whole of the community through the role of status people, such as elders, and through social sanction mechanisms, such as gossip. When, as in the city, peer groups exist without a surrounding controlling community they may become a community unto themselves. But what is learned in the peer group is still the same: sharing and caring within the group, collective responsibility, modulation of personal goals within a group context, attentiveness to the attitudes and opinions of others within the group, and moral relativism.

Sometimes groups of children act toward another child in ways that might seem abusive but really are not. For example, a mother left a three-month-old baby asleep, unattended, in an unlocked house while she went to the doctor. The house was entered by a group of preschool children who, while playing with the baby, dropped it causing fatal injuries. The mother might be judged neglectful by European standards, but because her older children were at school she had no one with whom she could leave the baby. By Polynesian standards, such a mother is unfortunate but not culpable. The parents of the young preschool children could also be judged neglectful but they, in the Polynesian way, might well have expected older children or other parents to have been watching the infant. And as their older siblings were at school, the preschool children could not operate as a Polynesian peer group should, with the older children teaching the younger ones what to do; the group's truncation produces a functional incompetence that may leave the children exposed to possible dangers or errors of judgment. We are not here arguing that older children should not go to school, but perhaps if the school were to accept the younger children the Polynesian peer group might continue to operate as such (though schools might need a major social reconstruction in order to accommodate interactive learning in a wider age span).

In a Polynesian setting adults can get free time to do the things they need to do on their own or in adult company because multiple parenting and the presence of a peer group take care of the children. But city environments are grossly deficient in child care provisions, especially from the Polynesian point of view. The result is often neglect: children are left locked in a house or car, or are given a dollar or two to amuse themselves downtown while parents go to the tavern. Furthermore, the strain placed upon adults by unaccustomed, unremitting child care can create either the preconditions or the flash point for actual child abuse. In every locality where a substantial number of Polynesians live each major facility—church, supermarket, tavern—should provide child care facilities. It is a welcome sign that in the city of Auckland some Polynesian groups are beginning to operate their own family-style clubs where food, entertainment, and liquor are all provided in a community setting.

In the cases of child abuse reported in the New Zealand study (Fergusson et al. 1972), we cannot find much that seems distinctive either about the type of injury, the explanations offered by the abusers, or the circumstances in which the abuse took place. There is the same sorry saga of children beaten with broomsticks, belts, and electric cords, of burns and scalds and cigarette injuries, of subdural hemorrhages and skull fractures, hematoma, multiple fractures, spiral fractures, and abrasions. The explanations have the same curious mixtures of evasiveness and naive forthrightness. Perhaps there is a slightly readier admission of adult loss of control while punishing the child for whining, dependent behaviors, persistent demands for attention, soiling, or refusal to eat. The surrounding circumstances simply show how quickly the universal preconditions of the battered-child syndrome can arise in any society that has ceased to maintain good standards of child care. Large families, poor living conditions, an intolerable degree of isolation, marital instability, strain, and alcohol—all compound in a generation to create the preconditions of child abuse. Perhaps it is less frequent that the abusive adult was abused as a child, but it is only a matter of time before this condition is added to all the others. What is the answer?

To us it seems that a strong hope lies in reconstruction. We believe that the Polynesian heritage rests upon Polynesian child rearing. We believe that a conscious and deliberate conservation of that pattern would prevent child abuse. We know of intact New Zealand Maori communities, old enclaves around which wider communities have grown. Within these communities child abuse is as unthinkable as it ever was. The first step in reconstructing a viable urban equivalent is for Polynesians to recognize the salient features of their child-rearing system so that they know what to protect. Time and again, when we have told Polynesian groups our analysis of the major features of Polynesian child-rearing style, they have said yes, that is how their childhood was; they recognize the pattern, they remember how nice it was. But in all the discussion of cultural preservation we have never heard the central role of child rearing acknowledged. Instead, the emphasis is on preservation of language, community ceremonial facilities, traditions, oratory, and song and dance. All these are important, but none of them will prevent disorganization from reaching down into the heart of family relationships.

It is easy to accept the thesis that an increase in child abuse and neglect is a natural concomitant of sociological disturbances created by migration, rapid urbanization, and other cultural changes. To do so is to admit helplessness. In the Polynesian context a preexisting child-rearing tradition is a major resource upon which people can draw to handle culture change constructively and creatively.

Many agencies and forces are pressing Polynesian families to switch to European child-rearing practices because they are considered to be better, easier to implement, more modern, or divinely ordained. Polynesians have few resources to resist such pressures, which come directly from medical practitioners, health workers, social workers, police, schoolteachers, and the media, and indirectly from other agencies. The most powerful purveyor of such influence is the surrounding European community. These pressures would have less impact if there were clearer psychological advantages in bringing children up one way in preference to another. On this question, however, the literature on child development is culture-bound and unhelpful. The literature of child abuse certainly does not suggest that European child-rearing styles are a model to emulate. The high frequency of child abuse among Polynesians in New Zealand suggests that when Maoris do follow the European model, the consequent strain is intolerable and children become the victims.

So little really needs to be done to bring a preventive perspective into the problem of child abuse and neglect among Polynesians. Because Maori and Pacific Island groups still have a community orientation through which prevention might work, certainly in some cases, there are networks into which information can be fed. There are real face-to-face groups whom one can ask how they would solve the problem. In addition to the visible resources— medical social workers, pediatric clinics, general hospitals, general practition- ers, public health nurses, youth aid and crime prevention officers, and all the machinery of European institutions—there is a wide and increasing array of Polynesian social structures, such as urban committees for community cen- ters, elders in positions of traditional authority (the Maori *kaumatua* and the Samoan *matai*), the Maori Women's Welfare Leagues, churches, and family networks. But before any real change can occur, the problem must be recog- nized and confronted by Polynesians themselves; to deal with it they must develop a strategy and must assess their own resources. More opportunities for collective living must be created for both Polynesians and Europeans, but especially for Polynesians because that kind of living is their background and, for many of them, their preference. As Helfer and Kempe (1974) emphasize, being judgmental about child abuse does not help the people who practice it.

A final cultural problem must be specifically tackled. Child abuse is abhorrent in every culture but more so in cultures that have no history of it. Western Europeans may be surprised when they are reminded of the history of child abuse in their own tradition (deMause 1975), but there are reminders of it all around us in laws designed to protect children from exploitation and abuse, in child welfare institutions, and in organizations designed to protect children, home, and family. While we may claim that the behavior of those who batter children is beyond our understanding, we have to some degree been desensi- tized to the phenomenon by both its historical and contemporary ubiquity. Polynesians have not been immunized until recently, and so their reaction to those who are caught up in the syndrome may be even more heavily judg- mental than that of Europeans. They may reject the offender with such statements as "A real Maori wouldn't do that." Again, the basic and funda- mental first principle in dealing with child abuse and neglect is to put one's judgments and feelings of horror to one side. Otherwise it is impossible to deal with the poignant and human realities of the situation.

REFERENCES

Beaglehole E., and P. Beaglehole
    1938 *Ethnology of Pukapuka*. Honolulu: Bishop Museum.
    1941 *Pangai: village in Tonga*. Wellington: Polynesian Society.
    1946 *Some modern Maoris*. Wellington: New Zealand Council for Educational Research.

Bernard, J.
1972 *The future of marriage.* New York: Bantam Books.

Bronfenbrenner, U.
1970 *Two worlds of childhood.* New York: Russell Sage Foundation.

Carroll, V., ed.
1970 *Adoption in eastern Oceania.* Honolulu: University of Hawaii Press.

deMause, L.
1975 Our forebears made childhood a nightmare. *Psychology Today* 9(April):85–88.

Fergusson, D. M., J. Fleming, and D. P. O'Neill
1972 *Child abuse in New Zealand.* Wellington: Government Printer.

Firth, R.
1936 *We the Tikopia.* London: Allen and Unwin.

Gallimore, R., J. W. Boggs, and C. Jordan
1974 *Culture, behavior and education: a study of Hawaiian Americans.* Beverly Hills, CA: Sage.

Goldman, I.
1955 Status rivalry and cultural evolution in Polynesia. *American Anthropologist* 57:680–697.

Helfer, R. E., and C. H. Kempe, eds.
1974 *The battered child.* 2nd ed. Chicago: University of Chicago Press.

Holmes, L. D.
1974 *Samoan village.* New York: Holt, Rinehart and Winston.

Howard, A.
1974 *Ain't no big thing: coping strategies in a Hawaiian-American community.* Honolulu: University of Hawaii Press.

Linton, R.
1936 *The study of man.* New York: Knopf.

Mead, M.
1928 *Coming of age in Samoa.* New York: William Morrow.

Oliver, D.
1974 *Ancient Tahitian society.* Canberra: Australian National University Press.

Ritchie, James E.
1963 *The making of a Maori.* Wellington: A. H. and A. W. Reed.

Ritchie, Jane
1957 *Childhood in Rakau.* Wellington: Victoria University.

1964 *Maori families.* Wellington: Victoria University.

1978 *Chance to be equal.* Cape Catley: Picton.

Ritchie, Jane, and James Ritchie
1970 *Child rearing patterns in New Zealand.* Wellington: A. H. and A. W. Reed.

1978 *Growing up in New Zealand.* Sydney: Allen and Unwin.

1979 *Growing up in Polynesia.* Sydney: Allen and Unwin.

1981 *Spare the rod.* Sydney: Allen and Unwin.

Rohner, R. P.
1975 *They love me, they love me not: a worldwide study of the effects of parental acceptance and rejection.* New Haven: HRAF Press.

State of Hawaii
> 1974   *A statistical report on child abuse and neglect in Hawaii.* Honolulu: Research and Statistics Office, Department of Social Services and Housing.
>
> 1975   *A statistical report on child abuse and neglect in Hawaii.* Honolulu: Research and Statistics Office, Department of Social Services and Housing.

Weisner, T. S., and R. Gallimore
> 1977   My brother's keeper: child and sibling caretaking. *Current Anthropology* 18(2): 169–190.

CONCLUSIONS 11

Jill E. Korbin

Principle: The Child Shall Be Protected Against All Forms of Neglect, Cruelty, and Exploitation

—United Nations Declaration of the Rights of
the Child, 20 November 1959

The foregoing consideration of child abuse and neglect within the context of diverse cultural groups affords us a perspective on this troubling aspect of human behavior. The preceding chapters have pointed out the importance of considering cultural variability in defining child abuse and neglect and have directed attention toward factors in the cultural milieu which can increase or decrease the likelihood that child maltreatment will occur.

The first task of our cross-cultural consideration was to explore definitions of child abuse and neglect. The chapters in this volume indicate that the issue is not as clear-cut as it might appear. There is no universally accepted standard for optimal child rearing or for abusive and neglectful behaviors. Child maltreatment, like other categories of behavior, must be defined by an aggregate of individuals, by a community or cultural group, to be meaningful. The authors have discussed cultural practices that Westerners criticize. Similarly, many of our Western child-training practices, regardless of how benign or even beneficial they seem to us, are equally open to criticism by other cultural groups.

In discussing culturally appropriate, but disparate, practices the authors stress the importance of considering behaviors within their cultural context, within the fabric of the society in which they occur. Thus, factors other than the overt act itself must be considered. Primary among them are the socialization goals of the cultural group, the intent and beliefs of the adults, and the interpretation children place on their treatment. In his autobiography, a young African speaks of the reassurance provided by his father prior to the initiation rite of circumcision. His father told him that all males of the group had survived the rite and that he, the son, would also. The son then recalled:

> However great the anxiety, however certain the pain, no one would have dreamed of running away from the ordeal . . . and I, for my own part, never entertained such thoughts. I wanted to be born, to be born again. I knew perfectly well that I was going to be hurt, but I wanted to be a man, and it seemed to me that nothing could be too painful if, by enduring it, I was to come to man's estate. [Laye 1954:113]

In accommodating cultural variation, regardless of how painful or how harmless a practice might appear to an outsider, we are not dealing with idiosyncratic harm to children outside the realm of culturally accepted practices. It is important to remember that no culture sanctions the extreme harm that befalls children, first described by Kempe and his colleagues as the "battered child syndrome" (Kempe et al. 1962). Were we to sample the range of cultures throughout the world, there might be closer agreement on the permissibility of physically harsh rites of passage and more universal condemnation of isolating small children to sleep alone or allowing an infant to cry unattended.

While definitions of child abuse and neglect legitimately vary across cultural boundaries, each of the groups discussed maintains concepts and definitions of behaviors that are beyond the standards of acceptable conduct. Although idiosyncratic child abuse and neglect may be defined differently by these groups and may occur with different frequencies, deviance in child care behavior is known cross-culturally as a possibility of human behavior.

The authors also discuss societal conditions such as poverty, food scarcity, and rapid socioeconomic change. These conditions are detrimental to both child and adult welfare and are frequently recognized by members of the various cultures as undermining previously high standards of care for some, if not all, children. Nevertheless, such conditions must be distinguished from harm inflicted or neglect perpetrated by individual parents or caretakers. Several chapters also point out the need to temper our condemnation of groups in which these conditions exist with an awareness of the parallels with past conditions in Western societies. The authors also indicate, however, that rapid socioeconomic change, with such consequences as social isolation and alcoholism, can increase the stress on individual parents so that child abuse and neglect increase.

The authors in this volume indicate that the kind of idiosyncratic child abuse and neglect of children which occurs in the United States and other

Western nations is relatively rare in cultures that do not provide a context conducive to its occurrence. When considering deviance cross-culturally, one must be cautious about a "romantization of the primitive" (Rohner 1975), such that deviant behavior is not recognized or is considered so rare as not to merit being reported in the literature. These papers suggest that children are subjected to a lower frequency of idiosyncratic child abuse and neglect—that they come to harm as the result of an individual parent's out-of-control discipline or pathology less frequently than in Western nations. The authors do not claim, however, that all is idyllic for children in these cultures. Children in many technologically less developed societies suffer insults to their health and development which could be prevented or cured with antibiotics, improved sanitation systems, better nutrition, and the like. Whereas children in urban settings may be subject to increased dangers from automobiles, fires in substandard homes, and other concomitants of urban life, children in less developed societies face the risk of rolling into the fire while sleeping, being harmed by animals, and so on. Children in many of the cultures discussed herein are subjected to considerable physical pain in the process of acquiring their adult status. As the LeVines point out, parents may see the cultural necessity for physically harsh initiation rites, but they may privately wonder if their own pain was worth it and may hope that their grandchildren will be spared—but only if their adult status as members of the group is ensured. It is also worthwhile to consider the question posed by Langness: Are these painful rites somehow an expression of hostility toward children which cannot be expressed by individual parents?

Reports of the rarity of child abuse and neglect in these cultures may be met with a measure of skepticism. It is well documented that the reported incidence of child maltreatment increases dramatically as public and professional awareness of the problem is enhanced and mandatory reporting laws are put into effect. What is telling, however, is that when child abuse and neglect occur in these far-removed cultures the incidents bear an unfortunate resemblance to child maltreatment in Western nations. The preceding discussions of these diverse societies propose that certain factors in the cultural context can act either to increase the incidence of child abuse and neglect, or to diminish the likelihood of their occurrence. These factors can be briefly summarized into general principles:

1. *Cultural value of children.*—If a culture values its children because they are the bearers of tradition, because they perpetuate the family or lineage, and because of their economic contributions, they are likely to be treated well. In some of the groups discussed infants are so valued that they are considered capable of suicidal revenge, of wandering off into the forest if they do not feel

that they are wanted and being cared for properly. Children are valued for the psychological pleasure they bring adults as well as for their economic contributions to the household. In most Western nations, children's economic participation in family and community life has decreased, making children expensive consumers and diminishing their contributions as producers (Logan 1979). By recent estimates it will cost individual parents over $200,000 to raise a child, without a college education (*Los Angeles Times*, Oct. 20, 1980). As incomprehensible as it would be to members of most of the cultures discussed in this book, children make such necessities as finding housing difficult in some parts of the United States (*Los Angeles Times*, Feb. 6, 1977, V:1).

2. *Beliefs about specific categories of children.*—A cultural group may value children highly, but not necessarily all children. Some children may be considered inadequate or unacceptable by cultural standards and thus fail to receive the same standard of care accorded to children in general. The preceding chapters reveal how different cultural contexts place certain children at increased risk of abuse or neglect. Depending on the cultural context, adopted children, illegitimate children, stepchildren, orphans, females, children who result from a difficult pregnancy or painful labor, retarded or deformed children, or children who display behaviors and characteristics not valued by their parents and culture may be at increased jeopardy.

3. *Beliefs about age capabilities and developmental stages of children.*—Cultures vary in terms of the age at which children are expected to behave in certain ways. If children are not considered competent, to "have sense," until seven or eight years of age, for example, then punishment before that age for wrongdoing would be pointless. It would be in direct opposition to the age-inappropriate expectations of very small children and infants that are so often implicated in child abuse and neglect in Western nations.

4. *Embeddedness of child rearing in kin and community networks.*—Children, who are by nature too immature to care for themselves, are particularly vulnerable to a "we/they" dichotomy. All the preceding chapters point out that a network of concerned individuals beyond the biological parents is a powerful deterrent to child abuse and neglect. This shared responsibility for child rearing acts in many ways to reduce the likelihood of child maltreatment. If a wide network of individuals is concerned with the well-being of the group's children, general standards of child care are more likely to be ensured. An extended network further helps to guarantee that someone will intervene when standards of child care are violated. A network of individuals provides alternative caretakers, thus relieving one or two biological parents of the entire burden of child care. If a child is not wanted or is not being treated well by his or her biological parents, there are likely to be mechanisms for redistributing such children through temporary or permanent adoption or fosterage. It must

be remembered here, however, that the preceding chapters also note that, within some contexts, children who are adopted or fostered, and not among kin, are at increased risk of maltreatment.

As modernization and exposure to Western society increase, the authors note a decrease in what Westerners would define as child abuse. It is well to be aware, however, that at the same time there is an increase in what these same cultures would traditionally define as abusive or neglectful. Thus, children will increasingly be put into separate beds or perhaps separate rooms to spend the night, will be allowed to cry without being attended to, will be subjected to the dangers of the evil eye or chilling, and will be left with strangers rather than with known kinsfolk or neighbors. The benefits of such changes are clearly an empirical matter, as several of the contributors have noted, rather than an ethical issue.

The foregoing chapters analyze cultures that are, for the most part, far removed from those Western nations that are most seriously grappling with the problems of child abuse and neglect. There are close parallels between the kinds of knowledge and principles that can be generated by examining far-removed and seemingly exotic cultures and diverse groups living within the borders of any one country, which we refer to as subcultural or ethnic diversity (Korbin 1980). An ability to transcend cultural boundaries, at what may be called "cultural translation" (Spradley 1979) or "ethnic competence" (Green and Tong 1978), is equally important when conducting anthropological fieldwork in remote parts of the world or when providing services in multicultural communities in Los Angeles, London, or Honolulu.

A perspective from cultures very different from our own underlines the importance of the cultural context in definitions of child abuse and neglect and in identifying those factors that may be conducive to child maltreatment or, conversely, may prevent its occurrence. Anthropologists have only recently become involved in the relatively new field of child abuse and neglect (Green 1978; Fraser and Kilbride 1980; Korbin 1977, 1979, 1980; Rohner 1975). Much remains to be accomplished in applying cultural considerations to problems of child abuse and neglect. It is important for anthropologists to be conscientious about reporting cross-cultural deviance in child rearing so that the prevalence of child maltreatment and the conditions under which it occurs can be better illuminated. It is similarly important for practitioners in the field of child abuse and neglect to be aware of the body of knowledge that exists concerning cultural variation in child-rearing practices and its implications for differing definitions of child abuse and neglect. And it is important for all concerned with children's welfare to endeavor to translate cultural awareness into tangible strategies for behavior which respect the needs and dignity of children and the rights of diverse cultures.

REFERENCES

Fraser, Gertrude, and Philip Kilbride
    1981 Child abuse and neglect—rare but perhaps increasing phenomena among the
        Samia of Kenya. *Child Abuse and Neglect: The International Journal.* 4(4):
        227–232.

Green, James
    1978 The role of cultural anthropology in the education of social service personnel.
        Journal of Sociology and Social Welfare 5(2):214–229.

Green, James, and Collin Tong
    1978 *Cultural awareness in the human services.* Seattle: Center for Social Welfare
        Research, University of Washington.

Kempe, C. Henry, Frederic N. Silverman, Brandt F. Steele, William Droegmueller,
and Henry K. Silver
    1962 The battered child syndrome. *Journal of the American Medical Association*
        181:17–24.

Korbin, Jill E.
    1977 Anthropological contributions to the study of child abuse and neglect. *Child
        Abuse and Neglect: The International Journal* 1(1):7–24.

    1979 A cross-cultural perspective on the role of the community in child abuse and
        neglect. *Child Abuse and Neglect: The International Journal* 3(1):9–18.

    1980 The cultural context of child abuse and neglect. In *The battered child*, ed. C.
        Henry Kempe and Ray E. Helfer. 3d ed. Chicago: University of Chicago
        Press. Pp. 21–35.

Logan, Richard
    1979 Socio-cultural change and the perception of children as burdens. *Child Abuse
        and Neglect: The International Journal* 3(3–4):657–662.

Laye, Camara
    1954 *The dark child: the autobiography of an African boy.* New York: Farrar, Straus and
        Geroux.

Minturn, Leigh, and William W. Lambert
    1964 *Mothers of six cultures: antecedents of child rearing.* New York: John Wiley and
        Sons.

Rohner, Ronald P.
    1975 *They love me, they love me not: a worldwide study of the effects of parental acceptance and
        rejection.* New Haven: HRAF Press.

Spradley, James P.
    1979 *The ethnographic interview.* New York: Holt, Rinehart and Winston.

Whiting, Beatrice B.
    1971 Folk wisdom and childrearing. Paper presented at meeting of the American
        Association for the Advancement of Science.

Whiting, Beatrice B., ed.
    1963 *Six cultures: studies of child rearing.* New York: John Wiley and Sons.

Whiting, Beatrice B., and John W. M. Whiting
    1975 *Children of six cultures: a psycho-cultural analysis.* Cambridge: Harvard University
        Press.

Whiting, John W. M., and Irvin L. Child
    1953 *Child training and personality.* New Haven: Yale University Press.

INDEX

Designer: Linda Robertson
Compositor: Trend Western
Printer: Braun-Brumfield
Binder: Braun-Brumfield
Text: 10/12 Janson
Display: CO 48 pt. Bodoni Bold Caps